P9-DMH-236

WHEN PRISONERS COME HOME

Recent Titles

STUDIES IN CRIME AND PUBLIC POLICY

Michael Tonry and Norval Morris, *General Editors*

Making Crime Pay: Law and Order in Contemporary American Politics
Katherine Beckett

Community Policing, Chicago Style
Wesley G. Skogan and Susan M. Hartnett

Crime Is Not the Problem: Lethal Violence in America
Franklin E. Zimring and Gordon Hawkins

Hate Crimes: Criminal Law & Identity Politics
James B. Jacobs and Kimberly Potter

Politics, Punishment, and Populism
Lord Windlesham

American Youth Violence
Franklin E. Zimring

Bad Kids: Race and the Transformation of the Juvenile Court
Barry C. Feld

Gun Violence: The Real Costs
Philip J. Cook and Jens Ludwig

Punishment, Communication, and Community
R. A. Duff

Punishment and Democracy: Three Strikes and You're Out in California
Franklin E. Zimring, Gordon Hawkins, and Sam Kamin

Restorative Justice and Responsive Regulation
John Braithwaite

Maconochie's Gentlemen:
The Story of Norfolk Island & the Roots of Modern Prison Reform
Norval Morris

Can Gun Control Work?
James B. Jacobs

Penal Populism and Public Opinion: Lessons from Five Countries
Julian V. Roberts, Loretta J. Stalans, David Indermaur, and Mike Hough

Mafia Brotherhoods: Organized Crime, Italian Style
Letizia Paoli

When Prisoners Come Home:
Parole and Prisoner Reentry
Joan Petersilia

WHEN PRISONERS COME HOME

Parole and Prisoner Reentry

Joan Petersilia

2003

OXFORD
UNIVERSITY PRESS

Oxford New York
Auckland Bangkok Buenos Aires Cape Town Chennai
Dar es Salaam Delhi Hong Kong Istanbul Karachi Kolkata
Kuala Lumpur Madrid Melbourne Mexico City Mumbai Nairobi
São Paulo Shanghai Taipei Tokyo Toronto

Published by Oxford University Press, Inc.
198 Madison Avenue, New York, New York 10016

www.oup.com

Library of Congress Cataloging-in-Publication Data
Petersilia, Joan
When prisoners come home : parole and prisoner reentry / by Joan Petersilia.
p. cm. — (Studies in crime and public policy)
Includes bibliographical references and index.
ISBN 0-19-516086-X
1. Parole—United States. 2. Criminals—Rehabilitation—United States. I. Title. II. Series.
HV9304 .P464 2003
364.8'0973—dc21 2002011531

9 8 7

Printed in the United States of America
on acid-free paper

Preface

Never before in U.S. history have so many individuals been released from prison. The U.S. Department of Justice estimates that nearly 95 percent of the 1.4 million prison inmates now in prison will eventually be released and will return to communities—635,000 people in 2002 alone and at least that many in future years, as more inmates complete long prison terms. We know that most of those leaving prison today will be poorly educated, lack vocational skills, and struggle with substance abuse, physical disabilities, or mental illnesses. Few of these problems will have been addressed in prison.

As prison populations have increased, the costs of building and operating prisons have soared. To cap operating costs, policymakers in many states decided to run austere, no-frill prisons and to cut back funding for programs and services. Inmates released today will be less prepared for life on the outside, be offered less assistance in their reintegration, and face an increasing likelihood of being returned to prison for parole violations or new crimes.

But the other consequences of prisoner reentry are less well known. What does it mean for a large number of men, mostly racial minorities from the inner city, to be taken out of these communities, sent to prison for two to three years, and then be released back into these communities? At release, many are unable to find jobs and suitable housing. Some will be legally barred from voting, receiving public assistance, obtaining a driver's license, or retaining custody of their children. Many (more than two-thirds) will eventually return to crime and prison, where the cycle begins again.

What impact does this constant churning of large segments of the resident population have on those who remain there? What are the consequences for the victims, the community at large, and the families and children left behind? How does the stigma of a prison record and the anger that often accompanies imprisonment contribute to drug use and dealing, gang activities, and family violence? Ultimately, how will the reentry phenomenon affect the next generations' criminality, as serving a prison sentence in some communities has become an acceptable and virtually inevitable phase of growing up. Surely, this reduces the power of prisons to deter and ultimately contributes to higher levels of crime in the community. Law enforcement is already attributing rises in 2001 violent crime rates to the return of so many unrehabilitated prisoners to the streets.

Faced with these realities, what can we do? This year-long study and resulting book conclude that there is much that *can* be done. There exist promising in-prison and postprison programs that help ex-convicts lead law-abiding lives. Importantly, community-based organizations, local businesses, and faith-based organizations are showing themselves to be critical partners in assisting offenders with their transitions. Some states have made important beginnings, and their programs are reducing recidivism and saving money.

Current practices in most states fail to reflect this evidence about what works, and instead reflect political posturing designed to appear tough on crime. In the end, we all lose. Evidence suggests that fewer and fewer prisoners are succeeding, and ultimately the result is not just more crime, but enormous resource expenditures. The 12 reform recommendations made in this book appear to be the most pressing; they deserve serious attention and debate.

This book assembles and analyzes the relevant information pertaining to prisoner reentry: the systems, people, programs, and prospects for implementing a more effective and just system. Chapter 1, for readers in a hurry, summarizes the data and develops major themes and policy recommendations. Chapter 2 provides a profile of returning prisoners and presents data on the demographic and crime profiles of returning prisoners. Race and gender, literacy and education, physical and mental illness, marital and parenting relationships, and substance abuse are some of the items discussed. Chapter 3 discusses the early evolution of parole in the United States and its use in modern sentencing practices, and chapter 4 describes parole supervision (as distinguished from parole release) as it is practiced today. Chapter 5 documents the decline of inmate participation in prison work, treatment, and education programs. These trends are considered in light of the growing amount of research documenting what works, and the changing nature of inmates' characteristics. Chapter 6 discusses the growing number of citizens who have criminal records and the ways in which those records are increasingly being openly shared with the public. This chapter also reviews the evidence on how a criminal record affects an offender's right to vote, qualify for public assistance, find work, or retain his parental rights. Chapter 7 presents data on the number of parolees recidivating (variously defined), as well as on the contribution that parolees make to the overall level of crime in a community. This chapter also identifies the demographic and crime factors that are significant predictors of recidivism. Chapter 8 focuses on the current and potential roles that victims might play in managing prisoner reentry. It discusses the legal rights of victims to be notified of a parolee's release and to testify at parole hearings. It also discusses the crucial role they might play in enhancing community safety and offender rehabilitation. Chapter 9 offers 12 concrete policy suggestions for reforming parole and enhancing prisoner reintegration. These options are grouped into four areas: the in-prison experience, prisoner release and revocation policies, postprison services and supervision, and reentry partnerships and community-based collaborations. Chapter 10 contains my concluding remarks, which reflect on the political and practical challenges, as well as the potential payoffs, of enhancing reentry strategies.

This book is based on interviews with dozens of correctional officials, policymakers, scholars, and convicts. A list of people too long to name here gave their time and expertise to help inform me about prison and parole practices, and I am grateful to all of them.

Dozens of inmates and ex-inmates shared their perspectives with me. I am particularly thankful to David Valdez, Elvin LeBron, Dave Davis, Vincent McKinley, Albert Sasser, Gregory Brunson, Jack Miles, and the many others who wished to remain anonymous. Special thanks go to those who provided agency data for my analysis, including Tony Fabelo and Mike Eisenberg (Texas Department of Corrections), Joseph Lehman and Steve Aos (Washington Department of Corrections), Reginald Wilkinson and Edward Rhine (Ohio Department of Corrections), John Berecochea, Bubpha Chen, Regina Stephens, Sharon Jackson, Michael Aros, and Warden Jeanne Woodford (California Department of Corrections), David Cook and Steve Ickes (Oregon Department of Corrections), Laurent Lepoutre (BI Incorporated), Gerry Gaes (U.S. Bureau of Prisons), Deborah Mukamal and Terri Stevens (Legal Action Center), Eric Johnson (Search Inc.), Patrick Langan (Bureau of Justice Statistics), and Matthew Katz (American Correctional Association). Allen Beck, director of correctional statistics at the Bureau of Justice Statistics, is owed great gratitude. His help was especially important to this effort, as he helped me get the facts right. I remain eternally appreciative.

Several colleagues aided this book in important ways. Particularly notable in this regard were Jeremy Travis, Christy Visher, Amy Solomon, Michelle Waul, and Sarah Lawrence (all of the Urban Institute). The collegiality and encouragement of Jeremy Travis was invaluable in all aspects of this project. We co-chair the Reentry Roundtable, a group of nationally prominent researchers convened by the Urban Institute to discuss prisoner reentry issues. These discussions shaped my thinking for this book. I also wish to thank James Austin, Martin Horn, Joe Lehman, Susan Tucker, John Laub, Todd Clear, Beth Richie, Marc Mauer, Dale Parent, Rick Seiter, Carol Shapiro, Diane Williams, Chris Uggen, Shadd Maruna, Charles Terry, Ned Rollo, and Bruce Western.

Earlier drafts of this book were reviewed by Michael Tonry of Cambridge University, Kevin Reitz of the University of Colorado Law School, Faye Taxman of the University of Maryland, Daniel Glaser formerly of the University of Southern California, and Jonathan Simon of the University of Miami. Their insightful comments enhanced the final product.

A special thanks goes to my graduate students at the University of California, Irvine, who participated in several classes I taught on the subject of prisoner reentry. These students challenged and engaged me: Alan Mobley, Connie Stivers-Ireland, Kelly Bradley, Danielle Rudes, James Mowrey, Ryan Fischer, and Darcy Purvis.

This book could not have been undertaken without the financial support of the Smith Richardson Foundation, which allowed me time to work on the manuscript and funded my travel to conduct interviews and observe programs. I am particularly thankful to Mark Steinmeyer of that foundation for his sustained encouragement.

Finally and most important, I thank my husband, Steve Thomas, and my sons, Jeffrey and Kyle, for cheerfully tolerating the book's intrusion in our lives. You three are my life force, my reason for living.

To all of these individuals, and countless others who assisted me, I am forever grateful.

Contents

WHEN PRISONERS COME HOME

ONE

Introduction and Overview

The Emerging Importance of Prisoner Reentry to Crime and Community

One of the most profound challenges facing American society is the reintegration of more than 600,000 adults—about 1,600 a day—who leave state and federal prisons and return home each year. As of 2002, the nation's prison population exceeded 1.4 million, and despite all of the attention given to the death penalty and life-without-parole sentences, just 7 percent of all prisoners are serving death or life sentences, and only a fraction of inmates—about 3,000 each year—die in prison. Thus, 93 percent of *all* prison inmates are eventually released.

Moreover, although the average prison term served is now 2.5 years, many prison terms are short enough so that 44 percent of all those now housed in state prisons are expected to be released within the year. Although prisons currently take in about 20,000 more prisoners than they let out, it is expected that by 2004 the ratio of admissions to releases will be 1:1.

How we plan for inmates' transition to free living—including how they spend their time during confinement, the process by which they are released, and how they are supervised after release—is critical to public safety. This process is called *prisoner reentry* and, simply defined, includes all activities and programming conducted to prepare ex-convicts to return safely to the community and to live as law-abiding citizens.

Most of those released from prison today have serious social and medical problems. They remain largely uneducated, unskilled, and usually without solid family supports—and now they have the added stigma of a prison record and the distrust and fear that it inevitably elicits. About three-quarters of all prisoners have a history of substance abuse, and one in six suffers from mental illness. Despite these needs, fewer than one-third of exiting prisoners receive substance abuse or mental health treatment while in prison. And while the federal government has provided some states with additional funding to increase drug treatment in prison, the percentage of state prisoners participating in such programs has been declining, from 25 percent in 1991 to 10 percent in 1997 (Mumola 1999).

A significant share of the prison population also lives with an infectious disease. At the end of 1999, 2.3 percent of the state prison population was HIV-positive or had AIDS, a rate five times higher than that of the U.S. population. According to the National Commission on Correctional Health Care (2002), about one-quarter of *all* individuals living with HIV or AIDS in the United States pass through a correctional facility (prison or jail) during any given year. Public health experts believe HIV will continue to escalate within prisons and eventually affect prevalence rates in the general community, as we incarcerate and release more drug offenders, many of whom engage in intravenous drug use, share needles, or trade sex for drugs.

Few inmates have marketable employment skills or sufficient literacy to become gainfully employed. Fully one-third of all prisoners were unemployed at their most recent arrest, and just 60 percent of inmates have a GED or high school diploma (compared to 85 percent of the U.S. adult population). The National Adult Literacy Survey (NALS) has established that 11 percent of inmates, compared with 3 percent of the general population, self-reported having a learning disability (LoBuglio 2001).

Despite evidence that inmates' literacy and job readiness have declined since 1990, fewer inmates are participating in prison prerelease, educational, and vocational programs. Just over one-fourth (29 percent) of those released from prison in 1997 participated in vocational training programs (down from 31 percent in 1991), and only 35 percent participated in education programs (down from 43 percent in 1991). Just 13 percent of all inmates leaving prison in 1997 were involved in any pre-release education program. Sadly, reentry programs have been reduced or eliminated altogether at precisely the time when inmate needs suggest they should be enhanced.

Part of the problem is money. State and federal prisons now consume an increasing share of tax dollars. The Bureau of Justice Statistics (BJS) estimates that we spend about $31 billion a year to operate the nation's prisons, up from $5 billion in 1978. If one adds in jail, probation, and parole expenditures, the nation spends nearly $50 billion annually on corrections.

Corrections now consumes more than 4 percent of state budgets. Yet these dollars have not funded more programs but rather prison staff, construction, and rising health care costs. Prisoners are the only population group guaranteed free health care in the United States, and as the inmate population has increased in numbers, gotten older and sicker, an increasing share of the prison budget goes to health care. Medical budgets comprise, on average, 10–15 percent of a state's corrections' total operating budget, and that percentage is increasing each year. Prison treatment programs, on the other hand, comprise 1–5 percent of state prison budgets, and that percentage is decreasing each year.

It is not just that resources are scarce. Public sentiment and political rhetoric have also forced the reduction of many programs. During the 1990s, state legislatures and prison administrators eliminated certain privileges and programs that prisoners previously enjoyed. A number of new "no-frills" statutes were passed, eliminating smoking, weight-lifting equipment, hot meals, personal clothing, telephone calls, family days, and so forth. Proponents argue that reducing such privileges is deserved—after all, incarceration should be punitive. Former Massachusetts governor William F. Weld said that prisons should be a "tour through the circles of hell," where inmates should learn only "the joys of busting rocks" (cited in Worth 1995).

Treatment and work programs have also been affected by society's expectation that prison will be punishing and that prisoners should not receive free any services for which law-abiding citizens must pay. According to this "principle of least eligibility," prisoners should be the least eligible of all citizens for social benefits beyond the bare minimum required by law. Otherwise, as George Bernard Shaw put it, "If the prison does not underbid the slum in human misery, the slum will empty and the prison will fill" (1946, p. 286).

Taken to its extreme, this principle prohibits many institutional benefits for prisoners, such as education and work-training programs. In 1994, Congress eliminated Pell grants for prisoners, which paid their tuition for college courses taken while incarcerated. Scholarships to prisoners, according to congressional logic, were unfair to hard-working citizens who could not afford to pay for college. Although less than 1 percent of all Pell grant funds went to prisoners, the Pell program died, and prison college programs are now virtually extinct in most states.

The Pell controversy was but a small part of a huge and largely undocumented trend to drastically scale back all prison vocational and education programs. At least 25 states report having made cuts in vocational and technical training, the areas most likely to provide inmates with an alternative career when they leave prison. Most states now have long waiting lists for classes of any kind. Even in states where programs have not been cut, prison crowding has rendered them almost useless. Class size has increased so rapidly that the standard approach for elementary-level courses, according to one prison teacher, is "throw them the GED handbook and say 'let me know when you're finished.' You can't learn that way." In New Jersey, the percentage of inmates participating in prison programs declined from 34 percent in 1997 to less than 10 percent in 2001.

More punitive public attitudes, combined with diminishing rehabilitation programs, means that more inmates spend their prison time being idle. In California, for example, which has nearly 160,000 inmates—the second largest state prison population in the nation—nearly 20 percent of all inmates have no assignment to a correctional program during their *entire* prison stay. Yet, research shows that California inmates who spend more time in programs are less likely to return to prison and less likely to participate in prison violence. While some of this relationship is due to differences in how prisons select inmates for programs (i.e., the most motivated are given priority), the relationship between participating in prison programs and reduced recidivism has been repeatedly documented.

Ironically, as inmate needs have *increased* and in-prison programs *decreased*, parole supervision and services have also decreased for most prisoners. In 1977, just 4 percent of all prisoners released "maxed out," or served the maximum amount of time allowed by law for their criminal conviction. But by 1999, 18 percent—or nearly one-fifth of all exiting prisoners—maxed out, and they have no obligation to report to a parole officer or to abide by any other conditions of release. As former assistant attorney general Laurie Robinson recently noted, some of those being released without any parole supervision are "some of the baddest of the bad actors" (cited in Gest 2001, p. 216), having been convicted of a particularly violent crime, which makes them ineligible for early release consideration, or they have behaved poorly in prison, thereby forfeiting possible "good time" early release credits. It is being argued that, in some states (e.g., Massachusetts), those who are released on parole supervision are those who need it *least*, and those who are released unconditionally—or without parole supervision—need it *most*.

Some policymakers worry that prisoner *reentry* equates with prisoner *recidivism* and may serve to increase crime in the community.

As *Time* magazine reported in its story about prisoners coming home: "The looming fear is that their return—just at the time the country is fighting a recession and a war—will boost crime again, just as their incarceration helped bring it down. Already, crime increases in Boston, Chicago, and Los Angeles have been blamed on their return" (Ripley 2002, p. 58). When Los Angeles police chief Bernard Parks was asked to explain the nearly 25 percent increase in murder rates during 2000, he said: "Surely it is attributable to the fact that a wave of convicted offenders has recently hit the streets" (Landsberg 2000). Los Angeles County receives 3,000 new parolees a month, nearly one-third of all those released in California.

Some of those being released have been housed in "supermax," or maximum-security, prisons prior to release, where for close to 23 hours a day, they are deprived of all human interaction. Kurki and Morris (2002) estimate that 1.2 percent of all prisoners (about 17,000 in 2002) are now held in supermax prisons in the United States, and the number is increasing. In the words of the judge in the decisive case involving supermax confinement, such segregation "may press the outer borders of what most humans can psychologically tolerate" (*Madrid v. Gomez* 1995). As Haney (2002) wrote, "Few states provide any meaningful or effective decompression program for prisoners, which means that many prisoners who have been confined in these supermax units—some for considerable periods of time—are released directly into the community from these extreme conditions of confinement."

Prisoners who have not maxed out—about 80 percent of all releasees—will be released to parole supervision. Most of them will be given a bus ticket and told to report to the parole office in their home community on the next business day. Their "home" is usually defined as their last legal residence or, in some states, the county in which their current conviction occurred. If they live in a state that provides funds upon release (about one-third of states do not), they will be given $25 to $200 in gate money. Some states provide a new set of clothing at release, but these "extras" (e.g., shoes, toiletries, a suit) have declined over time. Sometimes, a list of rental apartments or shelters is provided, but the arrangements are generally left up to the offender to determine where to reside and how to pay for basic essentials such as food, housing, and clothing during the first months. Employment is also mostly left up to the offender. Few prisons have transitional case managers to assist offenders, and the current process places the offender almost solely in charge and accountable for her own transition plan. The notion is that convicts can "make it," if they so desire.

National statistics show that nearly 10 percent of all state parolees who are required to report to parole offices after release fail to do so. They avoid supervision, and their whereabouts remain unknown. In California, which supervises one out of five parolees nationwide, the abscond rate is a staggering 22 percent. Warrants are routinely issued for parole absconders, but scarce police and parole resources may mean that such warrants are given low priority.

Parole officials say that housing is the biggest need for parolees. Homelessness is increasing nationally and even more so in the inner cities. Convicts are increasingly moving into the most impoverished areas of the inner city. Lynch and Sabol (2001) found that two-thirds of all prisoners released in 1996 returned to the nation's "core counties," those counties that contain the central cities of metropolitan areas. Within those counties, they found that parolees live in just a few neighborhoods. Research in Brooklyn illustrates this growing phenomenon: 11 percent of the city blocks in Brooklyn account for 20 percent of the population but 50 percent of the parolees. In those neighborhoods, it is estimated that one out of eight parenting-age males is admitted to jail or prison each year. Jails house offenders serving short sentences or awaiting trial; prisons usually house those serving one or more years.

The concentration of ex-prisoners in already fragile communities causes sociologists to worry about the impact on the children and other young people in the community. The BJS reports that, on any one day, 2 percent of all minor children in the United States—and more than 7 percent of black children—had at least one parent in prison. The lifetime prevalence rates of children with parents in prison are much higher. Of course, in some cases, removing a parent can be beneficial to the child. But research shows that children always experience the loss of a parent as a traumatic event, and children of incarcerated parents are more likely to exhibit low self-esteem, depression, and disruptive behavior at home and in school. Children of incarcerated parents are also five times more likely to serve time in prison than children whose parents have not been incarcerated.

Elijah Anderson, a noted sociologist, says that imprisonment also has devastating effects on the community at large. He has documented how the criminal element has come to dominate public spaces in inner-city communities. The drug dealers, with their ostentatious displays of money and power, are socializing the young in these communities, and he estimates that by the fourth grade, "fully three-quarters of young residents have bought into the oppositional culture . . . where it is better to be feared than loved" (1999, p. 314). Youth see few positive role models and no positive sense of the future. Endemic joblessness and alienation results, fueling the violence in which they engage. Eventually, they get sent to prison, and the vicious cycle continues, with prison being almost a normative life experience for an increasing number of youth.

Prisoner reentry has emerged as a key policy issue not solely because of its impact on crime. Legal scholars say the effects have moved beyond the prisoner and the prison to include crucial social, political, and economic consequences for families and entire communities. While corrections officials were reducing services to inmates behind bars and after release, Congress and many state legislatures were passing a number of laws and regulations that *increase* the employment, welfare, and housing barriers they face postincarceration. Since 1980, the United States has passed dozens of laws restricting the kinds of jobs for which ex-prisoners can be hired, easing the requirements for their parental rights to be terminated, restricting their access to public welfare and housing subsidies, and limiting their right to vote.

Together, these collateral consequences remove the safety net upon which many poor citizens rely and also raise the broader question of how civil society itself is being shaped by the exclusion of these ex-felons and their families. The effects are thought to be profound. Recent analysis by Uggen and Manza (2001) suggests that if just 15 percent of the nearly 900,000 disfranchised felons in Florida—those unable to vote due to a felony conviction—had participated in the last presidential election, Albert Gore would have prevailed in Florida, and President George W. Bush would not have been elected.

Jeremy Travis (2002) of the Urban Institute notes that these new laws largely operate beyond public view, yet they have serious, adverse consequences for the individuals affected. He calls these restrictions "invisible punishments" and notes that they have now become instruments of "social exclusion," creating a permanent diminution in the social status of convicted offenders.

A growing number of people are also now required to register with the police upon release from prison. Originally begun for sex offenders, criminal registration is now required of many other classes of offense (e.g., arson, crimes against children, domestic violence, stalking). It is not known how many criminals are included on all such registries, but as of the end of 2001, there were more than 386,000 people listed in state sex-offender registries.

The expansion of legal barriers has been accompanied by an increase in the ease of checking criminal records due to new technologies and expanded public access to criminal records through the Internet. Historically, criminal record information was restricted to law enforcement personnel and others who could demonstrate a "need to know." Today, those restrictions have been lifted and, for all practical purposes, one's criminal past is public. In 29 states, anyone can obtain at least some type of criminal record information on anyone else. In 25 states, that information can be publicly accessed through the Internet.

Expanded restrictions and legal requirements now apply to a greater percentage of the U.S. population simply because of the explosion in the number of people convicted and imprisoned during the 1990s. Uggen and colleagues (2002b) estimate that, in 2000, 13 million Americans were ex-felons, that is, they had served or were currently serving a felony probation, parole, prison, or jail sentence. This equals 6.5 percent of the entire adult population, 11 percent of the adult male population, and an astounding 37 percent of the adult black male population. Furthermore, the Department of Justice reports that more than 59 million Americans have a criminal record on file in state repositories—29 percent of the nation's *entire* adult population.

The number of criminal history files maintained by state and federal repositories more than doubled in the 1990s. A Bureau of Justice Statistics survey (2002c) reported that more than 75 percent of criminal history records are now automated and shared electronically, although just 60 percent of the arrest entries have dispositions. The same report also noted that privacy concerns were an issue in the early 1990s, but the trend toward privacy began to reverse course in the mid-1990s as greater access to criminal records was provided at both the state and federal levels.

Victims' rights groups argue that greater public access to criminal records enhances public safety and feelings of safety, and it certainly does. Law enforcement is also better able to identify suspects when similar crimes occur. Gun dealers and prospective employers can quickly conduct background checks to assure that they are not selling guns to or employing dangerous persons. All of these are tangible benefits from greater access to criminal histories.

We have to weigh those benefits, however, against the number of lives disrupted and the families and communities—especially minority communities—which are affected. Ideally, we would target these policies specifically on those offenders who represent serious threats. There are many violent and chronic inmates coming out of prison today, and we need to use all available means to monitor them at release.

But today, these policies are applied equally to offenders representing very different public safety risks. As we have expanded the number of people and kinds of crimes that get sentenced to prison, more first-time drug offenders have these restrictions applied to them—sometimes for life. The BJS reports that just half of the current prison population was sent there for a violent crime; about 20 percent was sentenced for a drug crime, and another 30 percent was committed for nonviolent property or public order offenses. Forty-two percent of those now in prison for drug crimes had no prior incarcerations, although most of them had prior probation terms. These people, who perhaps should not have gone to prison in the first place, are now forever stigmatized and excluded from participating fully in legitimate society.

The stigma associated with a criminal past significantly affects one's chances of finding and keeping a job, personal relationships, and housing—and these difficulties ultimately also affect public safety. Holzer (1996) conducted surveys in four major U.S. cities and found that more than 60 percent of employers were unwilling to hire an applicant with a criminal record.

Parole agents have also become less "kind and gentle." Parole departments in most large urban areas have developed a prevailing culture that emphasizes surveillance over services. Parole officers believe that their caseloads now contain more dangerous offenders, and they are now authorized to carry weapons in three-fourths of the states. Parole officer training often provides minimal training on casework practices and service referrals, but numerous classes on arrests, searches, and other topics stressing law enforcement. Such training increasingly reinforces the image of parole officers as cops rather than social workers.

Not surprisingly, most released prisoners are rearrested and returned to prison. The Bureau of Justice Statistics recently released the most comprehensive study ever conducted in the United States of prisoner recidivism (i.e., an offender's return to crime). The study found that 30 percent—or nearly one in three—released prisoners were rearrested in the first six months, 44 percent within the first year, and 67.5 percent within three years of release from prison (Langan and Levin 2002). Comparing these recidivism rates with a nearly identical study conducted in 1983 (Beck and Shipley 1989), one finds some disturbing trends. Overall, rearrest rates increased slightly (about 5 percent), the time to first rearrest was shorter, and the overall percentage of serious crime arrests attributable to ex-prisoners has increased. The BJS estimates that this single cohort of inmates, released in 1994, was responsible for 4.7 percent of all arrests for serious crime in the ensuing three years (1994–1997). The number was even higher for violent crimes; for example, they were responsible for 8 percent of all the homicides and 9 percent of the robberies. The comparable figure for the 1983 prisoner releasees was 2.8 percent. Ex-convicts appear to be doing less well than their counterparts released a decade earlier, and they represent a continuing serious threat to public safety.

Such a high recidivism rate is one of the major factors linked to growing U.S. prison populations. In 1999, parole failures account for 35 percent of new prison admissions each year—up from 17 percent in 1980. In some states, it is much higher. For example, 67 percent of all California prison admissions in 1999 were parole violators rather than new court commitments.

No one believes that the current prison and parole system is working. Recent public opinion polls show an increasing dissatisfaction with the purely punitive approach to criminal justice (Greene and Schiraldi 2002; Hart Research Associates 2002). Americans are reconsidering the wisdom of harsh prison sentences as the centerpiece of the nation's crime strategy, especially for nonviolent offenders. The criminal justice system is increasingly viewed as ineffective at reducing recidivism, incredibly expensive, and destructive of the lives of both victims and offenders. Ultimately, overly punitive approaches to criminal punishment fall equally heavily on the offender's family and the community to which he returns.

How Did It Get Like This?

This troubling state of affairs is attributable, in large part, to a shift in American sentencing and corrections policy since the mid-1970s. The sentencing reform movement, which spawned truth-in-sentencing, mandatory penalties, and an ever-escalating reliance on incapacitation (or physical isolation of criminals), created in its wake dramatic prison population growth. Since 1970, the number of state and federal prisoners has grown by more than 700 percent, from about 196,000 in 1970 to 1.4 million at the end of 2001.

The classic model of indeterminate, treatment-oriented sentencing, with its reliance on the discretion of parole boards to set release dates, came under attack in the early 1970s, and by 2001, 16 states had abolished their parole boards and replaced them with fixed-term punishments. In 1977, discretionary parole releasees accounted for 88 percent of state prison releasees. By 2000, discretionary parole accounted for only 24 percent of all prison releasees, and mandatory parole releases had increased to 41 percent.

Rehabilitation was replaced as the core mission of corrections with programs designed to deter and incapacitate. As David Garland writes, "The assault on individualized treatment opened the floodgates for a period of change that has been with us ever since" (Garland 2001, p. 63). Even in states that maintained treatment programs, many were retained primarily as a means of keeping inmates manageable rather than as methods to reduce recidivism. Data show that between 1980 and 2000, only prison industry programs grew. Apparently, legislators looked more favorably upon programs that could generate goods and services that the state needed than on education and work programs that might reform inmates. Indeed, it was openly acknowledged, "It is the duty of prisons to govern fairly and well within their own walls. It is not their duty to reform, rehabilitate, or reintegrate offenders into society" (Logan 1993).

In several states, sentencing commissions and guidelines were instituted to determine how long inmates would serve, and this process brought about jurisdiction-wide uniformity in sentencing, reduced disparities in prison sentences, and resulted in greater certainty of punishment. Some believe such changes increased the deterrent and incapacitation value of prison sentences and contributed to some of the recent declines in U.S. crime rates. But those sentencing changes have also had profound impact on the way inmates do time and are released, and these results remain poorly understood.

A majority of inmates being released today have not been required to "earn release" but rather have been automatically released. Parole boards used to examine prisoners' "preparation" for release, including whether they had a place to live, a potential job, and family support. With determinate sentences, these factors are not relevant to release. When offenders have done their time, they are released, no matter what level of support is available to them or how prepared they are for release.

Victims too, having earned the legal right to testify at parole hearings and to request that certain conditions be applied to an inmate's release (e.g., protective orders), now find they have fewer parole hearings to attend. An inmate's release date is determined at sentencing and, assuming good prison behavior, he will be released on that date—regardless of whether he has suffered major depression or mental illness, or whether new information has become known about him while in prison.

We spent the last decade debating who should go to prison, for how long, and how we might pay for it, and we paid virtually no attention to how we would cope with prisoners after they left prison. If these ex-prisoners are unable to lead law-abiding lives, we all pay in terms of new crimes committed. The latest prison survey shows that 22 percent of all state prisoners—and fully 18 percent of inmates on death row—committed their most recent crime while on parole (Snell 2001). The human and financial costs of returning ill-prepared convicts to communities are staggering. Moreover, our failure to pay attention to parole services is unfortunate, since most inmates, at the point of release, have an initial strong desire to succeed. If we fail to take advantage of this mindset, we miss one of the few potential turning points to successfully intervene in offenders' lives.

Addressing the Problem

Prisoner reentry is an incredibly complex and multifaceted problem. It involves tackling some of the central issues in contemporary crime policy: sentencing, prisons, and prison release practices. It also requires us to revisit the effectiveness of rehabilitation programs and the government's responsibility in helping people acquire new living and work skills. If we decide to assist the 6 or 7 million convicts coming home in the first decade of the twenty-first century, we must also rethink which agencies should be involved. Some question whether parole officers, given their current law enforcement stance, can operate "helping" programs. Perhaps other social service agencies, or even the courts, should be more involved in delivering and monitoring rehabilitation. At an even broader level, some question whether state-initiated criminal justice policy—or any of its programs—can be a vehicle for remedying what is criminogenic in some urban communities. Perhaps nonprofit organizations, convict self-help groups, and faith-based programs hold the key to successful reentry initiatives. These are all good questions, and debates about them should be taking place.

Of course, inmates have always been released from prison, and corrections officials have long struggled with how to facilitate successful transitions. But the current situation is decidedly different. The sheer number of releasees dwarfs anything in our history; the needs of parolees appear more serious; and the corrections system retains few rehabilitation programs.

The heightened interest in prisoner reentry is generating many new programs and a flurry of legislative activity. As James Austin wrote: "Reentry has become the new buzzword in correctional reform" (2001, p. 314). The Urban Institute in Washington, D.C., has begun a comprehensive, multisite research study of reentry processes. The U.S. Department of Justice (DOJ) is supporting the Coming Home Initiative, which brings together a number of federal partners (e.g., Health and Human Services, Housing and Urban Development) to fund new state reentry programs for juveniles and adults. The DOJ is also supporting the Reentry Partnership Initiative and the Reentry Courts Initiative. The states of Washington, Pennsylvania, and Maryland have completely revised their approaches to offender reentry. All have developed new risk assessment instruments that tie prison programs with postrelease risks and needs.

Correctional leaders are encouraged by the newfound focus on prisoner reentry, calling it a much-needed sea change in philosophy and perhaps just what the nation requires to bring balance back to a corrections system that many believe has become too punitive. Burke (1995) wrote that reentry could serve as an "elevating goal" for corrections, since regardless of one's political preferences about who should go to prison or how long they should serve, they all return home. Public opinion polls also show that people across the political and ideological spectrum agree that the objectives of reentry policy should be to prevent recidivism and to help offenders reintegrate into society as responsible and productive citizens. Hence, there is a zone of consensus around the reentry issue, which may provide unique opportunities.

Yet at the same time, caution should be exercised and the lessons of the past remembered. The author is reminded of the intermediate sanctions movement of the 1980s and 1990s. Prisons were crowded, and a groundswell of political and popular support quickly emerged to implement intensive supervision probation and parole (ISP) programs. The federal government provided financial incentives to develop ISPs, and within a few years, hundreds of local programs emerged across the nation. Despite good intentions to deliver more effective programs, the dollars were insufficient to fund social services and were used instead to fund more surveillance, such as drug testing and electronic monitoring. In the end, the ISP programs that were supposed to reduce recidivism through more effective rehabilitation, ended up simply identifying the failures more quickly and revoking a greater number of ex-inmates to custody. A similar story can be told about juvenile diversion programs. Our nation has a history of implementing programs that are initially designed to help offenders but instead end up treating them more harshly. As Todd Clear wrote, "Why does it seem that all good efforts to build reforms seem inevitably to disadvantage the offender?" (Clear 1992, p. ix). A similar scenario could befall prison reentry initiatives.

What Is to Be Done? The Call for Reform

There is a compelling need to reform the systems to prepare convicts for law-abiding lives. First, we must reinvest in prison work, education, and substance abuse programs. We simply cannot reduce recidivism without funding programs that open up opportunities for ex-convicts to create alternatives to a criminal lifestyle. It simply cannot be done. Ironically, just as evidence was building that certain rehabilitation programs *do* reduce recidivism, state corrections departments had to dismantle those very programs due to budget constraints. The result is that relatively few inmates leaving prison today have received any education or vocational training to address these deficiencies, almost guaranteeing their failure at release. Those failures create a rising tide of parolees returning to prison, putting pressure on states to build more prisons, which in turn, takes money away from rehabilitation programs that might have helped offenders in the first place.

The cry for more programming is always met with public skepticism. The public simply does not believe that prison programs make a difference. This is an unfortunate legacy of the 1970s, the "nothing works" era. Today, however, there is ample scientific evidence showing that treatment programs can reduce recidivism, if the programs are well designed, well implemented, and targeted appropriately. In this case, the devil is not in the principle but in the details.

Effective programs include therapeutic communities for drug addicts and substance abuse programs with aftercare for alcoholics and drug addicts; cognitive behavioral programs for sex offenders; and adult basic education, vocational education, and prison industries for the general prison population. Each of these programs has been shown to reduce the recidivism rate of program participants by 8–15 percent. Even with these relatively modest reductions in subsequent recidivism, these programs pay for themselves in terms of reducing future justice expenditures. For example, prisoners who participate in vocational education programs have about a 13 percent lower likelihood of recidivism, and the programs cost about $2,000 per participant, per year. Analysts have estimated that such programs result in an average of $12,000 savings, per participant, down the line in saved criminal justice expenditures (Aos, Phipps, Barnoski, and Lieb 2001). Similar cost savings accrue for the other proven correctional programs. It is thus highly likely that investing in selected rehabilitation programs will generate several dollars' worth of benefits for every dollar spent. Of course, the more important social benefits of reduced recidivism cannot be measured in economic terms. There no longer exists any reasonable justification for not funding proven rehabilitation programs.

Second, we should reinstitute discretionary parole in the 16 states that have abolished it, and reverse the trend toward automatic mandatory release in the states that are moving in that direction. In 2001, three out of four inmates leaving prison were released automatically at the end of a set time period, the highest figure since the federal government began compiling statistics on the issue.

Abolishing parole was a politically expedient way to appease the public, which wrongly equated parole with letting inmates out early. But the public was misinformed when it labeled parole as lenient. On the contrary, recent research shows that inmates who are released through discretionary parole actually serve *longer* prison terms, on average, than those released mandatorily, and the difference is most pronounced for violent offenders (Hughes, Wilson, and Beck 2001). Prisoners released by a discretionary parole board also have higher success rates than those released through mandatory parole. Both of these results hold true even after statistically controlling for crime type, prior criminal history, and other demographics (Stivers 2001).

These data suggest that having to earn and demonstrate readiness for release and being supervised postprison may have some deterrent or rehabilitation benefits—particularly for the most dangerous offenders. Importantly, discretionary parole systems provide a means by which inmates who represent continuing public safety risks can be kept in prison, and discretionary parole also serves to refocus prison staff and corrections budgets on planning for release, not just opening the door at release.

No one would argue for returning to the unfettered discretion that resulted in unwarranted sentence disparities among offenders. But we have thrown the baby out with the bathwater, and we should be using inmate risk assessments and parole guidelines to structure and control discretion but not eliminate it. When states abolish discretionary parole or reduce the discretion of parole authorities, they replace a rational, controlled system of earned release for *selected* inmates with automatic release for nearly *all* inmates (Burke 1995). No-parole systems sound tough but remove a critical gatekeeping role, which can protect victims and communities. In the long run, no one is more dangerous than a criminal who has no incentive to straighten himself out while in prison and who returns to society without a structured and supervised release plan. As ironic as it may seem, it is in the interests of public safety that discretionary parole systems should be reinstituted.

Third, we must front-load postprison services during the first six months after release. Recidivism statistics show that two-thirds of people released from prison will eventually be rearrested. But recidivism data also show that the return to crime happens very quickly: nearly 30 percent of all released inmates are rearrested for a serious crime in the first six months. On the other hand, the risk of recidivism declines dramatically after three years, and after five years of arrest-free behavior, recidivism is extremely low. These data suggest that the first six months after release are extremely critical to eventual success, and we should concentrate our limited resources on that time period. At the same time, parole terms of longer than five years, for all but the most serious offenders, should be eliminated for parolees who have remained arrest-free during that time period. As logical as this sounds, parole services are not currently organized this way in most states.

Ideally, all inmates who have spent a considerable time period incarcerated (say, more than two years) would transition to a halfway house or day-reporting center. These centers would be used to establish a central location for parole agents, police, social service personnel, reentering offenders, and their families to share information and manage the reentry process. The format (whether reentry courts, reentry partnerships, or police-parole teams) matters less than the strategies adopted. Initially, parole officers will create alliances with social service agencies and community policing officers to ensure service delivery and accountability. During the critical first six months, these agencies will work to coordinate surveillance, drug testing and treatment, job training and placement, health and mental health services, family services, and transitional housing.

These formal agencies will apply incentives and graduated sanctions to promote positive behavior and to marshal resources to support prisoners' successful reintegration. Ultimately, however, they would use their energies and resources to facilitate *informal* social controls—those interpersonal bonds that link ex-inmates to churches, law-abiding neighbors, families, and communities. These informal social bonds are the strongest predictors of ultimate desistance from crime.

Fourth, we must establish procedures by which some convicts can put entirely their criminal offending in the past. The United States has the highest incarceration rate of industrial democracies, and yet unlike all other democracies, we have virtually no practical means of sealing or expunging adult criminal records. A criminal conviction—no matter how trivial or how long ago it occurred—scars one for life. In terms of this issue, we have the worst of both worlds: higher conviction and imprisonment rates combined with no legal way to move beyond their stigmatizing effects.

To be sure, there are valid reasons for wanting to know the criminal backgrounds of persons with whom we come in contact. Prior criminal record is a strong predictor of future criminality. But there are ways to simultaneously protect the public from those criminals who wish to continue committing crimes, while not allowing those same procedures to prevent criminals who wish to go straight from doing so. Establishing procedures to seal some adult criminal convictions seems especially urgent now, as public access to criminals' records is becoming more widespread via the Internet.

Current legal barriers and prohibitions are simply overly broad. For instance, employment applications ask whether or not you have "ever" been convicted of a crime. Research shows that persons answering "yes" to that question are unlikely to be hired, and if hired, seldom promoted. Similarly, 10 states *permanently* deny convicted felons the right to vote after a single felony conviction. Disfranchising felons for life is a custom unheard of in other democratic countries. Public housing and welfare benefits are also denied, sometimes for life, even for a 20-year-old record for a minor crime. Jobs, housing, and financial stability are necessary for convicts to refrain from crime and to establish the informal networks critical for long-term survival, as previously noted.

Protocols should be established that allow *some* offenders to put entirely their criminal offending in the past and be restored to complete citizenship. Ex-offenders should have an opportunity to show they are good risks through consideration of the circumstances of the crime, the severity of the sentence, or their rehabilitation. England's Rehabilitation of Offenders Act provides a good model. That act allows for persons convicted of a crime and sentenced to prison for less than 2.5 years to have that conviction "spent," or ignored, after a period of time has elapsed if no felony convictions occur during this time period. Individuals must remain conviction-free for a period of 7–10 years after the original conviction, but after that time period, they are not required to mention the original conviction on most job applications. The individual's criminal history legally "expires" after a given number of years. Moreover, the original conviction cannot be grounds for firing someone or denying them child custody, insurance, housing, or public financial benefits.

There are really few public safety risks in such a scheme, given that so few prisoners return to crime after 7–10 years of crime-free living. Yet, the benefits may be quite large, as a greater number of ex-convicts would be able to find stable housing and meaningful employment and to support their children. Those persons who establish a stake in the welfare of their community are also less likely to engage in illegal activities that will bring harm to others.

These, and the other policy recommendations made in this book, should receive high priority as the economy slows and the nation searches for ways to keep the crime rate down as nearly 600,000 inmates a year—1,600 a day—leave prison to return home. We would also do well to keep in mind the advice given by Mary Belle Harris, the first female federal prison warden in the United States, upon her retirement. She said, "We must remember always that the doors of prisons swing both ways" (1936, p. xiii). This is advice we should heed more than ever now.

TWO

Who's Coming Home?

A Profile of Returning Prisoners

Ex-prisoners are still mostly male, minority, and unskilled—yet in each of these areas, there are trends that signal significant changes. Today's inmate is likely to have been in custody several times before, has a lengthy history of alcohol and drug abuse, is more likely to be involved in gang activities and drug dealing, has probably experienced significant periods of unemployment and homelessness, and may have a physical or mental disability. Most of them have young children, with whom they hope to reunite after release, although in most cases, their children will have infrequently visited them during their incarceration. A significant number of inmates will have spent weeks, if not months, in solitary confinement or supermax prisons, devoid of human contact and prison program participation. Recognizing the unique needs of returning prisoners and the abilities of communities to supervise and assist them must precede any reform efforts.

Increases in Number of Prisoners and Parole Releasees

The public is now quite familiar with the tremendous growth in U.S. prison populations since the early 1970s. The per capita rate of imprisonment in America hovered at about 110 per 100,000 from 1925 to 1973, with little variation. Starting in 1973, the rate of imprisonment began to grow steadily, so that by the end of 2000, there were an estimated 478 prison inmates per 100,000 U.S. residents, equivalent to 1 in every 109 men and 1 in every 1,695 women. These rates vary dramatically by race. In 2000, 1 in every 29 black males was sentenced to at least a year's confinement, compared with 1 in every 82 Hispanic males, and 1 in every 223 white males (Beck and Harrison 2001).

The United States has a higher per capita incarceration rate than any other industrialized democracy. However, simply comparing imprisonment rates across countries fails to account for differences in the level and nature of crime and criminals in a society. James Lynch (2002) recently completed such an analysis and found that the propensity to incarcerate for violent crimes is *not* different in the United States when compared with other institutionally similar countries, but for property and drug crimes, the United States incarcerates more of those convicted and for longer periods than other similar nations. In fact, no other nation treats people who commit nonviolent (especially drug) crimes as harshly as does the United States.

As a natural, predictable consequence of increased levels of imprisonment, more people leave prison to return home, typically under some form of criminal justice supervision. In 1997, just 3 percent of federal prisoners and 8 percent of state prisoners had life or death sentences. Some offenders with life sentences may eventually be released, and some offenders not serving life sentences may never be released (e.g., older offenders who have very long sentences). It is estimated that 93 percent of all prison inmates will eventually return home.

As figure 2.1 shows, in 2000, there were similar numbers admitted to prison (625,225) as released (606,225). If the capacity to manage reintegration had kept pace with the flow of released prisoners, then the reentry phenomenon today would be no different than in times past. Unfortunately, parole programs and release mechanisms have weakened, while offenders' needs for services and supervision have grown.

Sentence Length and Prison Time Left to Serve

Not only are more people being sent to prison, but "three strikes" and other mandatory minimums and truth-in-sentencing laws have increased the average length of prison terms served since the mid-1970s. Among all state prison inmates released from prison for their first time on their current offense, the average (mean) time served in prison was 29 months in 1999, 7 months longer than for those released in 1990 (Hughes, Wilson, and Beck 2001). This longer time in prison translates into a longer period of detachment from family and other social networks, posing new challenges to the process of reintegration.

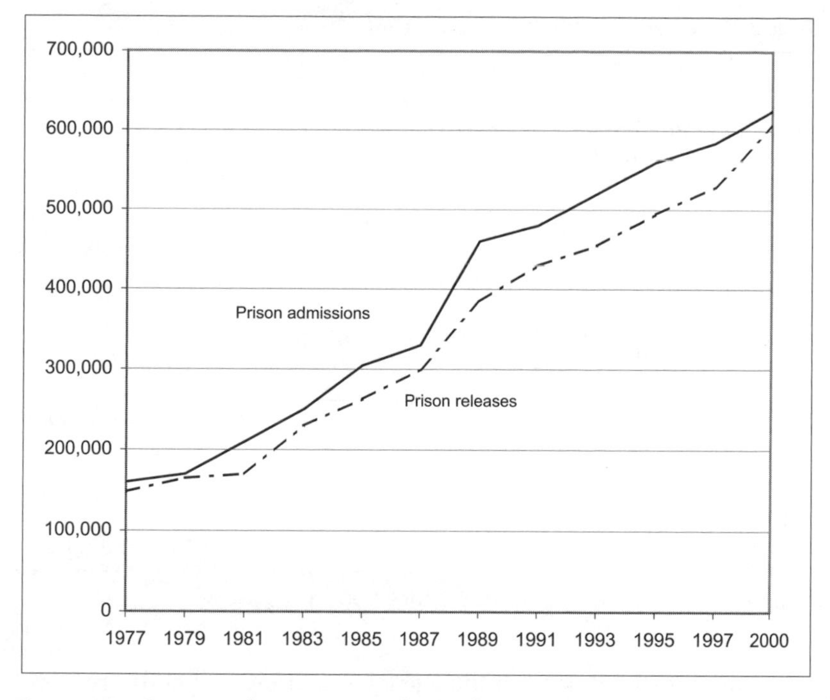

Figure 2.1. Sentenced prisoners admitted and released from state and federal prisons, 1977–2000.

Yet while many inmates serve long prison sentences, a significant number are released within a few months, especially if they have been returned to prison for a technical violation. The Bureau of Justice Statistics estimates that 44 percent of all state (and 27 percent of all federal) prisoners have less than one year left to serve on their sentences (see table 2.1).

Demographic and Crime Profiles of Returning Prisoners

Most of what we know about U.S. prisoners and parolees comes from the BJS, the statistical arm of the U.S. Department of Justice. Since the early 1980s, the BJS has reported on the number of persons entering and exiting parole through its National Corrections Reporting Program. The BJS also conducts the Annual Parole Survey (APS), which provides a count of the number of persons under parole supervision, and the Census of State and Local Probation and Parole Agen-

Table 2.1. Sentence length for inmates, 1997

	State	Federal
Offender characteristic		
Life sentence or death sentence	8%	3%
For those not serving life or death sentences, median sentence length	*Length in years*	
All offenders	5	7
Drug offenders	3	8
Violent offenders	7	9
Sentence time remaining	*Percentage of inmates*	
Less than 1 year	44	27
1 to 5 years	38	42
More than 5 years	18	31
Number of inmates	1,059,607	89,072

Source: Government Accounting Office 2001.

cies, which gathers data on the agencies' staffing, expenditures, and programs. Finally, the BJS conducts the Survey of Inmates in State Adult Correctional Facilities (usually done every five years), which asks inmates about their personal backgrounds, substance abuse histories, criminal histories, and other related matters.

Age, Gender, Race

Age The average age of state prisoners released to parole was 34 years in 1999, slightly older than the average of 31 years in 1990 (see table 2.2). As sentence lengths increase, the average age of prisoners also increases. But the average age misses a critical point: there are a greater number of older parolees now being released. In 1999, an estimated 109,300 state prisoners aged 40 or older were paroled—26 percent of all entrants to parole. There were about 44,000 parolees aged 55 or older. This number more than doubled in the 1990s. According to the BJS, the majority of elderly state prisoners (61 percent) are incarcerated for violent offenses.

The costs of incarcerating older offenders is estimated at $69,000 per year, or three times the $22,000 average it costs to keep younger, healthier offenders in prison. Age is also negatively correlated with

Table 2.2. Demographic characteristics of state parole entrants, 1990 and 1999

Characteristic	Percentage of entrants	
	1990	1999
Gender		
Male	92.1	90.1
Female	7.9	9.9
Race/origin		
White non-Hispanic	34.2	35.4
Black non-Hispanic	48.8	47.3
Hispanic	16.3	16.1
Other	0.7	0.7
Age at prison release		
17 or younger	0.2	0.1
18–24	23.4	16.3
25–29	26.6	19.0
30–34	22.2	19.7
35–39	13.9	19.2
40–44	7.3	13.5
45–54	4.9	10.2
55 or older	1.5	2.1
Mean age	31 yrs.	34 yrs.
Education		
8th grade or less	16.6	11.0
Some high school	45.4	39.8
High school graduate or GED	29.6	42.2
Some college or more	8.2	7.0

Source: Hughes et al. 2001.

recidivism. The older an offender is at release, other factors held constant, the lower the rate of recidivism (Gendreau, Little, and Goggin 1996).

Gender Prisoners and parolees are mostly male, and always have been. However, women constitute the most rapidly growing, and least violent, segment of the U.S. prison population. Females now comprise 9.9 percent of state parole entrants, up from 7.9 percent in

1990. Two-thirds of women parolees are minorities, and nearly half were convicted of drug offenses (42 percent in 1999, up from 36 percent in 1990). Almost all female prisoners are classified as low risk on prison classification instruments.

In many ways, the war on drugs has hit females harder than males. During the decade after passage of mandatory sentencing for drug convictions in 1986, the number of women incarcerated for drug crimes rose by 888 percent (Mauer, Potler, and Wolf 1999). Mandatory sentencing laws required judges to sentence men and women who committed the same offense to the same punishment. Extenuating circumstances often could not be fully considered. The federal sentencing guidelines, for example, do not permit judges to consider the role of women in caring for children, the subordinate roles women play in many crimes, nor the fact that women are much less likely than men to commit new crimes after being released. Three years after full implementation of the federal sentencing guidelines, the number of women in federal institutions nearly doubled (Raeder 1993).

Female offenders have different needs than male offenders, as 57 percent of women in state prison report prior physical or sexual abuse, and they have higher rates of drug addiction and infectious disease than their male counterparts (Harlow 1999). Nearly half of all female prisoners ran away from home as youth, and a quarter of them had attempted suicide. Most had never earned more than $6.50 an hour (Donziger 1996). Despite these unique needs, there are fewer prison and parole programs to assist them and their children.

Race Race is a critical dimension of the reentry discussion. About one-third of parole entrants are white, 47 percent are black, and 16 percent are Hispanic, who may be of any race—hence, about two-thirds of all returning prisoners are racial or ethnic minorities. This is approximately three times the percentage of minorities in the general population of the United States. As the National Trust for the Development of African-American Men declared: "In many prisons, one feels as if there is an invisible sign on the front door that reads 'Only Black and Hispanics Need Apply'" (2002).

In terms of inmates *in* prison (as distinguished from parole releases), Hispanics represent the fastest growing minority group. Hispanics comprise 9.4 percent of the U.S. population, but are 16 percent of the current prison population. In 1985, they were 11 percent of the prison population. These increases reflect a rate twice as high as the increase for black and white inmates (Walker, Spohn, and DeLone 2002). With little information about the number of Asian and Native American prisoners, it appears their representation is not substantially greater than their representation in the general population.

Minority families and their communities are feeling the consequences of imprisonment and release in unprecedented ways. Bonczar and Beck (1997) calculated that in 1991, a black male had a 29 percent chance of being incarcerated at least once in his lifetime, six times higher than the chance for a white male. Beck and Harrison (2001) estimated that nearly 10 percent of black males and 3 percent of Hispanic males in their late twenties and early thirties were in prison at the end of 2000. There are now more young black men between the ages of 20 and 29 under the control of the nation's criminal justice system (including probation and parole) than the total number in college.

Pettit and Western (2001) have calculated the percentage of blacks and whites experiencing different life events in the United States. Table 2.3 contains these results. These life event differences are particularly dramatic with respect to prison incarceration: fully 20 percent of black males will experience a prison term before reaching age 35, whereas this is the case with fewer than 3 percent of white males. White men are also more likely than black men to obtain a bachelor's degree and be married, whereas they are less likely to have been in military service.

Table 2.3. Percentage of U.S. black and white men experiencing life events by age 35

Life event	Whites	Blacks
All men		
Prison incarceration	2.9	20.3
Bachelor's degree	29.7	13.5
Military service	17.3	26.7
Marriage	83.0	69.4
Noncollege men		
Prison incarceration	5.3	29.9
High school diploma/GED	74.5	56.0
Military service	17.8	23.3
Marriage	83.8	67.3

Source: Pettit and Western 2001.

Serving a prison term is becoming almost a normal experience in some poor, minority communities. In fact, some communities are so severely affected by crime and imprisonment that they no longer even recognize it as a problem. Kurki (2000) reports that, during a Minnesota focus group on reentry, she asked a black man how his father's imprisonment during his childhood might have affected him negatively, and he answered that he had never really thought about it. Another man in that same focus group noted: "The criminal justice system has disrupted our families, kept women and men apart, and forced us to focus on just surviving rather than succeeding. . . . other people are getting ahead and we're just dealing with the system."

There are a number of reasons for the overrepresentation of racial minorities in prison, including overt discrimination, policies that have differential racial effects, and racial differences in committing the kinds of crimes that lead to imprisonment. However measured, rates of criminal offending among black Americans for many crime categories are much higher than comparable rates of offending among whites (Blumstein 2001; Tonry 1995). Especially for the crimes of homicide and armed robbery, black rates of offending have been eight and ten times the white rate. Blumstein (2001) found that, except for drug crimes and some property crimes, differential black imprisonment rates are explained almost entirely by differential rates of offending.

It is with respect to drug crimes that the United States stands alone in its punitive response and where the minority disproportionality is most evident. Michael Tonry (1995) argues that the war on drugs had a remarkably disproportionate effect on black American males. As shown in figure 2.2, the rate of prison drug admissions for black persons has escalated sharply over the past 15 years. While white drug admissions increased more than 7-fold between 1983 and 1998, Hispanic drug admissions increased 18-fold, and black drug admissions increased more than 26-fold.

Iguchi and colleagues note that these numbers are particularly disproportionate because, during that time period, Hispanics and blacks each made up only 11–12 percent of the U.S. population, while 72 percent of the U.S. population was white. Furthermore, past-month prevalence numbers in the 1999 National Household Survey indicate that only a slightly higher proportion of blacks than Hispanics and whites reported current use of illegal drugs (blacks 7.7 percent, Hispanics 6.8 percent, and whites 6.6 percent) (Iguchi et al. 2002).

The differential impact of the war on drugs is due more to drug-

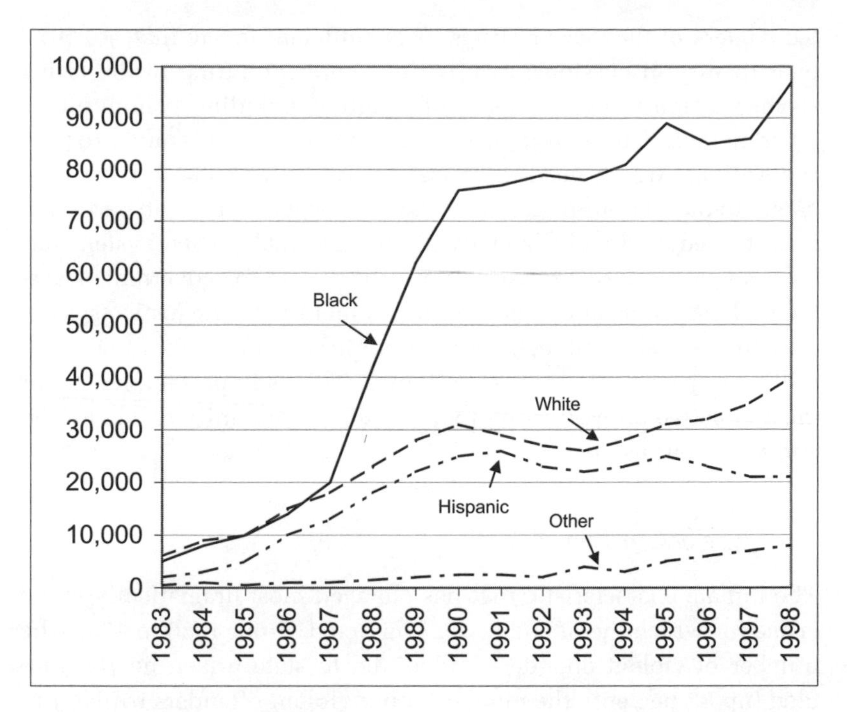

Figure 2.2. State and federal prison drug admissions by race, 1983–1998. *Source*: Iguchi et al. 2002.

law enforcement and sentencing than to higher patterns of minority drug use. Critics argue that whereas the police are *reactive* in responding to robbery, burglary, and other index offenses, they are *proactive* in dealing with drug offenses. Walker and his colleagues conclude: "There is evidence to suggest that police target minority communities—where drug dealing is more visible and where it is thus easier to make arrests—and tend to give less attention to drug activities in other neighborhoods" (Walker, Spohn, and DeLone 2002, p. 16).

It is also true that while the conviction rate for powdered cocaine is higher for whites and lower for minorities, minorities are much more likely to be convicted for crack-related offenses, which carry penalties that are one hundred times greater than those involving equivalent amounts of powdered cocaine. So many minority inmates, especially in the federal prison system, are serving long mandatory prison terms because they handled crystalline cocaine instead of powdered cocaine.

This is not the place to debate the racial disparities issue or the effectiveness of the war on drugs. It is sufficient to say that, for prisoner reentry discussions, race is the "elephant sitting in the living room." It affects every aspect of reentry, including communities, labor markets, family welfare, government entitlements, and program innovations, which need to be culturally appropriate. It eventually cuts into our notions of democracy, voting rights, and civic participation. Moreover, involvement with the criminal justice system has been shown to lead to distrust and disrespect for government systems. Greater alienation and disillusionment with the justice system also erodes residents' feelings of commitment and makes them less willing to participate in local activities. This is important, since our most effective crime-fighting tools require community collaboration and active engagement.

Type of Conviction Crime

The inmate characteristic that has changed most dramatically is the crime for which the offender was convicted. From 1980 to 1997, the number of violent offenders committed to state prison nearly doubled (up 82 percent); the number of nonviolent offenders tripled (up 207 percent); while the number of drug offenders increased 11-fold (up 1,040 percent) (Greene and Schiraldi 2002). Nonviolent offenders accounted for 77 percent of the growth in intake to America's state and federal prisons between 1978 and 1996.

As we think about reentry policies, it is also important to separate the in-prison population from the prison release population. People committed to prison for violent crimes serve longer prison terms on average than those committed for nonviolent or drug crimes. Violent offenders eventually get out, but not as quickly, and so their proportion in prison release cohorts is smaller. Nonviolent and drug offenders receive shorter sentences, and so they recycle back to the community faster than violent offenders. Hence, their proportion in prison release cohorts is larger. For this reason, analysts studying prisoner reentry examine prison release cohorts when the information is available, as in-prison data overrepresent the seriousness of the inmate population.

As shown in figure 2.3, drug offenders comprise an increasing percentage of state prison releases. Nearly 33 percent (177,000) of state prisoners released in 1999 were drug offenders (up from 26 percent in 1990 and 11 percent in 1985) (Hughes, Wilson, and Beck 2001). Sixteen percent of those being released from state prison were con-

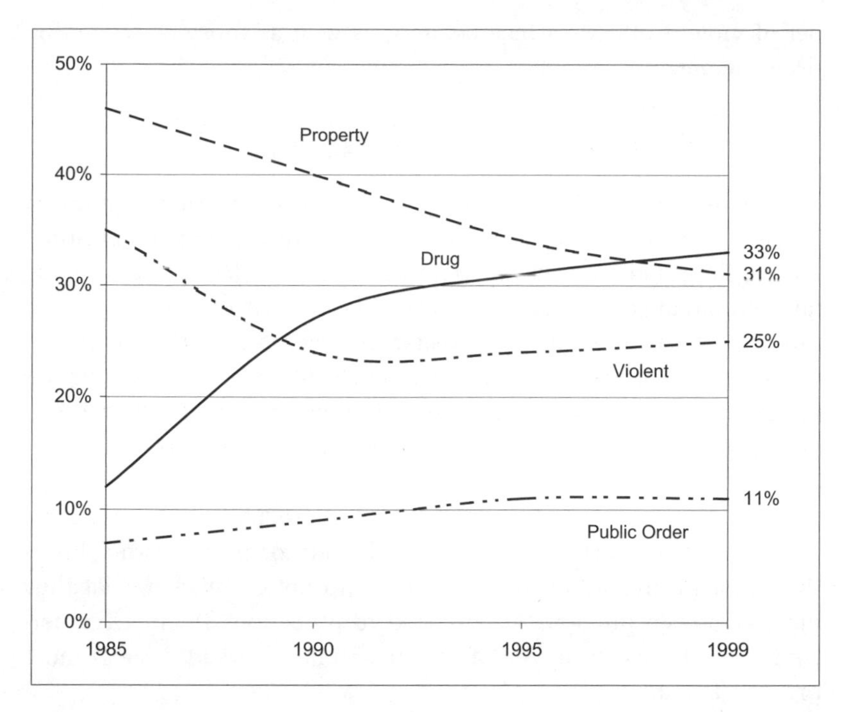

Figure 2.3. Releasees from state prison by conviction offense. *Source*: Hughes et al. 2001.

victed of drug possession, and 17 percent were convicted of drug trafficking. Inmates being released from federal prisons are even more likely to have been convicted of drug crimes: fully 60 percent of them were imprisoned for drug offense convictions.

Of course, some drug offenders are serious and belong in prison. The fact remains, however, that some fraction of imprisoned drug law violators are neither major drug traffickers nor persons who have committed other serious felonies. At present, it is impossible to know how many low-level "drug only" offenders are behind bars. We do know that between 1980 and 1998, the number of persons incarcerated for drug offenses in California increased 25-fold, with incarceration for simple possession outstripping incarceration for sales (Beatty, Holman, and Schiraldi 2000).

It is also important to note in figure 2.3 that 25 percent of *all* those released in 1999—more than 110,000 prisoners—were convicted of violent crimes (e.g., rape, robbery, assault). Blumstein and Beck's (1999) analyses show that the increase in prison populations has been caused by increases in *both* the length of sentence and the number of violent offenders incarcerated, as well as those convicted on drug charges.

Prior Criminal Record and Status at Arrest

Of course, it is not just a prisoner's current conviction crime that causes us concern; we also care about an inmate's prior criminal record. Repeated criminal convictions not only reflect disdain for the law, but having a prior criminal record is also one of the best predictors of parolee recidivism: the greater the prior record, the greater the recidivism (Gendreau, Little, and Goggin 1996). So, as we consider the public safety risks of releasing inmates to the community, it is useful to consider both their current crime and prior criminal history.

Table 2.4 shows that 44 percent of those being released from prison have *not* served a prior juvenile, jail, or prison term; this is their first incarceration. It is important to note, however, that they may have been previously sentenced to probation. Twenty-five percent of all those coming out of prison will have served three or more prior incarcerations.

Table 2.5 shows the status of prisoners when they were arrested for the crime that led to their current conviction. This table reveals that more than half (54 percent) of those being released from prison were on some conditional status (probation, parole, escape) when they were arrested for their most recent crime.

Literacy and Educational Attainment

While illiteracy and poor academic performance are not direct causes of criminal behavior, people who have received inadequate education or who exhibit poor literacy skills are disproportionately found within prisons. Among adult state prisoners, 19 percent are completely illiterate and 40 percent are functionally illiterate, compared to 4 percent and 21 percent, respectively, of the nonincarcerated public (Rubinstein 2001).

In terms of formal education levels, table 2.2 reveals that just 49 percent of state parole entrants in 1999 had a high school diploma or some college (compared to 85 percent for the adult population as a whole). Fifty-one percent of inmates were not high school graduates, and 11 percent of those being released had an eighth-grade education or less. Research consistently shows an inverse relationship between

Table 2.4. Prior incarcerations for state prison releasees, 1999

Number of prior incarcerations (jail or prison)	Violent	Property	Drug	Public order	Other crimes	All crime types combined
0	53%	38%	42%	35%	40%	44
1	19	20	23	22	42	21
2	10	10	10	11	11	10
3–5	11	19	16	18	0	15
6+	7	14	10	14	8	10

Note: Includes prior incarcerations in juvenile facilities.

Source: Bureau of Justice Statistics 2002b.

Table 2.5. Status when arrested for current crime, state prison releasees, 1999

	Most serious offense					
Criminal justice status at arrest	Violent	Property	Drug	Public order	Other crimes	All crime types combined
None	62%	38%	43%	31%	27%	46%
On probation	19	30	28	34	47	26
On parole	19	31	28	34	27	28
Escapee	0.5	0.9	0.5	1.1	0	0.7

Source: Bureau of Justice Statistics 2002b.

recidivism and education: the higher the education level, the less likely the person is to be rearrested or reimprisoned (Gottfredson, Wilson, and Najaka 2002).

It is promising that a larger percentage of parole entrants have a high school degree or have earned their general equivalency diploma (GED) than was the case in 1990. Yet, the percentage with "some college" has declined slightly. The decline of inmate college programs is likely due to the elimination of Pell grants to fund such programs.

Pell grants were popular in the 1970s and 1980s as a way for disadvantaged populations to receive funds to attend college. In 1994, the U.S. Congress specifically eliminated inmates from receiving federal Pell grants. The provision was designed to ameliorate the notion that prisons had become places of leisure and that inmates were given access to higher education at the expense of law-abiding taxpayers. Yet, inmates eligible for federal tuition assistance never received support at the expense of those in the free world. Pell grants were noncompetitive, need-based federal funds available to all qualifying low-income individuals who wished to attend college. Less than one-tenth of 1 percent of the total Pell annual budget was spent on inmate higher education (Rubinstein 2001).

Still, this financial support was perceived to be important to corrections. In 1990, there were 350 higher education programs for inmates. By 1997, there were just eight. In 2000, the Federal Bureau of Prisons modified its rules to make inmates responsible for their own college tuition costs. According to one study, higher education for inmates now faces "virtual extinction" (Corrections Compendium 1994, p. 10). Several states, including California, Florida, and Michigan, have no state-financed college programs for inmates. In most others, the programs generally serve only a small fraction of the prison population and tend to rely on charitable donations or the inmates themselves for financial support.

There is some evidence of a rebound in public sentiment for support of education programs in prison. Recent research examining the impact of prison education programs on recidivism rates in Maryland, Minnesota, and Ohio found that inmates who took any classes were 23 percent less likely than other convicts to be reimprisoned. That study concluded that every dollar spent on prison education yields more than two dollars in savings from avoiding reincarceration alone (Schmidt 2002). There are methodological problems with this study, in that there are key differences among inmates who enroll in education programs and those who do not, and many of these differences are related to recidivism. But many prison wardens also believe that prison education programs help maintain order in the prison because they offer inmates hope, occupy their waking hours, and work well into the prison reward system, since inmates are generally offered access to classes only if they behave well.

Physical Impairment and Mental Conditions

By any indicator, prison inmates and releasees are less healthy—both physically and mentally—than the population at large. Some felons are born with conditions that increase their probability of becoming involved with crime (e.g., attention deficit disorder). For others, their risky lifestyles, poor access to health care, and substance abuse histories take a heavy toll on their physical and mental health.

The BJS's publication *Medical Problems of Inmates* reported that nearly one-third of all state inmates and a quarter of federal inmates reported having some physical impairment or mental condition (see table 2.6) (Maruschak and Beck 2001). Ten percent of state inmates and 5 percent of federal inmates reported a learning disability, such as dyslexia or attention deficit disorder. Moreover, 13 percent of prisoners reported having two or more of these conditions.

These estimates are thought to underrepresent these conditions, however, since they were derived from personal interviews with inmates where they were asked a series of questions related to their physical and mental health. For example, the question in the Survey of Inmates in State and Federal Correctional Facilities asked: "Do you have . . . a learning disability, such as dyslexia or attention deficit disorder?" The accuracy of the estimates in table 2.6 therefore depends on the ability of inmates to recognize and report such problems. Yet, for most of these conditions, inmate self-reports are the only source of information, since most prison systems lack comprehensive and accessible data on the health status of their inmates.

Maruschak and Beck (2001) compared the rates of some physical impairments in the prison population with that in the general population and found the prevalence of speech disabilities among state inmates (3.7 percent) is more than three times higher than in the general U.S. population (1 percent). The percentage of inmates with impaired vision (8.3 percent) is more than twice as high as in the U.S. population (3.1 percent). The percentage with impaired hearing is lower among inmates (5.7 percent) than in the U.S. population (8.3 percent).

Because some of these differences result from differing age and

Table 2.6. Percentage of state and federal prison inmates with physical impairments or mental conditions

Physical or mental impairment	State inmates	Federal inmates
Any condition	31	23
Learning	10	5
Speech	4	2
Hearing	6	6
Vision	8	8
Mental	10	5
Physical	12	11
Condition limits ability to work	21	18

Source: Maruschak and Beck 2001.

gender distributions (e.g., a higher percentage of inmates are middle-aged and male), Maruschak and Beck further compared these conditions with U.S. population figures, standardizing for differences in age and gender. Even with these controls, they found that prisoners had higher rates of speech and vision impairments and slightly lower rates of hearing impairments.

The BJS survey also asked inmates if any of these conditions limited their ability to work and then compared the prisoner estimates with similar estimates from the National Adult Literacy Survey (NALS). Twenty-one percent of state and federal inmates reported having some condition that limited their ability to work (compared to 12 percent of the general U.S. population). This is an important consideration for reentry practices, since getting a job is one of the common requirements of parole release.

Researchers have long noted that inmates with disabilities have a harder time adjusting to prison, and their disabilities make them easy prey for other inmates. The BJS survey also asked inmates whether they had been injured in a fight since their admission to prison. Based on these self-reports, the BJS concluded that 7 percent of state inmates can be expected to be injured in a fight while in prison. The risk of being in a fight while in prison also increases with time served: inmates serving 5 years or more have a 16 percent chance of being injured in a fight while in prison (Maruschak and Beck 2001).

Wiebe and Petersilia (2000) used these self-report data to examine whether those who reported various physical and mental conditions were more likely to be injured while incarcerated. After controlling for a number of factors previously found to be related to the risk of prison injury and victimization (e.g., age, race, criminal history, past physical and sexual abuse, institutional factors, work assignment), they found that inmates reporting a mental disability were 1.4 times more likely to be injured while in custody. With regard to sexual assault, inmates reporting physical or mental disabilities were three times more likely to be sexually assaulted while incarcerated. Both of these results were statistically significant. Certainly, the very real pains of imprisonment—psychological and physical—affect the prospects of successfully transitioning to the free community.

Mental Illness

Persons with mental illness are increasingly criminalized and processed through the corrections system instead of the mental health system. In 1955, the number of mental health patients in state hospitals had reached a high of 559,000. New antipsychotic drugs were developed in the 1950s, and by prescribing them to people with mental illness, many could remain in the community rather than being placed in mental hospitals. This community-based alternative seemed more humane and less expensive than committing people to state hospitals. This fundamental change in mental health policy, known as deinstitutionalization, shifted the focus of care of persons with mental illness from psychiatric hospitals to local communities. As a result, states closed many of their mental hospitals, and by 2000, fewer than 70,000 persons remained in such facilities.

Unfortunately, persons with mental illness living in the community sometimes stop taking their medication. Sometimes, individuals cannot afford to buy the medicine. Sometimes, the medicines have uncomfortable side effects, and if patients think they are doing better, they stop taking the medication. Without the medication, the symptoms of mental illness return. If these people then begin committing crimes, they come to the attention of law enforcement. Since there are now fewer mental health hospitals, and we have more stringent criteria for involuntary commitment, many of them wind up in prison. Prison is not the place for a seriously mentally ill criminal. By and large, almost everyone agrees with that proposition in principle but not in practice. In recent years, a growing number of seriously mentally ill people has been sent to prison. Ultimately, most of them will be released to the community.

Few studies have directly measured the number of persons with mental illness in prison, and estimates vary widely on the proportion of inmates with various mental illnesses. Part of the problem in estimating prevalence rates results from differences in defining serious mental illness and in using assessment tools for research purposes. The BJS used prisoners' self-reports to examine rates of mental illness. Ditton (1999) reported that more than 16 percent of the state prison inmates reported in a personal interview an emotional illness or an overnight stay in a mental hospital or mental health facility. It is also clear that substance abuse problems and mental disorders often go hand in hand, particularly among correctional populations. It is estimated that 13 percent of the prison population has both a substance abuse and a mental health problem.

Because of the methodological issues involved in using inmate self-reports to establish the prevalence of mental health conditions, the National Commission on Correctional Health Care commissioned research from Veysey and Bichler-Robertson (2002) to establish the prevalence of psychiatric disorders in correctional settings. This paper concludes that the prevalence of certain mental health disorders in inmate populations is remarkably greater than that of the overall U.S. population. Their results are in table 2.7.

Despite the high prevalence of mental disorders in persons released from prisons, 75 percent of the parole administrators responding to a 1995 national survey reported that they do not have special programs for mentally ill clients. Administrators also note that mental disorders in parolee populations are likely to be ignored unless offenders' psychiatric symptoms are an explicit part of their offense, are specified in their release plans, or are obvious at the time of discharge.

There are also relatively few public mental health services available, and studies show that even when they are available, mentally ill parolees fail to access available treatment because they fear institutionalization, deny that they are mentally ill, or distrust the mental health system. A recent review of the topic concludes that overall persons with mental illness on parole are an underidentified and underserved population, and most parole officers are unable to handle the problems of these offenders successfully (Lurigio 2001).

One further point deserves mentioning. People with mental illness have no higher incidence of violent and nonviolent serious crime than the general population with the same age and socioeconomic circumstances. But Monahan (1996) reports that people who are both mentally ill and abusing drugs or alcohol (the "dually diagnosed") *do* have a higher incidence of committing violent and serious crimes. Treating them at release is a particularly high priority.

Table 2.7. Lifetime prevalence of mental illness in state prisoners versus U.S. population

Disease	State prisoners	U.S. population
Schizophrenia/other psychotic disorders	2.3–3.9%	.8%
Major depression	13–19	18
Anxiety disorder	22–30	NA
Bipolar (manic) disorder	2–4	1.5
Posttraumatic stress disorder	6–12	7
Dysthymia (less severe depression)	8–13	7

Source: National Commission on Correctional Health Care 2002.

Interestingly, a period of incarceration sometimes has positive consequences for the health status of a prisoner—in part, because adequate health care is constitutionally required and because the food and living environment are more conducive to better health outcomes than many situations in the community. Yet the consequences for a prisoner's mental health may be adverse. Haney (2002) notes that prisons do not, in general, make people "crazy." However, psychologists agree that, for some people, prison can produce negative, long-lasting change. Those prisoners who are mentally ill have a tougher time adjusting to prison life, and their symptoms may become more bizarre and threatening. They often are placed in segregation or, increasingly, held under supermax conditions. Haney, an expert on the psychological effects of imprisonment, says that, for persons who are mentally ill or developmentally disabled, "the rule-bound nature of institutional life may have especially disastrous consequences. Yet, both groups are too often left to their own devices to somehow survive in prison and leave without having had any of their unique needs addressed."

Prisoners with mental illness often refuse to take their medication (or are not prescribed the right dosage or medication) and then enter a vicious cycle in which their mental disease takes over, often causing hostile and aggressive behavior to the point that they break prison rules and end up in segregated units as management problems. The result, increasingly, is placement in punitive isolation or supermax facilities, where they are kept under conditions of unprecedented levels of social deprivation for unprecedented lengths of time. Haney concludes that such confinement creates its own set of psychological pressures, which, in some instances, uniquely disable prisoners for free world reintegration.

Kurki and Morris (2002) estimate that 1.2 percent of all prisoners (about 17,000) are now held in supermax units in the United States, and the number is increasing. Many of these prisoners are released directly from long-term isolation into free world communities. Haney recommends that strict time limits be placed on the use of punitive isolation and that all prisoners subjected to such conditions be provided with effective decompression programs in which they are reacclimated to the nature and norms of the free world.

As the proportion of prisoners with mental illness grows, in combination with the increasing use of maximum-security facilities, more prisoners with mental illness will surely find themselves in supermax conditions, and they will eventually be released to the community. The human and public safety consequences are severe, and serious thought should be given to mobilizing community resources to better support people with mental illness who return to the community from prison.

Employment

Employment remains one of the most important vehicles for hastening offender reintegration and desistance from crime, and there is fairly strong evidence to indicate that an individual's criminal behavior is responsive to changes in employment status (i.e., un-employment is associated with higher crime commission rates and more arrests). For a complete review, see Bushway and Reuter (2002).

In the survey of prison and jail inmates, the BJS asked inmates to self-report whether they were employed in the month prior to their arrest. As expected, prisoners in both federal and state facilities have poor employment histories. Thirty-one percent of state prisoners reported that they were unemployed in the month before their arrest, whereas this was the case with 27 percent of federal prisoners. During 1997, the year of this survey, just 7 percent of Americans over the age of 18 reported being unemployed. The prison survey also revealed that 5 percent of state prisoners and 3 percent of federal prisoners had *never* been employed (Government Accounting Office 2000).

Empirical evidence demonstrates that prisoners will have an extremely hard time finding employment after release. There is a serious stigma attached to a criminal history—particularly a prison record—in the legal labor market, and ex-offenders are often shut out from legitimate jobs. Surveys of employers reveal a great reluctance to hire felony offenders. Kling (2000) found that even if ex-prisoners are able to find a job, there is a substantial impact on future earnings (about 30 percent lower), and firms willing to hire ex-offenders tend to offer lower wages and fewer benefits. The impact of a prison record on future employment is discussed fully in chapter 6.

Employment prospects for ex-prisoners are further complicated by the fact that many of them have already developed behavior patterns that make holding a job quite difficult. Criminologists have documented that, over time, ex-offenders become "embedded" in criminality, and they gradually weaken their bonds to conventional society (e.g., attachment to parents, commitment to jobs and school).

After years of engaging in a criminal lifestyle, reestablishing these bonds becomes very difficult.

Detachment from conventional society is one of the primary reasons that job-training programs have not produced the positive outcomes for which proponents had hoped. After reviewing the results of such programs, Bushway and Reuter conclude:

> The overwhelming evidence from thirty years and billions of dollars of government spending is that it is very difficult to change an individual's employment status and earnings level (and therefore their crime participation), especially for those individuals most embedded in criminal activity. We believe the primary reason is that they themselves need to be motivated to work before things like job skills can make a difference; although unemployment may have contributed to their criminal activity, a job opportunity (and job skill training) by itself does not solve the problem. (Bushway and Reuter 2002, p. 221)

Newer job-training programs are focusing on both the individual-and community-level forces that operate to dissuade citizens from engaging in, and from returning to, crime.

Marital and Family Relationships

Marriage and Family

Legal employment and marriage are the two most prominent ties to conventional society for adults. A solid marriage can give a prisoner emotional support upon release, an immediate place to live, motivation to succeed, and possibly financial assistance until he gets his feet on the ground. On the other hand, marriage can also produce dynamics that contribute to family violence, substance abuse, and economic pressure. Strained marriages often end during imprisonment. Research reveals that prisoners are less likely to be married than persons who are not in prison, but these differences are partially due to age differences in the prison versus the general population. Just 17 percent of state prisoners and 30 percent of federal prisoners are married, compared to 61 percent of the U.S. general adult population.

Reviews of prisoners' family relationships yield two consistent findings: male prisoners who maintain strong family ties during imprisonment have higher rates of post-release success, and men who assume husband and parenting roles upon release have higher rates of success than those who do not (Hairston 2002). Presumably, female family relationships are similarly important, but there exist no data on that.

In a recent study of people's experiences during the first 30 days after release from jail or prison, the Vera Institute of Justice found that families provided critical support early on. A majority of the offenders lived with family and ate with them, and some received financial support as well. Family members helped to locate work and encouraged abstinence from drugs and compliance with treatment. The Vera study also found that people with strong family support had lower levels of recidivism. Offenders whose families accepted and supported them also had a higher level of confidence and were more successful and optimistic for their future (Nelson, Deess, and Allen 1999).

Some states (e.g., New York) have begun to realize the critical role that families can play in rehabilitation and are trying to include families as natural supports in rehabilitation and parole programs. For a review, see Shapiro (2001). Unfortunately, at the same time, we are also seeing policies that serve to sever ties between family members and inmates (e.g., greater restrictions on visitation). As Hairston recently concluded: "The correctional policies and practices that govern contact between prisoners and their families often impede, rather than support, the maintenance of family ties" (2002, p. 17).

Part of the move to make prisons "tougher" has included reducing the visits of children and family members. Of course, this is also done for security reasons, as family visits are one of the main ways that drugs and other contraband enter the prisons. But in terms of reentry, limiting family visits has significant implications for cutting the very contacts the inmate needs to succeed on the outside. As one parolee told the author, "If you come out of prison without a real support system of family and friends, nine out of ten times, you won't make it." Given what we know about the positive impact of family members on recidivism, we should be encouraging rather than discouraging family visitation.

Parenting and Contacts with Children

One of the most dramatic effects of the increase in the number of prisoners, particularly women, has been the impact on their children. There were about 72 million minor children living in the United States in 1999, and it has been determined that 2.1 percent of them had at least one parent in state or federal prison (Mumola 2000). That means that an estimated 1.5 million minor children had a parent in prison on any one day, a 50 percent increase since 1990.

As expected, there are more minority parents in prison than white parents. In terms of minor children, nearly 7 percent of African-American children, 3 percent of Hispanic children, and 1 percent of white children living in the United States had a parent incarcerated on any given day. It is important to recall that this is an estimate of the number of children with parents incarcerated on any *one* day. If one considers the lifetime probability of children having a parent in prison, the figure is much higher. More than 10 million children in the United States have parents who were imprisoned at some point in their children's lives. In some ways, children are the unseen victims of the prison boom and the war on drugs.

The BJS reports that, in 1997, 65 percent of women in state prison and 59 percent of women in federal prison had minor children. The majority were single mothers, with an average of two children, who prior to their arrests were the custodial parents. According to these parents, the children they left behind were young; nearly 60 percent were under 10 years old. Most commonly, grandparents become the caregivers (53 percent of the time for state prisoners). About 10 percent of the children of mothers in state prisons and 4 percent of the children of mothers in federal prisons were in foster care (Mumola 2000).

Certainly, sometimes, children are better off separated from a parent who commits a crime, especially if the parent has been abusive or involved with illegal substances. We know that children who grow up with parents who are criminally involved have a high probability of engaging in delinquent behavior. In their meta-analysis of 34 prospective longitudinal studies of the development of antisocial behavior, Lipsey and Derzon (1998) found that having an antisocial parent or parents was one of the strongest predictors of violent or serious delinquency in adolescence and young adulthood. Certainly, removing the negative influence of a parent can result in both positive and negative outcomes for the children, but we have virtually no data on this.

Most imprisoned mothers plan to reunite with their children at release, and they cite separation from their children as one of the most difficult aspects of imprisonment. A parent's imprisonment is also a traumatizing event for most children. Studies have indicated that children may suffer from separation anxiety and depression, are preoccupied with their loss, and experience a pervading sense of sadness (Parke and Clarke-Stewart 2001). Boys are more likely to exhibit externalizing behavior problems, while girls are more likely to display internalizing problems.

An important determinant of a child's adjustment to a parent being in prison is regular contact with the incarcerated parent. Children who visit their parents more often and under better visiting conditions exhibit fewer adjustment problems. Some prisoners resist the idea of being visited by their children, thinking that the visit will produce negative reactions in the children, but there is no evidence of any long-term negative responses (Parke and Clarke-Stewart 2001). Visiting can calm children's fears about their parents' welfare as well as their concerns about the parents' feelings for them.

While visits and phone calls are one way to assist many children, they are increasingly difficult to maintain. According to the BJS, 54 percent of mothers in state prison report having *no* personal visits with their children since their admission. Geographical distance to a prison, lack of transportation, the relationship of the prisoner with the children's caregiver, and the inability of a caregiver to bring a child to a correctional facility are the reasons most often cited for a lack of visits (Covington 2002). Visitation hours are often scheduled at inconvenient times, usually during the day, when most caregivers are working. And due to the greater security and contraband concerns of prison officials, the conditions are often cumbersome and uncomfortable for visitors. As one inmate told the author:

> In my own experience, I have noticed that prison officials often disrespect visitors, the huge majority being women and children, [who are] treated as bad, if not worse, than convicts while undergoing the visiting process. The prisoners have lots of legal protections concerning how they are handled; the visitors do not. They are patronized, made to wait exorbitant amounts of time, told what types of clothing is permitted, and generally treated as burdens rather than human beings. My own mother's experience at one California facility was so bad I told her to never come see me there again.

The primary method of contact between parents and their children is mail, closely followed by telephone, and least by personal contact. All types of visitation between parents and their children wane as time goes by. Children are most likely to visit their mothers in the first year and less likely to do so after this initial period. Recent analysis by Lynch and Sabol (2001) shows that all types of contacts with children (i.e., calls, letters, visits) decrease as the length of time served in prison increases, and both calls and letters from family members have declined since 1991 (see figure 2.4).

With prisons often in remote locations (especially female prisons), phone calls are often the only practical means to keep in touch with family members. But prison phone calls have become very expensive, often $1 to $3 a minute. Maryland prisoners, for example, have to pay more than $10 for a 10-minute long-distance call (local calls are 85 cents each, but may increase shortly to $2). Despite the fact that technology has lowered the costs of long distance to the general public in recent years, and rates of less than 20 cents per minute are widely advertised, the rates charged to families of prisoners remain high and are increasing.

The higher cost of prisoner phone calls is attributed to the fact that they are collect calls, but the prisoner has no choice because most states only allow prisoners to make collect calls. A recent report on the Maryland situation concluded: "The margin of profit is so

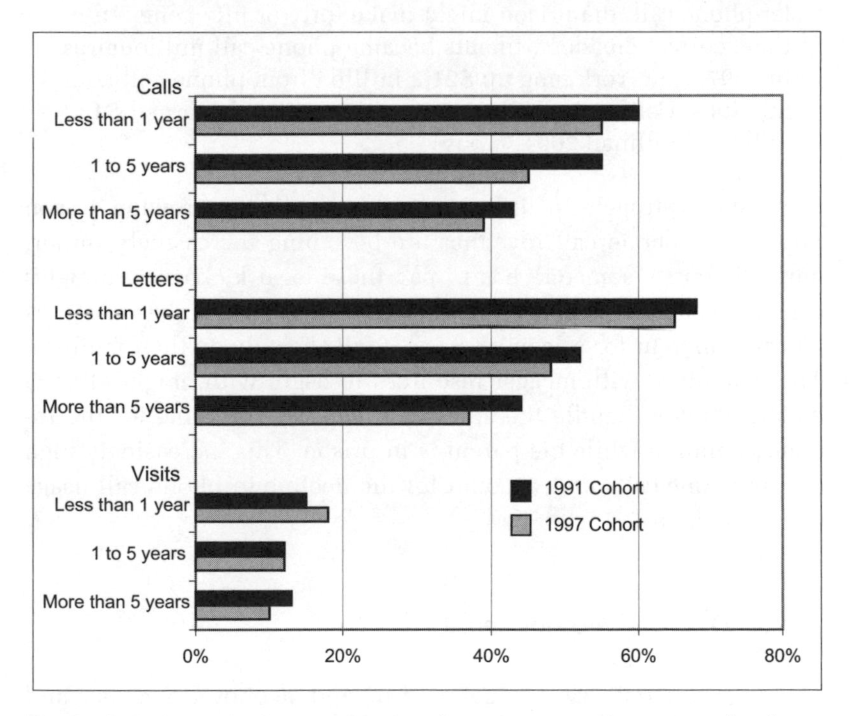

Figure 2.4. State inmates releasing in next year: Percentage having weekly contact with children, by method and length of stay, 1991 versus 1997. *Source*: Lynch and Sabol 2001.

great that the telephone company is able to pay 'commissions' to the State equal to 42 percent of the total billed price of the calls" (Maryland Justice Policy Institute 2002). Not only are the prices high, but in states such as California, calls are interrupted about every 20 seconds by a mechanical robotic voice, which comes on the line and says, "This is a call from a California prison inmate."

Inmate telephone calls have become an important source of revenue for both the prison and the company supplying them. A pay phone at a prison can generate as much as $15,000 a year—about five times the revenue of a typical pay phone on the street. It is estimated that inmate calls generate a billion dollars or more in revenues each year, and as Hallinan writes, prisons get kickbacks from these calls:

> AT&T estimated that inmates place $1 billion a year in long-distance phone calls. But unlike you and me, the inmates don't get to pick their long-distance carrier—the prison does. And so AT&T and its competitors learned that the way to get inmates as customers was to give the prison a legal kickback: on a one-dollar phone call, the prison might make forty or fifty cents. In no time, corrections departments became phone-call millionaires. In 1997, New York rang up $21.2 million from phone-call commissions. California made $17.6 million. Florida earned $13.8 million. (Hallinan 2001, p. xiv)

As states struggle to find funding to support a growing prison population, phone call revenues are becoming increasingly important. Of course, someone has to pay these legal kickbacks. Inmates can not usually afford these charges, since they may make as little as 25 cents an hour for prison work, so it falls heavily on their families. These families, with meager resources to begin with, might already be struggling to handle the additional expense of caring for the inmate's children while the parent is in prison. This increasingly high cost of phone calls may account for the decline in phone call usage shown in figure 2.4.

Drug and Alcohol Abuse

There are different ways to define drug and alcohol use, abuse, and involvement. There are no studies that systematically measure the prevalence of alcoholism, drug abuse and drug dependency/addiction disorders in correctional facilities, as defined by the American

Psychological Association's *Diagnostic Statistical Manual.* Nevertheless, there can be no doubt that substance abuse disproportionately affects prisoners, that sustained treatment is rare, and that continued use contributes to recidivism.

Twenty-one percent of all state prisoners at the end of 1999 had drug convictions as their most current offense. In 1999, drug offenders in both state and federal prisons reported crack and powdered cocaine as the drugs most commonly involved in the current conviction, followed by heroin, other opiates, and marijuana (Government Accounting Office 2000). But a much higher percentage of prisoners are drug addicted or drug involved. Inmates were asked to self-report their involvement with various substances, and these reports were used to compile the information in table 2.8. Nearly two-thirds of inmates (59 percent) reported using drugs in the month before they committed their current crime, and more than one-third (34 percent) said they were under the influence of drugs at the time they committed their crime. Fewer prison inmates (25 percent) reported that they were "alcohol dependent" prior to imprisonment but 36 percent of inmates reported abusing alcohol at the time of their most recent crime.

Whether or not prison is the answer for the drug user or drug seller is the subject of much public debate, as is the appropriate method of effective treatment. We do know that the vast majority of prison inmates with substance abuse problems do not receive treatment in prison. Of the soon-to-be-released group members who were using

Table 2.8. Self-reported substance abuse among reentering state prisoners

	Percentage of reentering inmates
Drug/alcohol use	74
Drug use	
In month before offense	59
At time of offense	34
Intravenous use in past	22
Alcohol abuse	
Binge drinker	42
Alcohol dependent	25
At time of offense	36

Note: Reentering inmates are those expected to be released within the next 12 months.

Source: Beck 2000.

drugs or alcohol in the month prior to their incarceration, only 18 percent of the drug users and 22 percent of the alcohol abusers had participated in treatment since prison admission (Beck 2000). According to the National Center on Addiction and Substance Abuse (1998), states spend 5 percent of their prison budget on drug and alcohol treatment; the Bureau of Prisons spends less than 1 percent. Chapter 5 discusses the extent of drug and alcohol treatment within prisons.

Of course, lack of treatment for substance-abusing prisoners endangers the public. Alcohol is linked more closely with violent crimes than are drugs. More than 20 percent of inmates in state and federal prisons for violent crimes were under the influence of alcohol—and no other substance—when they commited their crimes. In contrast, at the time of their crimes, only 3 percent of violent offenders were under the influence of cocaine or crack alone, only 1 percent under the influence of heroin alone. Continued criminality is also highly related to substance use and abuse. More than 40 percent of first-time offenders have a history of drug use. The proportion increases to more than 80 percent with five or more prior convictions.

Releasing substance abusers from prison without treatment maintains the market for illegal drugs and keeps drug dealers in business. As the National Center on Addiction and Substance Abuse put it, "Release of untreated drug- and alcohol-addicted inmates is tantamount to visiting criminals on society" (1998, p. vii). The cost-benefit analysis shown in table 9.1 suggests that even if we spent an average of $3,100 per year per offender for substance abuse treatment for inmates, it would pay for itself in terms of savings in justice system and victim costs.

AIDS and Other Infectious Diseases

Prisoners have significantly more medical problems than does the general population, due to lifestyles that often include crowded or itinerant living conditions, prior intravenous (IV) drug use, poverty, and high rates of substance abuse. In fact, in prisons, "older" persons are commonly considered to be 50 years or older, in part because the health of the average 50-year-old prisoner approximates the average health condition of persons 10 years older in the free community (McDonald 1999).

When examined in terms of the prevalence of infectious disease among the prisoners, some 2–3 percent of individuals in the prison population are HIV-positive or have AIDS, a rate five times higher than the general population. However, there is considerable variation in HIV-positive rates across states: 50 percent of all known prison cases are concentrated in New York, Florida, and Texas. Eighteen percent of all U.S. prisoners are infected with hepatitis C, nine to ten times the rate of the general population (Hammett, Harmon, and Maruschak 1999). The Centers for Disease Control found the rate of prison inmates with tuberculosis (TB) to be six times that of the general population.

Communicable diseases move quickly among prisoners because they live in close quarters, and there have been recent outbreaks that caused public health officials to worry (e.g., TB in three Alabama state prisons in 1999 and in South Carolina in 2000). Public health experts predict that these rates will continue to escalate within prisons and eventually make their way to the streets, particularly as we incarcerate more drug offenders, many of whom engage in intravenous drug use, share needles, or trade sex for drugs.

According to an analysis conducted for Congress by the National Commission on Correctional Health Care, during 1997, between 20 and 26 percent of the nation's individuals living with HIV or AIDS, 29–32 percent of the people with hepatitis C, and 38 percent of those with tuberculosis were released from a correctional facility that year (see table 2.9).

HIV/AIDS is rising rapidly among women, and women in state prisons are now more likely than men to be infected with HIV (3.4 percent of female inmates compared to 2.1 percent of male inmates). HIV infection rates among females are predominantly related to injecting drugs, crack use, and prostitution for drugs. Female crack smokers tend to have more sex partners, are more likely than other female drug users to exchange sex for drugs, and have a higher prevalence of HIV infection in comparison to other female drug users. Officials report, however, that HIV rates in prison leveled off in 2002, and AIDS-related prison deaths have declined.

Interestingly, incarcerated inmates may have greater access to medical care than those with similar sociodemographic characteristics not serving time in a correctional facility. Prison inmates have access to free health care as result of the 1976 U.S. Supreme Court case *Estelle v. Gamble* (1975). *Estelle* concluded that inmates have a constitutional right to reasonable, adequate health services for serious medical needs. However, the Court also made clear that such a right did not mean that prisoners have unqualified access to health

Table 2.9. Infectious disease among people passing through state and federal correctional facilities, 1997

Condition	Est. number of prison releasees with condition	Total number in U.S. population with condition	Releasees with condition as percentage of total population with condition
AIDS	39,000	247,000	16
HIV infection	112,000–158,000	503,000	22–31
Total HIV/AIDS	151,000–197,000	750,000	20–26
Hepatitis B infection	155,000	1–1.25 million	12–16
Hepatitis C infection	1.3–1.4 million	4.5 million	29–32
Tuberculosis	12,000	32,000	38

Source: Hammett et al. 2002.

care. Lower courts have held that the Constitution does not require that the medical care provided to prisoners be perfect, the best obtainable, or even very good. The courts have supported the principle of least eligibility and said that prison conditions—including the delivery of health care—must be a step below those of the working class and people on welfare. As a result, prisoners are denied access to medical specialists, second opinions, prompt delivery of medical services, technologically advanced diagnostic techniques, the latest medications, and up-to-date medical procedures.

On average, prisoners draw heavily on available health care services while incarcerated. One reason for this is that prisoners are generally in worse health than nonincarcerated persons. The cost of providing health care services in the prisons has been increasing rapidly in recent years. A survey by the National Commission on Correctional Health Care found that state departments of correction budgeted $2.3 billion in 1995 to support inmate health care services, or approximately $2,308 per inmate. This is an increase of 160 percent in the per-prisoner expenditure over 1982 (estimated at $883 per prisoner). A recent survey found that this per-inmate cost is increasing and is now closer to $3,300 per inmate (American Correctional Association 2000). Medical budgets comprised, on average, 10 percent of corrections agencies' total operating budgets in 1999. But in states where inmates have higher health care needs, the costs are much greater. For example, California spends 16 percent of its entire corrections budget on health care.

Prisoners are the only U.S. citizens with a constitutional right to health care. But upon release, most are unable to access programs to maintain any health benefits accrued during imprisonment or to access some of the medications they previously were prescribed. Many return to unhealthy lifestyles and have the potential for spreading disease (particularly, tuberculosis, hepatitis, and AIDS). In New York City, for example, a major multidrug-resistant form of tuberculosis emerged in 1989, with 80 percent of all cases being traced to jails and prisons. By 1991, the Rikers Island jail had one of the highest TB rates in the nation. In Los Angeles, an outbreak of meningitis in the county jail moved into the surrounding neighborhoods.

Public health experts have begun to work more closely with corrections officials to collaborate on health-related reentry programs. Whether this capacity exists and whether criminal justice supervision could increase the likelihood of healthy outcomes are open questions. For an excellent review, see Rossman (2002).

Geographical Concentration

Finding housing and jobs for ex-prisoners has always been difficult, but it appears to be worse now. Evidence by Lynch and Sabol (2001) has found that prisoners are increasingly being released to a small number of urban "core counties." Within these core counties, ex-prisoner concentrations are even more pronounced because releasees are increasingly focused in a few neighborhoods within these core counties.

Lynch and Sabol found that, of all offenders in Ohio prisons, 20 percent resided in Cuyahoga County, which contains the city of Cleveland (which accounts for 12 percent of the state's population), before they were incarcerated. They report further that just 3 percent of all Cuyahoga County's census block groups accounted for most of those sent to Ohio's state prisons. They found also that in these "high-rate block groups," the estimated one-day incarceration rate averaged about 1.5 percent of the resident population. But, for black men between the ages of 18 and 19, the estimated one-day incarceration rate was between 8 and 15 percent. They documented a similar concentration in Brooklyn, New York, where 11 percent of the city blocks accounted for 20 percent of the Brooklyn population, but 50 percent of the parolees in the city.

Further analyses revealed that repeat offenders (those who had previously failed on parole) were increasingly concentrated in these core counties. In 1984, an estimated 42 percent of subsequent releasees (offenders released for at least the second time on an original sentence) returned to a core county. By 1996, this increased to an estimated 75 percent. These "churners" were primarily convicted of drug crimes, and the Lynch and Sabol analysis suggests that these are exactly the offenders who are being increasingly concentrated in core communities.

These data have wide-ranging implications. If most parolees remain unemployed and homeless, the social characteristics of neighborhoods begin to change in ways that affect crime rates. There are "tipping points," beyond which communities are no longer able to exert positive influences on the behavior of residents. Norms start to change, disorder and incivilities increase, out-migration follows, and crime and violence increase.

Elijah Anderson vividly illustrates the breakdown of social cohesion in socially disorganized communities. Moral authority increasingly is vested in street-smart young men for whom drugs and crime are a way of life. Attitudes, behaviors, and lessons learned in prison are transmitted into the free society. Anderson concludes that as "family caretakers and role models disappear or decline in influence, and as unemployment and poverty become more persistent, the community, particularly its children, becomes vulnerable to a variety of social ills, including crime, drugs, family disorganization, generalized demoralization and unemployment" (Anderson 1990, p. 4).

Prison gangs have growing influence in inner-city communities. Joan Moore notes that most California prisons are violent and dangerous places, and new inmates search for protection and connections. Many find both in gangs. Inevitably, gang loyalties are exported to the neighborhoods. The revolving prison door strengthens street gang ties. Moore commented, "In California . . . I don't think the gangs would continue existing as they are without the prison scene" (Moore 1996, p. 73). Moore also found that state-raised youth, whose adolescence involved recurring trips to California juvenile detention facilities, were the most committed to the most crime-oriented gangs. She warns that, as more young people are incarcerated earlier in their criminal careers, larger numbers of youths will come out of prison with hostile attitudes and will exert strong negative influences on neighborhoods.

Several criminologists have begun to explore the focus of reentry well beyond families to include the social ecology and place-based conditions of everyday life where offenders reside. They explore the counterintuitive notion that crime rates go *up* in those neighborhoods where the greatest concentration of offenders returns and in those that send a lot of people to prison.

Rose and colleagues (1999) explored the direct effects of offenders going to prison and returning to their home communities after one year in prison. They theorized that the aggregate impact of high levels of incarceration would be damaging to networks of social control and would decrease the legitimacy of formal social control. In their model, when public control occurs at high levels, informal controls function less effectively. The result is more crime. They tested their theory in Tallahassee, Florida, and found support for the proposition that spatial concentrations of incarcerated individuals promote higher-than-expected rates of crime. Using the "neighborhood" as the level of analysis, they found that low rates of prison admissions were associated with no drop in crime the following year; moderate rates of admissions were associated with moderate drops in crime; and higher rates of admission—after a tipping point was reached of about 1.5 percent of the neighborhood's total population—had a strong, positive relationship to crime in the following year. This result supports the idea that high rates of admitting people to prison can destabilize informal networks of social control and lead to increases in crime.

Conclusions

It is clear that prisoner reentry is not just about the greater number of prisoners returning home, although that certainly challenges parole authorities to provide more services with fewer resources. But this chapter has revealed that the average inmate coming home will have served a longer prison sentence than in the past, be more disconnected from family and friends, have a higher prevalence of substance abuse and mental illness, and be less educated and employable than those in prior prison release cohorts. Each of these factors is known to predict recidivism, yet few of these needs are addressed while the inmate is in prison or on parole. To understand the philosophies and programs that influence parole and prison today, it is useful to appreciate their evolution and use in modern sentencing practices, which is the subject of the next chapter.

THREE

The Origins and Evolution of Modern Parole

Parole is often misunderstood, and the general public confuses it with probation. Parole is similar to probation in that both refer to the supervision of an offender who lives and works in the community. Offenders on parole, however, have served prison terms and been released to the community under parole supervision. But since its beginnings, parole has come under attack, and demands for reform have been continuous.

Beginning in the late 1970s, state after state began abolishing discretionary parole boards, and by 2002, 16 states had done so, and three out of four inmates being released from prison were released automatically at the end of a prescribed prison term, rather than through a parole hearing. Proponents hoped that abolishing parole would reduce disparities in prison time served, and it has. Proponents also hoped that abolishing parole would tie the hands of parole boards, which were often accused of letting inmates out early. Recent research shows, however, that inmates actually serve *longer* prison terms in states retaining discretionary parole, and those states' parolees have higher success rates. Retaining discretionary parole may serve to refocus prison staff and corrections staff on planning for release, not just opening the door at release. Importantly, discretionary parole systems also provide a means by which inmates who represent continuing public safety risks can be kept in prison. The last state to abolish parole was Wisconsin in 1999, and several states are now reconsidering the wisdom of reducing parole boards' discretionary authority.

Early European Foundations and Growth of Parole

Parole comes from the French word *parol*, referring to "word," as in giving one's word of honor or promise. It has come to mean an inmate's promise to conduct herself in a law-abiding manner and according to certain rules in exchange for release. Parole is part of the general nineteenth-century trend in criminology that progressed from punishment to reformation.

Chief credit for developing the early parole system is given to Captain Alexander Maconochie (1787–1860), who was in charge of the English penal colony at Norfolk Island, off the coast of Australia. Maconochie criticized definite prison terms and developed a system of rewards for good conduct, labor, and study. Through his classification procedure, called the "mark system," prisoners could progress through stages of increasing responsibility and ultimately gain freedom. The five stages in his system were (1) strict imprisonment, (2) labor on government chain gangs, (3) freedom within a limited area, (4) a ticket of leave on parole, resulting in a conditional pardon, and (5) full restoration of liberty. He assumed that prisoners should be prepared for a gradual, conditional release to full freedom.

In 1840, Maconochie was given an opportunity to apply these principles as superintendent of the Norfolk Island penal settlement in the South Pacific. Under his direction, task accomplishment, not time served, was the criterion for release. Marks of commendation were given to prisoners who performed their tasks well, and they were released from the penal colony as they demonstrated a willingness to accept society's rules.

Norval Morris notes that Maconochie was a true visionary. Up until his time, prison sentences carried no element of positive conditioning. Inmates served their prison terms working as convicts for the state or as indentured laborers for free citizens. When their terms were completed, they were freed. During the prison term, harsh physical punishment ensured obedience. Maconochie found this system ineffective and reprehensible. He believed that criminals would not change for the better by deterrent brutality but rather through education or training. Maconochie wrote, "When a man keeps the key of his own prison he is soon persuaded to fit it to the lock" (cited in Morris, 2002, p. 178).

Inmates were given marks as rewards for work and good behavior, and the marks were withdrawn for misbehavior. A ticket of leave (i.e., furlough) and a small house and farm were positive incentives when sufficient marks had been earned. Maconochie believed that time in prison should not be "time defined" but should be "work defined." The exact sentence an inmate would serve should always be indeterminate, dependent upon the completion of a defined amount of work and the prisoner's behavior during confinement. In that sense, inmates could actively participate in the termination of their sentences. He also believed that "freedom must be tested in the laboratory of the world and not the unreal world of the prison; hence supervision of conformity until full autonomy was achieved and free citizenship regained" (cited in Morris 2002, p. 182).

Morris notes that, in just four years, Maconochie transformed what was one of the most brutal convict settlements in history into a controlled, stable, and productive environment. Inmates released from his prison reportedly achieved such success upon release that they came to be called "Maconochie's Gentlemen." His ideas provided the foundation for work furlough, parole, and indeterminate sentencing. Maconochie's principal biographer, Sir John Barry, wrote: "Maconochie formulated the conceptions on which modern penology is based, and he put them into practical operation" (cited in Morris 2002, p. 184).

Returning to England in 1844 to campaign for penal reform, Maconochie tried to implement his reforms when he was appointed governor of the new Birmingham Borough prison in 1849. However, he was unable to institute his reforms there because he was dismissed from his position in 1851 on the grounds that his methods were too lenient.

Sir Walter Crofton attempted to implement Maconochie's mark system when he became the administrator of the Irish prison system in 1854. Crofton felt that prisons should be directed more toward reformation and that tickets of leave should be awarded to prisoners who had shown achievement and positive attitude change. After instituting strict imprisonment, Crofton began transferring offenders to "intermediate prisons," where they could accumulate marks based on work, good behavior, and educational improvement. Eventually, they were also given tickets of leave and released on parole supervision.

Most significant, in terms of Crofton's historical contribution, was his requirement that parolees submit monthly reports to the police. In Dublin, a special civilian inspector helped those released find jobs, visited them periodically, and supervised their activities. The modern-day parole officer had thus been born.

The Genesis of American Parole

By 1865, American penal reformers were well aware of the reforms achieved in the European prison systems, particularly in the Irish system. At the Cincinnati meeting of the National Prison Association in 1870, a paper by Crofton was read, and specific references to the Irish system were incorporated into the Declaration of Principles, along with other reforms, such as indeterminate sentencing and classification for release based on a mark system. Because of Crofton's experiment, many Americans referred to parole as "the Irish system."

Zebulon Brockway (1827–1920), a Michigan penologist, is given credit for implementing the first parole system in the United States. He proposed a two-pronged strategy for managing prison populations and preparing inmates for release: indeterminate sentencing coupled with parole supervision. He was given a chance to put his proposal into practice in 1876, when he was appointed superintendent at a new youth facility, the Elmira Reformatory in New York. He instituted a system of indeterminacy and parole release and is commonly credited as the father of both in the United States. His ideas reflected the tenor of the times: the beliefs that criminals could be reformed and that every prisoner's treatment should be individualized.

On being admitted to Elmira, each inmate (males between the ages of 16 and 30) was placed in the second grade of classification. Six months of good conduct meant promotion to the first grade, while misbehavior could result in being placed in the third grade, from which the inmate would have to work his way back up. Continued good behavior in the first grade resulted in release. Paroled inmates remained under the jurisdiction of authorities for an additional six months, during which the parolee was required to report on the first day of every month to his appointed volunteer guardian (from which parole officers evolved) and provide an account of his situation and conduct. Written reports became required and, after being signed by the parolee's employer and guardian, were submitted to the institution.

Indeterminate sentencing and parole spread rapidly through the United States. In 1907, New York became the first state to formally adopt all of the components of a parole system: indeterminate sentences, a system for granting release, postrelease supervision, and specific criteria for parole revocation. By 1927, only three states (Florida, Mississippi, and Virginia) were without a parole system, and by 1942, all of the states and the federal government had such systems.

The percentage of U.S. prisoners released on discretionary parole rose from 44 percent in 1940 to a high of 72 percent in 1977, after which some states began to question the very foundations of parole, and the number of prisoners released in this fashion began to decline. As shown in figure 3.1, discretionary parole boards released just 24 percent of state prisoners in 1999. This is the lowest figure since the federal government began compiling statistics on this issue. This has important practical implications since, over time, a growing number of inmates are automatically released after they have served a preset number of months. The number of months to be served is usually based on a combination of their prior record and crime seriousness, not their suitability for release based on various risk criteria.

Mandatory parole now surpasses discretionary parole releases. Mandatory parole is basically a matter of bookkeeping: one calculates the amount of time served plus good time and subtracts it from the prison sentence imposed. When the required number of months has been served, prisoners are automatically released, conditionally, to parole supervision for the rest of the sentence. Parole supervision generally lasts one to three years, but can last much longer in some states (e.g., Texas parole terms are often ten to twenty years). Manda-

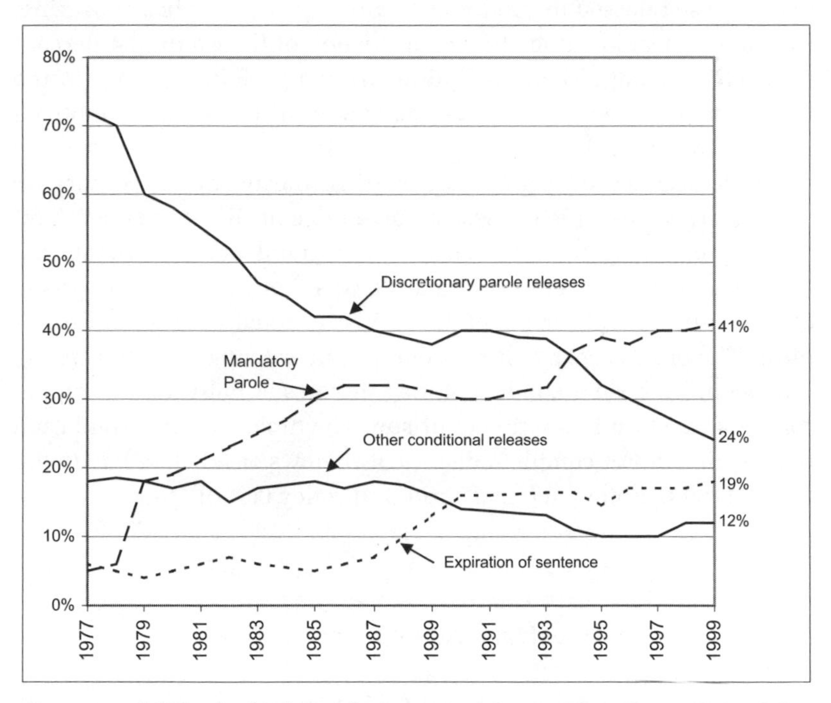

Figure 3.1. Method of release from state prison, 1977–1999. *Note*: Other conditional releases include commutations, pardons, and deaths. *Source*: Hughes et al. 2001.

tory parole is used by federal jurisdictions and states with determinate sentences and parole guidelines.

Figure 3.1 also shows a significant increase in the number of prisoners released through expiration of sentence, or "maxing out." This refers to inmates who are released without any further correctional supervision and who cannot be returned to prison for any remaining portion of a sentence for a current offense. These prisoners have been incarcerated until the end of their legally imposed sentence. In 1999, 19 percent—or nearly one in five inmates—left prison after their sentence had expired, without any parole supervision or reporting requirements. Sometimes, prisoners who have maxed out are the more serious inmates, as they may not have gained good time in states that grant it nor been granted early parole in states that still utilize discretionary parole boards. But in determinate-sentencing states, once inmates have served their full court-imposed prison sentence, the state must release them outright, with no further reporting requirements.

If one adds up those released at the expiration of sentence and those released on mandatory parole, there is a growing imbalance between those released discretionarily, through a parole board hearing, and those released automatically at the end of their term (24 percent versus 60 percent). The implications of this profound change in the way inmates are returned to the free community has gone unnoticed and undebated by the U.S. public.

Parole seemed, during the first half of the twentieth century, to make perfect sense. First, it was believed to contribute to prisoner reform, by encouraging participation in programs aimed at rehabilitation. Second, the power to grant parole was thought to provide prison officials with a tool for maintaining institutional control and discipline. The prospect of a reduced sentence in exchange for good behavior encouraged better conduct among inmates. Finally, release on parole, as a "back end" solution to prison crowding, was important from the beginning. For complete historical reviews, see Petersilia (1996), Simon (1993), Rothman (1980), and Bottomley (1990).

Early Twentieth-Century Parole: The Conflict between Growth and Adaptation

The tremendous growth in parole as a concept, however, did not imply uniform development, public support, or quality practices. As Bottomley writes, "It is doubtful whether parole ever really operated consistently in the United States either in principle or practice" (1990, p. 326). Moreover, parole-as-rehabilitation was never taken very seriously, and from its inception, prison administrators used parole primarily to manage prison crowding and reduce inmate violence.

Despite its expanded usage, parole was controversial from the start. A Gallup poll conducted in 1934 revealed that 82 percent of U.S. adults believed that parole was not strict enough and should not be granted as frequently. Today, parole is still unpopular, and a 1998 survey shows that 80 percent of Americans favor making parole more difficult to obtain. A comparable percentage is opposed to granting parole a second time to inmates who previously have been granted parole for a serious crime. On the other hand, the public significantly underestimates the amount of time inmates serve, so their lack of support for parole may reflect that misperception.

Nonetheless, over time, the positivistic approach to crime and criminals—which viewed the offender as "sick" and in need of help—began to influence parole release and supervision. The rehabilitation ideal, as it came to be known, affected all of corrections well into the 1960s and gained acceptance for the belief that the purpose of incarceration and parole was to change the offender's behavior rather than simply to punish. As Rhine (1996) notes, as the rehabilitative ideal evolved, indeterminate sentencing in tandem with parole acquired a newfound legitimacy. It also gave legitimacy and purpose to parole boards, which were supposed to be composed of "experts" in behavioral change, and it was their responsibility to discern that moment during confinement when the offender was rehabilitated and thus suitable for release.

Mid–Twentieth-Century Parole: The Conflict between Release and Rehabilitation

Parole boards, usually composed of political appointees, used to have broad discretion to determine when an offender was ready for release—a decision limited only by the constraints of the maximum sentence imposed by the judge. Parole boards—usually composed of no more than 10 individuals—also had the authority to rescind an established parole date, issue warrants and subpoenas, set conditions of supervision, restore offenders' civil rights, and grant final discharges. In most states, they also ordered the payment of restitution or supervision fees as a condition of parole release.

In the early years, there were few standards governing the decision to grant or deny parole, and decision-making rules were not made public. One of the long-standing criticisms of paroling authorities is that their members are too often selected based on party loyalty and political patronage rather than on professional qualifications and experience.

In *Conscience and Convenience* (1980), David Rothman discusses the issue of discretionary decisions by parole boards. He reports that, in the early twentieth century, parole boards considered primarily the seriousness of the crime in determining whether to release an inmate on parole. However, there was no consensus on what constituted a serious crime. Instead, according to Rothman, "each member made his own decisions. The judgments were personal and therefore not subject to debate or reconsideration" (Rothman 1980, p. 173). These personal preferences often resulted in unwarranted sentencing disparities or racial and gender bias. As Rhine and colleagues observed, "No other part of the criminal justice system concentrates such power in the hands of so few" (Rhine et al. 1991, pp. 32–33).

Regardless of criticisms, the use of parole release grew, and instead of using it as a special privilege to be extended to exceptional prisoners, it began to be used as a standard mode of release from prison, routinely considered upon completion of a minimum term of confinement. What had started as a practical alternative to executive clemency and then come to be used as a mechanism for controlling prison growth gradually developed a distinctively rehabilitative rationale, incorporating the promise of help, assistance, and surveillance (Bottomley 1990, p. 325).

By the mid-1950s, indeterminate sentencing coupled with parole release was well entrenched in the United States, such that it was the dominant sentencing structure in every state, and by the late 1970s, more than 70 percent of all inmates released were released as a result of a parole board's discretionary decision. In some states, essentially everyone was released as a result of the parole board's decision making. For example, throughout the 1960s, more than 95 percent of all inmates released in Washington, New Hampshire, and California were released on parole. Indeterminate sentencing coupled with parole release was a matter of absolute routine and good correctional practice for most of the twentieth century. But all that was to change starting in the late 1970s, when demands for substantial reforms in parole practices increasingly began to be heard.

Modern Challenges and Changes to Parole

The pillars of the American corrections systems—indeterminate sentencing coupled with parole release, for the purposes of offender rehabilitation—came under severe attack and basically collapsed during the late 1970s and early 1980s. This period in penology has been well documented elsewhere, and the history will not be repeated here. For an excellent review, see Reitz (2000).

In summary, attacks on indeterminate sentencing and parole release centered on three major criticisms. First, there was little scientific evidence that parole release and supervision reduced subsequent recidivism. In 1974, Robert Martinson and his colleagues published the now-famous review of the effectiveness of correctional treatment and concluded: "With few and isolated exceptions, the rehabilitative efforts that have been reported so far have had no appreciable effect on recidivism" (Lipton, Martinson, and Wilks 1975, p. 20). Of the 289 studies they reviewed, just 25 (9 percent) pertained to parole, and yet their summary was interpreted to mean that parole supervision (and all correctional rehabilitation programs) did not work.

The National Research Council reviewed the Martinson study and basically concurred with its conclusions (Sechrest, White, and Brown 1979). Martinson's study is often credited with giving rehabilitation the coup de grace. As Holt (1998) notes, once rehabilitation could not be legitimized by science, there was nothing to support the "readiness for release" idea and, therefore, no role for parole boards or indeterminate sentencing.

Second, parole and indeterminate sentencing were challenged on moral grounds as unjust and inhumane, especially when imposed on unwilling participants. Research (e.g., Glaser 1969) showed there was little relationship between in-prison behavior, participation in rehabilitation programs, and postrelease recidivism. If that were true, then why base release dates on in-prison performance? Prisoners argued that not knowing their release dates held them in "suspended animation" and contributed one more pain to their imprisonment.

Third, indeterminate sentencing permitted authorities to use a great deal of uncontrolled discretion in release decisions, and these decisions often were inconsistent and discriminatory. Since parole boards had a great deal of autonomy and their decisions were not subject to outside scrutiny, critics argued that it was a hidden system of discretionary decision making and led to race and class bias in release decisions.

It seemed as if no one liked indeterminate sentencing and parole in the 1970s, and the time was ripe for change. Crime control advocates denounced parole supervision as being largely nominal and ineffective; social welfare advocates decried the lack of meaningful and useful rehabilitation programs. Several scholars, including James Q. Wilson, Andrew von Hirsch, Norval Morris, and David Fogel, began to advocate alternative sentencing proposals.

Wilson argued that if there were no scientific basis for knowing the probability of rehabilitation, then the philosophical rationale for making it the chief goal of sentencing should be abandoned. He urged instead a revival of interest in the deterrence and incapacitation functions of the criminal justice system. He wrote: "Wicked people exist. Nothing avails except to set them apart from innocent people." He urged the abandonment of rehabilitation as a major purpose of corrections:

> Instead we could view the correctional system as having a very different function—to isolate and to punish. That statement may strike many readers as cruel, even barbaric. It is not. It is merely recognition that society must be able to protect itself from dangerous offenders. It is also a frank admission that society really does not know how to do much else. (Wilson 1985, p. 193)

Von Hirsch (1976) provided a seemingly neutral ideological substitute for rehabilitation. He argued that the discredited rehabilitation model should be replaced with the simple, nonutilitarian notion that sentencing sanctions should reflect the social harm caused by the misconduct. Indeterminacy and parole should be replaced with a specific penalty for a specific offense. He believed that all persons committing the same crimes "deserve" to be sentenced to conditions that are similar in both type and duration, and that individual traits, such as rehabilitation or the potential for recidivism, should be irrelevant to the sentencing and parole decisions. He proposed abolishing parole and adopting a system of "just deserts" sentencing, where similar criminal conduct would be punished similarly.

Fogel (1975) advocated for a "justice model" for prisons and parole, where inmates would be given opportunities to volunteer for rehabilitation programs, but that participation would not be required. He criticized the unbridled discretion exercised by correctional officials, particularly parole boards, under the guise of "treatment." He recommended a return to flat time/determinate sentencing and the elimination of parole boards. He also advocated abolishing parole's surveillance function and turning that function over to law enforcement.

The Call to End Rehabilitation and Discretionary Parole

These individuals had a major influence on both academic and policy thinking about sentencing objectives. Together, they advocated a system with less emphasis on rehabilitation and the abolition of indeterminate sentencing and discretionary parole release. Liberals and conservatives endorsed the proposals. The political Left was concerned about excessive discretion that permitted vastly different sentences in presumably similar cases, and the political Right was concerned about the leniency of parole boards. As Reitz wrote, once the belief in rehabilitation lost force, "all the virtues of indeterminacy could be recast as vices" (2000, p. 228). A political coalition resulted, and soon incapacitation and "just deserts" replaced rehabilitation as the primary goal of American prisons. Even rank-and-file Americans abandoned their faith in rehabilitation. In 1970, a Harris poll found that 73 percent of Americans thought that the primary purpose of prison should be rehabilitation. By 1995, only 26 percent did (Hallinan 2001).

With that changed focus, indeterminate sentencing and parole release came under serious attack, and calls to abolish parole were heard in state after state. In 1976, Maine became the first state to eliminate parole. The following year, California and Indiana joined Maine in establishing determinate sentencing legislation and abolishing discretionary parole release from prison. California's 1977 Determinate Sentencing Law also amended the state's penal code to declare that the ultimate goal of imprisonment was "punishment" and not "rehabilitation."

By the end of 2002, 16 states had abolished discretionary release from prison by a parole board for nearly all offenders. Another 5 states had abolished discretionary parole for certain violent offenses or other felony crimes. In addition, in 21 states, parole authorities were operating under what might be called a sundown provision, in that they had discretion over a small and decreasing parole-eligible population. By the end of 2002, just 16 states still gave their parole boards full authority to release inmates through a discretionary process (see table 3.1).

Table 3.1. Status of parole release in the United States, 2002

	Parole board has full release powers	Parole board has limited release powers	If parole board powers are limited, crimes ineligible for discretionary release	Discretionary parole abolished (year)
Alabama	√			
Alaska	√			
Arizona				√ (1994)
Arkansas		√		
California			only for indeterminate life sentence	√ (1977)
Colorado	√			none 1979–1985
Connecticut		√	murders, capital felonies	
Delaware				√ (1990)
Florida		√	certain capital/life felonies	
Georgia		√	several felonies	
Hawaii		√	punishment by life without parole	
Idaho	√			
Illinois				√ (1978)
Indiana				√ (1977)
Iowa		√	murder 1, kidnapping, sexual abuse	
Kansas				√ (1993)
Kentucky	√			
Louisiana		√	several felonies	
Maine				√ (1976)
Maryland		√	violent, or death penalty sought	
Massachusetts		√	murder 1	
Michigan		√	murder 1, 650+ grams cocaine	
Minnesota				√ (1980)
Mississippi				√ (1995)
Missouri		√	several felonies	
Montana	√			
Nebraska		√	murder 1/life, kidnap/life	

Nevada	√			
New Hampshire		√	Murder 1	
New Jersey	√			
New Mexico		√		
New York		√	“violent felony offenders”	
North Carolina				√ (1994)
North Dakota	√			
Ohio				√ (1996)
Oklahoma	√			
Oregon				√ (1989)
Pennsylvania	√			
Rhode Island	√			
South Carolina	√			
South Dakota		√	none with life sentence	
Tennessee		√	murder 1/life, rapes	
Texas		√	none if on death row	
Utah	√			
Vermont	√			
Virginia				√ (1995)
Washington				√ (1984)
West Virginia		√	no life without mercy	
Wisconsin			no life without parole	√ (1999)
Wyoming	√			
U.S. parole (federal)				√ (1984)
TOTAL	16	19		16

Source: Petersilia 1999b; Hughes et al. 2001; Association of Parole Authorities, International 2001.

Likewise, at the federal level, the Comprehensive Crime Control Act of 1984 created the U.S. Sentencing Commission. That legislation abolished the U.S. Parole Commission, and parole was phased out from the federal criminal justice system in 1997. Offenders sentenced to federal prison, while no longer eligible for parole release, are now required to serve a defined term of "supervised release" following release from prison.

A recent state survey found that the unfavorable reputation that parole experienced in the early 1990s has now diminished, and there is little desire to further eliminate parole (American Correctional Association 2001).

Even in states that did not formally abolish parole or restrict its use to certain serious offenses, the sentencing reform movement produced a significant diminution of parole boards' discretionary authority to release. Mandatory minimum-sentencing policies now exist in every state, and the federal government and 24 states have enacted "three strikes and you're out" laws, which require extremely long minimum terms for certain repeat offenders. These different sentencing regimes all have had the effect of removing discretion from the dispositional stage of the sentencing process. Offender-based systems were replaced with offense-based systems.

Perhaps most significantly, 27 states and the District of Columbia have established truth-in-sentencing laws, under which people convicted of selected violent crimes must serve at least 85 percent of the announced prison sentence. To satisfy the 85 percent test (to qualify for federal funds for prison construction), states have limited the powers of parole boards to set release dates, or of prison managers to award good time and gain time (time off for good behavior or for participation in work or treatment programs), or both. As a result, violent offenders' postrelease oversight time has decreased to 15 percent of the imposed sentence. Truth-in-sentencing laws effectively eliminate not only parole but also most "good time."

Assessing the Impacts of Discretionary Parole Release

One of the presumed effects of eliminating parole or limiting its use is to increase the length of the prison term served. After all, parole release is widely regarded as "letting them out early." Overall, time served in prison has increased in recent years, and recent Bureau of

Justice Statistics figures show that among all state inmates released from prison for the first time on their current offense, the average (mean) time served in prison increased from 22 months in 1990 to 29 months in 1999. Released inmates also served an average of 5 months in local jails prior to their admission to prison. Thus, inmates released in 1999 had been incarcerated a total of 34 months—6 months longer than released inmates in 1990. These longer prison terms are expected to continue as the effects of truth-in-sentencing laws take hold.

At first glance, these longer prison terms might be seen as evidence that abolishing parole boards resulted in keeping inmates behind bars longer. After all, that is what proponents of abolishing parole hoped for. That interpretation, however, would be wrong. Important recent analyses published by the BJS reveal a relationship between type of release (mandatory versus discretionary) and the length of time spent in prison prior to release (Hughes, Wilson, and Beck 2001). Contrary to expectations, the length of time served in prison is greater in states having discretionary parole. For violent offenses, men served 60 months prior to discretionary release compared to 48 months for men who received a mandatory sentence with automatic parole. Similar trends were found for women: for violent offenses, women served 45 months prior to discretionary release compared to 36 months for women who received automatic parole. For all offense types combined, the mean (average) total time served for those released from state prison for first releases in 1999 through discretionary parole methods was 35 months, whereas for those released mandatorily, the average (mean) time served in prison was 33 months.

Analysis by Stivers (2001) confirmed that discretionary parole was associated with longer prison terms served, even when offense, prior record, age, gender, and conviction crime type were statistically controlled. For almost every offense type, those released discretionarily served longer prison terms than those released mandatorily, and the difference was most pronounced for violent offenders.

Important new data also show that, in every year between 1990 and 1999, state prisoners released by a parole board had higher success rates than those released through mandatory parole (Hughes, Wilson, and Beck 2001). Figure 3.2 shows that more than half (54 percent) of those released on discretionary parole successfully completed their parole terms, compared to one-third (33 percent) of mandatory releases.

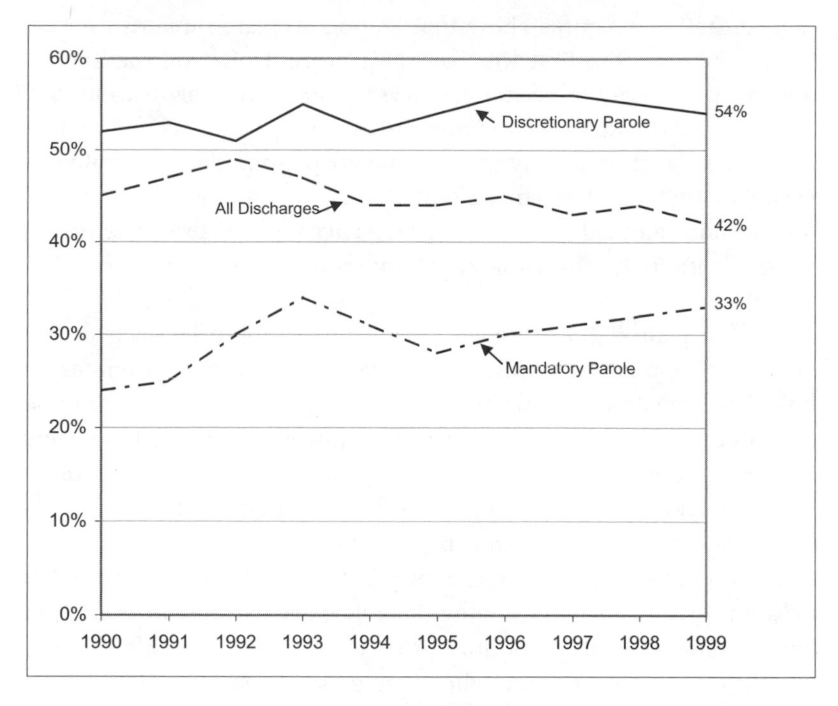

Figure 3.2. Percentage successful among state parole discharges, 1990–1999.

The figure 3.2 results, which show higher success rates among discretionary parole releases, may be interpreted in two ways. Perhaps those released discretionarily are less serious in their crimes or criminal record to begin with, and hence are released early in states using discretionary parole release. Or, it may mean that having to earn and demonstrate readiness for release and being supervised postprison have some deterrent and rehabilitation benefits.

The second interpretation seems to have merit. Using logistic regression, which controlled for offense type, prior record, age, ethnicity, education, and gender, Stivers (2001) discovered a consistent and significant relationship between parole success and method of release. She found that those released from prison via discretionary parole were more than twice as likely to complete their parole period successfully than those released mandatorily. This finding was consistent across all offense types.

These scientific findings buttress the arguments made by advocates of parole. They argue that discretionary release ultimately leads to greater public safety, since it encourages both inmates and prison officials to focus more heavily on reintegration programs. Further research on the effects of discretionary versus mandatory parole release should be given highest priority.

Parole Guidelines and Risk Prediction Instruments

Release practices have changed dramatically even in the 16 states that still authorize parole authorities to use their discretion to release inmates. Nearly all of these states have further restricted parole by setting specific standards that offenders must meet to be eligible for release, and most of them now use formal risk prediction instruments or parole guidelines to structure the parole decision-making process. Since the 1970s, corrections has developed risk assessment instruments or parole guidelines in an attempt to make the parole release decision more rational and accurate in terms of recidivism prediction.

Parole guidelines are usually actuarial devices, which objectively predict the risk of recidivism based on crime and offender background information. The guidelines produce a "seriousness" score for each individual by summing points assigned for various background characteristics (higher scores mean greater risk). Inmates with the least serious crimes and the lowest statistical probability of reoffending would then be the first to be released and so forth.

Many guidelines are based on the U.S. Parole Commission's salient factor score (SFS), which has been in use since 1981. The salient factors are (1) number of prior convictions/adjudications, (2) number of prior commitments of more than 30 days, (3) age at current offense, (4) recent three-year incarceration-free period, (5) probation/parole/confinement/escape violation at the time of the current offense or during the present confinement, (6) heroin/opiate dependence, and (7) if an older offender.

The SFS places the offender in one of four risk categories: very good, good, fair, or poor. Parole officials consider this score in deciding whether parole is to be granted and, if so, what level of supervision will be required. Several SFS validation studies have been conducted using large samples of inmates released in various years, and results show that the SFS provides a reliable means of differentiating the higher-risk offenders from the lower-risk ones and predicts recidivism more accurately than subjective methods.

Despite these advantages, few states currently rely primarily on parole guidelines or risk prediction instruments for release decisions. As noted, parole boards have either been abolished or have lost decision-making jurisdiction over a growing percentage of offenders. Moreover, using the guidelines or actuarial instruments requires validating the risk factors and revising the weights, updating minimum-time-served calculations, and accounting for the growing number of offenders returned to prison for technical violations. In most states, the research capacity to do these tasks does not exist. However, Ohio, Virginia, Pennsylvania, Washington, and Maryland report using risk assessment instruments for those offenders for whom they still retain discretionary authority, although in each of these instances, the risk assessment score is strictly advisory.

Another reason that generic parole guidelines have fallen into disuse in some states is that they primarily measure static, criminal history items and provide little information on criminogenic needs. Researchers have called attention to more dynamic factors or criminogenic needs that should be targeted by treatment providers, and have urged that these items be included in the next generation of risk assessment instruments.

Level of Service Inventory–Revised

The most popular and respected of the newer risk assessment instruments is the Level of Service Inventory–Revised (LSI-R) (Andrews and Bonta 1995). Unlike parole guidelines, this risk assessment procedure was not originally designed to assist in parole release decision making but rather to make effective treatment program decisions after release. It is now being used to do both.

The LSI-R scale includes both criminal history items and measures of offender needs, such as substance abuse, employment, and special needs accommodations. The tool has been proven to be both reliable and valid. The LSI-R is administered during a standardized, one-hour, semistructured interview, and it objectively evaluates predictors of program success (such as residence, family ties, employment) and predictors of program failure (such as prior convictions, prior failures to appear, drug use, prior violations of sentence). It includes 54 items ranging from static, criminal history variables to more dynamic items, such as the offender's present employment and financial situation. Scoring of the instrument follows the Burgess 0–1 method, where the presence of a risk factor is scored as 1. Scores are then totaled to give a risk-needs score. The LSI-R can be further analyzed into its subcomponents, many of which reflect dynamic aspects of the offender's situation (e.g., living accommodations). High scores on the subcomponents suggest criminogenic needs or areas to target for intervention.

Results of the LSI-R provide the parole officer and supervisor a numeric estimate of each client's risks and needs, which makes it possible to assign clients to appropriate services (i.e., substance abuse counseling, cognitive restructuring, anger management, life skills). Because many of the risks and needs factors are dynamic (i.e., changeable), the test can be given repeatedly over time to reflect either positive changes or negative changes in the areas being measured. The LSI-R is being used in more progressive corrections departments to identify treatment goals for staff who counsel offenders, run treatment programs, and in general attempt to reduce the risk of future criminal behavior. The state of Washington is using the LSI-R within the prison system to tie inmate needs with postprison services.

Politics and Parole Decisions

An interesting, and potentially dangerous, development has occurred in recent years regarding parole releases. Even in some states retaining discretionary parole, a greater proportion of eligible prisoners are waiving their parole hearings and choosing instead to finish their sentences behind bars and then be released unconditionally from prison.

An example comes from Massachusetts. Massachusetts retains a system of discretionary parole for most inmates, but since 1990, the Massachusetts Parole Board has been releasing fewer inmates who come before it. Parole decisions are made extremely conservatively—recall that Willie Horton was released in Massachusetts. The parole board does not want another situation like that on its watch. In 1990, 70 percent of state inmates who went before the board were paroled as compared with 38 percent in 1999. The decline in parole grant rates has discouraged inmates from going before the parole board. As Bradley and Oliver write:

> Inmates are more likely now to opt to "pay their dues" behind bars than they were in 1990. . . . these inmates are choosing

> to entirely forego [*sic*] parole eligibility by passing the Board and the controlled, supervised release it provides. This is particularly worrisome when considered in light of the three-fold increase in the percentage of male DOC inmates discharged directly from maximum security over this same time period. *The result is that the inmates who pose the greatest threat to public safety are denied parole, while minor offenders, least in need of supervision, are under the watchful eye of a parole officer.* (Bradley and Oliver 2001, p. 4; italics mine)

A report on the Massachusetts situation concludes: "The joke is on us, however. The very thing the public wants—community safety—is jeopardized when inmates are released without the supervision and the support of parole" (Bradley and Oliver 2001, p. 5). The Massachusetts legislature is now considering a proposal that would provide some amount of postprison supervision to *every* released prisoner.

Conclusions

Parole has experienced dramatic changes in the past 25 years. Discretionary parole release was once the mechanism by which more than 95 percent of U.S. prisoners returned home. At the end of 2002, that figure had fallen to less than one-fourth. The majority of inmates (59 percent) are now released automatically and mandatorily, without ever appearing before a parole board. Proponents had hoped that determinate sentencing, with less room for discretionary and individual judicial preferences, would make sentencing more consistent across offenders and offenses—and it has. But it was also thought that it would lengthen the time inmates spent behind bars—and it has not. Perhaps more important, recent research suggests that inmates who max out—and leave prison without parole supervision—have higher failure rates than those who are released with parole requirements.

Common sense and empirical evidence call for reinstating discretionary parole release for inmates. Parole release decisions should be made by a professional parole board, which should be guided by objective risk prediction instruments or parole guidelines to make release decisions. Inmates should be given incentives to participate in prison programs, since research shows that regardless of their initial incentive to become involved, some positive effects will accrue for some people. No one is more dangerous than a criminal who has no incentive to straighten himself out while in prison and who returns to society without a supervised transition plan. As ironic as it may seem, it is in the interests of public safety that discretionary parole systems be reinstituted.

FOUR

The Changing Nature of Parole Supervision and Services

Parole consists of two parts: *parole boards*, which have the authority to decide when to release prisoners, and *parole field services*, whose parole officers supervise offenders after their release. Regardless of whether inmates are released through a discretionary or mandatory process, the majority will still be subject to some sort of postprison or parole supervision. This period is designed both to aid offenders' readjustment to society and to monitor their movements. Each parolee will likely be assigned to a parole agent who has the job of assuring that the parolee abides by his parole conditions or is returned to custody, if appropriate. The major criticisms of parole release (e.g., unwarranted discretion and ineffectiveness) have also been leveled at parole field supervision and have caused major changes and reforms there as well.

Parole officers, historically committed to providing counseling and brokering community resources to assist parolees, have become more surveillance oriented. The public's tough-on-crime stance has demanded it, and the practical considerations of high parole caseloads combined with scarce resources have left parole officers with few alternatives. Drug testing, house arrest, and electronic monitoring are now common parole supervision techniques. Of course, such techniques seldom contribute to rehabilitation; they just help identify the failures more quickly.

Growth in Parole Populations

As shown in figure 4.1, there were 725,527 persons on parole at the end of 2000. Parolees represented 11 percent of the nearly 6.5 million persons who were under correctional control (in jail or prison, on parole or probation) at that time. Four states (California, New York, Pennsylvania, and Texas) supervised more than half of all state

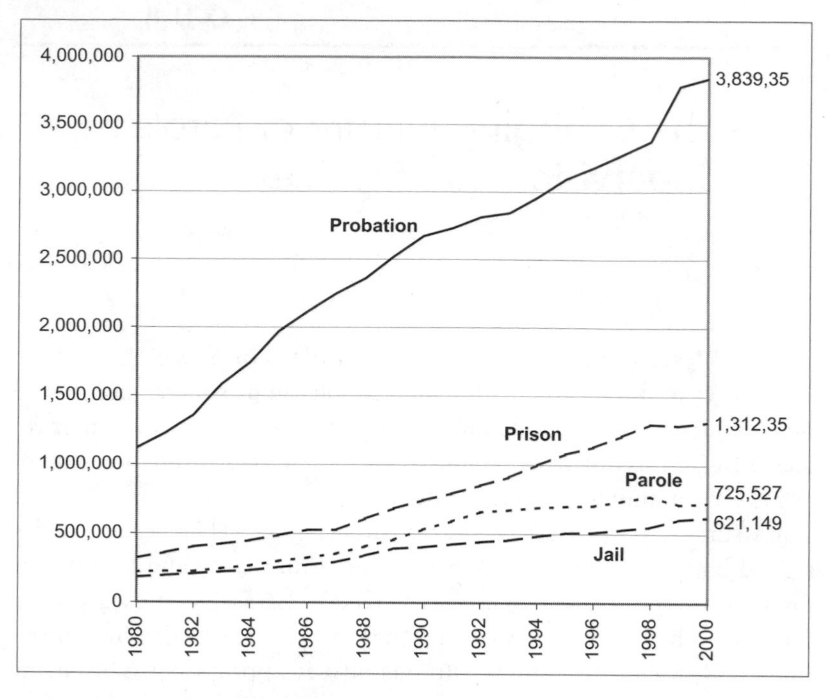

Figure 4.1. Adult correctional populations in the United States, 1980–2000. *Note*: Data include state and federal prisoners and parolees. *Source*: Beck and Harrison 2001; Bureau of Justice Statistics 1997.

parolees. The District of Columbia has, by far, the greatest number of its resident population on parole supervision. In 2000, nearly 1.2 percent of all its residents were on parole on any given day, compared to a national average of 0.3 percent.

The disproportionate number of criminals serving sentences in the community is not new. There have always been more people convicted of crimes in the United States than prison cells to hold them. In fact, despite mandatory minimum sentences, "three strikes and you're out" legislation, and other tough-on-crime policies of the 1990s, the absolute number of offenders serving sentences in the community is larger than ever before in our history (the probation population is up 41 percent since 1990), and the percentage of the total correctional population under community supervision (versus incarceration) declined only slightly in that period—from 74 percent to 71 percent.

The truth is that, as the U.S. population has grown, more citizens are being arrested and convicted, and all corrections populations (in prisons and jails, on probation and parole) have grown simultaneously (see figure 4.1). The number of offenders under correctional supervision is now so large that the U.S. Department of Justice estimates that 3.1 percent of *all* U.S. adult residents, or 1 in every 32 adults, was under some type of correctional control in 2000. Most of those (2.2 percent) are serving sentences in the community on probation or parole.

Administration of Parole Field Services

One of the first and continuing reforms in parole field services has been to make them more independent of parole boards. Since the mid-1960s, states increasingly have moved parole field services away from being an arm of the parole board and into a separate agency. The parole field service is housed under a separate agency in 40 states (80 percent), usually in the state's department of corrections. Parole boards have responsibility for supervising parolees in only 10 states.

Regardless of their administrative relationship, parole board directives heavily influence how parole agents carry out their duties and responsibilities. When setting the conditions of release, parole boards are prescribing the goals it expects parole agents to pursue in the period of supervision. A recent survey by the Association of Parole Authorities, International (APAI) shows that most parole boards are responsible for ordering community service, restitution, supervision fees, sex offender registration, and treatment program participation. In addition, some parole boards also mandate drug testing, intensified supervision (such as the lifetime supervision of sex offenders in Colorado and of child molesters in Rhode Island), and participation in victim mediation programs.

In most states, the decision to revoke parole ultimately rests with the parole board. As such, parole boards set implicit and explicit criteria about which types of parole violations will warrant return to prison and, therefore, heavily influence the types of behavior that parole officers monitor and record. If, for example, failing a drug test is not a violation that will result in revocation to prison or any serious consequence by the parole board, parole agents will not administer drug tests as frequently, since no consequence can be guaranteed.

In this way, parole boards and parole field services are functionally interdependent.

Striking a Balance between Services and Supervision

Persons released from prison face a multitude of difficulties in trying to reenter the outside community successfully. They remain largely uneducated, unskilled, and usually without solid family support systems—and now they have the added burden of a prison record and the distrust and fear that it inevitably elicits. As Irwin and Austin write: "Any imprisonment reduces the opportunities of felons, most of whom had relatively few opportunities to begin with" (Irwin and Austin 1997, p. 133).

Research has shown that parolees want the same things in life as the rest of us, although most believe they will not succeed. Most aspire to a relatively modest, stable, conventional life after prison: "When I get out, I want to have my kids with me and have a good job so I can support them."

The public, too, would like them to succeed. But what assistance are parolees given as they reenter our communities? Sadly, while inmates' needs for services and assistance have increased, parole in some states (if not most) has retreated from its historical mission to provide counseling, job training, and housing assistance. Except in relation to sex offenders, the help and control that ex-convicts receive once released has been largely constant or decreasing.

An ethnographic study of parole officers in California concludes that while rehabilitation remains in parole's rhetoric, as a practical matter, parole services are almost entirely focused on control-oriented activities. Agents have constructed an image of the prototypical parolee as someone who generally chooses to maintain an involvement with crime, who needs no more than an attitude adjustment to get on the "right track," and who does not need the agent to provide intervention and services to facilitate reform. As Lynch observes: "In this way, while parole may talk of the need and capability for reform among their clientele, the agency can absolve itself of the responsibility to provide it." Even when traditional rehabilitative tools are available to agents—for example, drug treatment and counseling—they "are treated as rehabilitative in discourse, but are often used for coercive control in practice" (Lynch 1999, p. 857).

Parole Services and Conditions

Of course, the help parolees receive differs vastly, depending on the state and jurisdiction in which they are being supervised. But as states put more and more of their fiscal resources into building prisons, fewer resources are available for parole services. Oklahoma senators estimate that the state pays $36 million annually to incarcerate parole failures, half of whom are on waiting lists to enter rehabilitation programs required by their parole conditions (Hinton 2001). And, as noted earlier, the public has become less tolerant and forgiving of past criminal transgressions and more fearful of particular offenders (for example, sex offenders). This sentiment has translated into both stricter requirements for release and stricter supervision and revocation procedures once released.

In California, for example, there are few services for parolees. There are only 200 shelter beds in the state for more than 10,000 homeless parolees, 4 mental health clinics for 18,000 psychiatric cases, 750 beds in treatment programs for 85,000 drug and alcohol abusers. Under the terms of their parole, offenders are often subjected to periodic drug tests, but they are rarely offered any opportunity to get drug treatment. Of the approximately 130,000 substance abusers in California's prisons, only 3,000 are receiving treatment behind bars. And of the 132,000 inmates released last year in California, just 8,000 received any kind of prerelease program to help them cope with life on the outside (Little Hoover Commission 1998). As Schlosser reported:

> Inmates are simply released from prison each year in California; given nothing more than $200 and a bus ticket back to the county where they were convicted. At least 1,200 inmates every year go from a secure housing unit at a Level 4 prison—an isolation unit, designed to hold the most violent and dangerous inmates in the system—right onto the street. One day these predatory inmates are locked in their cells for twenty-three hours at a time and fed all their meals through a slot in the door, and the next day they're out of prison, riding a bus home. (Schlosser 1998, p. 76)

All parolees are required to sign an agreement to abide by certain regulations. Seeing that the parolee lives up to this parole contract is the principal responsibility of the parole agent. Parole agents are equipped with legal authority to carry and use firearms; to search places, persons, and property without the requirements imposed by the Fourth Amendment (the right to privacy); and to order arrests without probable cause and to confine without bail. The power to search applies to the household where a parolee is living and businesses where a parolee is working. The ability to arrest, confine, and, in some cases, reimprison the parolee for violating conditions of the parole agreement makes the parole agent a walking court system.

Conditions generally can be grouped into standard conditions applicable to all parolees and special conditions that are tailored to particular offenders. Special conditions for substance abusers, for example, usually include periodic drug testing. Standard conditions are similar throughout most jurisdictions, and violating them can result in a return to prison. Common standard parole conditions include:

- reporting to the parole agent within 24 hours of release
- not carrying weapons
- reporting changes of address and employment
- not traveling more than 50 miles from home or not leaving the county for more than 48 hours without prior approval from the parole agent
- obeying all parole agent instructions
- seeking and maintaining employment or participating in education/work training
- not committing crimes
- submitting to search by the police and parole officers

Special conditions are those imposed on certain parolees but not all. For example, sex offenders may be required to participate in sex offender therapy, register as sex offenders, and refrain from entering child safety zones. Substance abusers may be required to submit to urinalysis and participate in substance abuse treatment. Persons convicted for driving under the influence may be required to refrain from operating a motor vehicle and to participate in counseling for alcohol abuse. A person convicted of embezzlement may be required, as a condition of parole, not to seek employment as a bookkeeper. A person convicted of domestic assault may be required, as a condition of parole, not to contact his spouse or other injured family members. Generally, a special condition of parole is invalid only if it has all three of the following characteristics: (1) has no relationship to the crime, (2) is related to conduct that is not in itself criminal, and (3) forbids or requires conduct that is not reasonably related to the future criminality of the offender or does not serve the statutory ends of parole (del Carmen et al. 2000).

Some argue that we have created unrealistic parole conditions. Boards were asked in 1988 to indicate from a list of 14 items what were standard parole conditions in their state. The most common, of course, was "obey all laws." However, 78 percent required "gainful employment" as a standard condition; 61 percent required "no association with persons with criminal records"; 53 percent required "all fines and restitution paid"; and 47 percent required parolees to "support family and all dependents." None of these can consistently be met by most parolees (Rhine et al. 1991). Increasingly, the most common condition for probationers and parolees is drug testing. In 1999, all states' parole agencies reported testing for drugs, more than 2 million parolees were tested during the year, and about 1 percent had their parole revoked as a result of a dirty drug test. Of all parolees revoked and sent to prison in 1997, 8 percent were revoked as a result of a positive test for drug use (see table 7.2).

Parole Classification and Specialized Caseloads

Most jurisdictions rely on a formal approach to classification and case management for parolee supervision. Such systems recognize that not all offenders are equal in their need for supervision. A parole survey found that 90 percent of the states use a classification system for assigning parolees to different levels of supervision (Rhunda, Rhine, and Wetter 1994).

Most often, this assignment is based on a structured assessment of parolee risk and an assessment of the needs or problem areas that have contributed to the parolee's criminality. By scoring information relative to the risk of recidivism and the particular needs of the offender (in other words, a risk-need instrument), a total score is derived, which then dictates the particular level of parole supervision (for example, intensive, medium, minimum, or administrative). Each jurisdiction usually has established policy that dictates the contact levels (minimum times the officer will meet with the parolee). These contact levels correspond to each level of parole supervision. The notion is that higher-risk inmates and those with greater needs will be seen most frequently. These models are described as management tools and are not devised to reduce recidivism directly.

Larger parole departments also have established specialized caseloads to supervise certain types of offenders more effectively. These offenders generally pose a particularly serious threat to public safety or present unique problems that may handicap their adjustment to supervision. Specialized caseloads afford the opportunity to match the unique skills and training of parole officers with the specialized needs of parolees. The most common specialized caseloads in the United States are those that target sex offenders and parolees with serious substance abuse problems, although, as shown in table 4.1, just 3 percent of all parolees are supervised on specialized caseloads.

Caseload Assignment and Costs

Individual cases are assigned to parole officers and comprise officers' caseloads. Table 4.1 shows that 85 percent of all U.S. parolees are supervised on regular caseloads, averaging 66 cases to one parole officer, in which they are seen (face to face) less than twice per month. Officers also may initiate "collateral" contacts, such as inquiring of family members or employers about the parolee's progress. Many parole officers are frustrated because they lack the time and resources to do the kind of job they believe is maximally helpful to their clients. Parole officers often complain that paperwork has increased, their clients have more serious problems, and their caseloads are much higher than the 35–50 cases that had been considered the ideal caseload for a parole officer. However, there is no empirical evidence to show that smaller caseloads result in lower recidivism rates.

A national demonstration project evaluating the effects of reducing caseload size for probationers and parolees conducted by Petersilia and Turner (1993) showed *higher* recidivism rates for offenders supervised on smaller caseloads—officers were able to watch them more closely and uncover more of their misdeeds. But this research also found that where offenders both received surveillance and participated in relevant treatment, recidivism was reduced 20–30 percent. Program evaluations in Texas, Wisconsin, Oregon, and Colorado have produced similarly encouraging results. There now exists solid empirical evidence that ordering offenders into treatment and requiring them to participate reduces recidivism (Gendreau, Little, and Goggin 1996). The first order of business, therefore, must be to allocate sufficient resources so that the designed programs (incorporating both surveillance and treatment) can be implemented. Sufficient monetary resources are essential to obtaining and sustaining judicial support and achieving program success.

Table 4.1. Parole caseload supervision level, contacts, and annual costs

Caseload type	Percentage of all parolees	Average caseload size	Face-to-face contacts (per month)	Annual supervision costs ($)
Regular	85	66:1	1.7	1,806
Intensive	14	25:1	5.6	4,113
Electronic Monitoring	1	13:1	3.5	5,715
Specialized	3	32:1	4.7	4,938

Note: Percentage of all parolees does not add to 100 percent since some parolees may be on more than one type of caseload (e.g., intensive supervision with electronic monitoring). State and federal information combined.

Source: Camp and Camp 2001.

High-quality parole supervision costs money, and we should be honest about that. We currently spend less than $2,000 per year per parolee for regular supervision. It is no wonder that recidivism rates are so high. Effective substance abuse programs are estimated to cost at least $12,000 to $14,000 per year. These resources will be forthcoming only if the public believes the programs are both effective and punitive.

Legal Liability of Parole Officers and Supervisors

One important implication of an increasingly litigious society, larger caseloads, and the reduction in the quality of client supervision is the increased potential for lawsuits arising from negligent supervision by a parole officer of her clients. Lawsuits of this type stem from allegations of nonperformance and improper performance of official responsibilities. As del Carmen and colleagues write:

> There was a time when probation/parole officers were insulated from litigation. Those days are gone and are likely to be gone forever. Judicial officers (judges and prosecutors) are vested with absolute immunity, but probation/parole officers enjoy only qualified immunity. . . . Probation/parole officers, therefore, are susceptible to liability lawsuits in whatever they do that is related to their job. (del Carmen et al. 2000, p. 2)

This affects their desire to take chances on an offender who is relapsing, although it is now recognized that frequent relapses are a part of the journey toward recovery.

Under certain circumstances, not only may offenders file civil suits against an officer but also even victims of crimes may potentially assert a civil claim against an officer. Although negligent supervision cases are not new, the 1990s saw an increase in suits filed against individual probation and parole officers.

In a 1986 Alaska case, the Alaska Supreme Court ruled that state agencies and their officers might be held liable for negligence when probationers and parolees under their supervision commit violent offenses. The courts have further ruled in *Taggart v. State* and *Sandau v. State* on the issue of the responsibility of a parole officer toward a third party injured by a parolee. In both cases, the parole board for the state of Washington and several parole officers were sued by victims of crimes committed by two persons who were being supervised on parole. For a review, see del Carmen et al. (2002).

The plaintiffs alleged that certain parole officers were negligent in recommending to the parole board that the parolees be placed on parole, that the parole board was negligent in granting parole, and that certain other parole officers were negligent in supervising the parolees while they were on parole. The court disagreed that parole officers were entitled to absolute immunity for all of their actions but gave them qualified immunity, saying that parole officers are immune from liability for allegedly negligent parole supervision if their actions are in substantial compliance with the directions of superiors and guidelines.

However, in both *Taggart* and *Sandau*, the court observed that parole officers had failed to perform certain responsibilities as required by agency policies and directives (e.g., regular drug testing, field contacts). Thus, parole officers are increasingly at risk through tort actions filed by victims harmed by the crimes committed by their offender-clients. Some have argued that the upside of these lawsuits is that this legal threat eventually forces states to invest more heavily in parole supervision.

As del Carmen and colleagues observe, these legal developments have important implications for the reporting of technical violations, since once the matter (e.g., a dirty drug test) has been brought to the attention of supervisors, individual parole officers will have discharged their responsibilities and not be held liable. Individual parole officers are less likely to use their discretion, since by doing so they expose themselves to legal risks should the offender commit a new crime. The parole supervisor, in turn, is mandated to report to the parole board any technical violations and will do so since the board enjoys more immunity than the parole supervisor in the field.

Parole administrators admit to formally reporting a greater number of discovered violations since the courts began to intervene, as no one wants to expose themselves and their agencies to negligent supervision lawsuits. Parole boards, in turn, now have a written report of a violation and, not wanting to risk a lawsuit for negligent supervision, may be more likely to revoke to custody. This litigious environment certainly is related to the growing number of parolees who are returned to prison for technical violations. As will be discussed more fully in chapter 7, the number of offenders reincarcerated for violating parole or other release conditions has increased more than sevenfold since 1980 and is a major reason that prison populations continue to increase even as crime rates decline.

Violations of Conditions and Parole Revocation

If parolees fail to live up to their conditions, they can be revoked to custody. Parole can be revoked for two reasons: (1) the commission of a new crime, or (2) the violation of the conditions of parole (a technical violation). Technical violations pertain to behavior that is not criminal, such as the failure to refrain from alcohol use or remain employed.

In either event, the violation process is rather straightforward. Given that parolees are technically still in the legal custody of the prison or parole authorities, and as a result maintain a quasi-prisoner status, their constitutional rights are severely limited. When parole officers become aware of violations of the parole contract, they notify their supervisors, who rather easily can return a parolee to prison. This ease with which inmates can be pulled back into prison worries some observers.

Parole boards are administrative bodies and often have no legal training. In most states with discretionary release, parole hearings are secret with only board members, the inmate, and correctional officers present. Often no published criteria guide decisions, and prisoners are given no reason for the denial or granting of parole. On the other hand, parole boards can quickly remove dangerous offenders from the streets at the first sign that they are returning to criminal activity (e.g., through drug use), without the time and expense of a full criminal trial. Some worry that, as discretionary parole release wanes in the United States, the ability of the justice system to quickly incapacitate those who continue to violate the law diminishes.

While parole revocations are an administrative function that is typically devoid of court involvement, parolees do have some rights in revocation proceedings. Two U.S. Supreme Court cases, *Morrissey v. Brewer* (1972) and *Gagnon v. Scarpelli* (1973), are considered landmark cases of parolee rights in revocation proceedings. Among other things, *Morrissey* and *Gagnon* established minimum requirements for the revocation of parole, forcing boards to conform to some standards of due process. Parolees must be given written notice of the nature of the violation and the evidence obtained, and they have a right to confront and cross-examine their accusers. For a complete review, see del Carmen and colleagues (2000).

Rehabilitation versus Surveillance

Historically, parole agents were viewed as paternalistic figures, who mixed authority with help. Officers provided direct services (for example, counseling) and also knew the community and brokered services (for example, job training) for needy offenders. As noted earlier, parole was originally designed to make the transition from prison to the community more gradual and, during this time, parole officers were to assist the offender in addressing personal problems and searching for employment and a place to live. Many parole agencies still do assist in these service activities. Increasingly, however, parole supervision has shifted away from providing services to parolees and more toward providing surveillance activities, such as drug testing, monitoring curfews, and collecting restitution.

A recent survey of 21 parole agencies shows that 14 provide job development help, 8 offer detoxification services, and 12 offer substance abuse treatment, yet all do drug testing (Camp and Camp 2000). Historically, offering services and treatment to parolees was commonplace, but such services are dwindling.

There are a number of reasons for this shift. First, a greater number of parole conditions are being assigned to released prisoners. In the federal system, for example, between 1987 and 1996, the proportion of offenders required to comply with at least one special supervision condition increased from 67 percent of entrants to 91 percent

(Adams and Roth 1998). Parolees in state systems also are being required to submit more frequently to drug testing, to complete community service, and to make restitution payments.

Parole officers work for the corrections system, and if paroling authorities are imposing a greater number of conditions on parolees, then field agents must monitor those conditions. As a result, contemporary parole officers have less time to provide other services, such as counseling, even if they are inclined to do so.

It is also true that the slowing economy experienced across the United States has reduced the number of treatment and job training programs in the community at large, and, given the fear and suspicion surrounding ex-convicts, these persons usually are placed at the end of the waiting lists. These programs are also nervous about the legal liability and exposure of placing addicts and convicts into treatment and work programs with others. Brokering services to parolees, given the scarcity of programs, has become increasingly difficult. If there is one common complaint among parole officers in the United States, it is the lack of available treatment and job programs for parolees.

At the end of the 1960s, when the country had more employment opportunities for blue collar workers than it does now, there was some movement to reduce the employment barriers, and studies revealed a full-time employment rate of around 50 percent for parolees (Simon 1993). We discuss the employment issue more fully in chapter 6, but let it suffice to say for now that low employment rates are a combination of the structural barriers we impose regarding their employment, the stigma that others place on their convict status, and their lack of motivation and training to keep and maintain a job. If one adds the fact that services are not made available to most parolees because parole supervision has been transformed ideologically from a social service to a law enforcement system, it is no wonder that full-time employment among parolees is relatively rare.

Feely and Simon (1992) argue that, over the past few decades, a systems analysis approach to danger management has come to dominate parole, and it has evolved into a "waste management" system, rather than one focused on rehabilitation. In their model, those in the dangerous class of criminals are nearly synonymous with those in the larger social category of the underclass, a segment of the population that has been abandoned to a fate of poverty and despair. They suggest that a "new penology" has emerged, one that simply strives to manage risk by use of actuarial methods. Offenders are addressed not as individuals but as aggregate populations. The traditional correctional objectives of rehabilitation and the reduction of offender recidivism have given way to the rational and efficient deployment of control strategies for managing (and confining) high-risk criminals. Surveillance and control have replaced treatment as the main goals of parole.

Newly hired parole officers often embrace the surveillance versus the rehabilitation model of parole, along with the quasi-policing role that parole has taken on in some locales. In the 1980s, social work was the most common educational path for those pursuing careers in parole. At the end of 2002, the most common educational path was criminal justice studies, an academic field spawned in the 1960s to professionalize law enforcement. Parole agents began to carry concealed firearms in the 1980s. Firearms are now provided in most jurisdictions and represent a major investment of training resources, agent time, and administrative oversight.

The programming innovations likewise represent a theme of control and supervision rather than service and assistance. Parolees are held more accountable for a broader range of behavior, including alcohol and substance abuse, restitution, curfews, and community service.

Technology and Parole Supervision

There can be no doubt about the ever-increasing role of technology in the field of probation and parole. As James Gondles, president of the American Correctional Association, wrote: "Technology is changing the face of our profession. . . . In many cases, those who break the law are becoming more sophisticated. . . . as a result, we must keep up with them" (2000, p. 6).

Hand-held computers, global positioning satellites, geographic information systems, electronic kiosks, concealed weapons detection and other methods to increase officer safety, and voice and face recognition technologies are now being tested by parole and law enforcement agencies nationwide. These technologies are changing the nature of reporting to parole officers, the manner in which drug and alcohol tests are taken, officer safety, and tracking and locating parolees within geographical boundaries.

When the Cold War ended, government and private technology research centers across the country began looking for new partners outside the defense arena. Law enforcement was an early beneficiary of the technology, with various methods introduced to increase officer safety. But with more than 1.4 million inmates and more than 600,000 prisoners being released each year, corrections surveillance and monitoring began to attract attention, and now corporate giants like AT&T and TRW are developing and testing new products for correctional uses. There are so many new technologies and they are emerging so quickly that the National Institute of Justice, part of the U.S. Department of Justice, maintains the National Law Enforcement and Corrections Technology Center (NLECTC) to share information and answer questions.

Florida, New Jersey, and Michigan are now using global positioning satellites (GPS) to track offenders on community supervision. Their GPS systems are connected to satellites owned by the U.S. government. These satellites orbit above the earth, constantly transmitting the precise time and their position in space. GPS receivers can determine whether offenders are in the community 24 hours a day, as well as the direction and speed they are moving.

One of the most important benefits of satellite tracking is the increased protection it offers crime victims. For instance, when the court orders a sex offender to have no contact with the victim, exclusionary boundaries can be set at an appropriate distance around the victim's residence and place of employment. If the perimeters are broken, an early warning can be sent to the victim. It can send an alarm if the offender is in an area where he is not allowed (exclusion zone), or if he leaves an area in which he must stay (inclusion zone). With GPS, everything is archived, so if it is necessary to know an offender's whereabouts in the past, that information is available. A Florida chief judge who is using the system indicated that it appears to be the "ultimate means of protecting the community" (Wilkinson 2000, p. 235). The cost per day to place an offender on Florida's GPS system is $9.25, compared to $3 per day for regular electronic monitoring.

A recent survey of correctional officers in Florida showed that they are very supportive of the GPS system, and believe it is ideal for violent (particularly, domestic violence) offenders and sex offenders but may be a waste of money for drug offenders (because the offender could be using narcotics in her own home, and GPS would have no way of indicating that a violation had occurred). Fabelo (2000) worries that such devices will expand the net of state control and reduce the rehabilitation efforts of probation and parole. There is no doubt that corrections technology will accelerate in the coming years and will allow community corrections the option of becoming more surveillance oriented.

Conclusions

Once a parolee arrives at parole headquarters to check in, he will find a very different organization than existed prior to the 1980s. Parole officers will likely be armed with weapons and a list of conditions the parolee must follow. Most of these conditions are related to prohibited behavior (e.g., no drug use), but others require work or treatment participation. The parole officer may or may not, depending on the jurisdiction, be able to offer much help in finding a job or treatment program. Parole caseloads have risen while resources have declined. The parolee, however, will be responsible for adhering to the conditions, and the parole system will be increasingly intolerant of his failure. Part of this intolerance reflects the public's and system's perceptions that those coming out of prison today are a more hardcore group, requiring surveillance more than services.

This situation will not change until parole shows that it can deliver services that work, and programs will not have an opportunity to work without sufficient funding and research. There are proven rehabilitation programs that can both reduce recidivism and save money. This is the subject to which we now turn. But implementing these programs is neither easy nor inexpensive. The key is to bring greater balance to the handling of parole populations by singling out those offenders who present different public safety risks and different prospects for rehabilitation.

FIVE

How We Help

Preparing Inmates for Release

We must accept the reality that to confine offenders behind walls without trying to change them is an expensive folly with short-term benefits—winning battles while losing the war. It is wrong. It is expensive. It is stupid.

—Former U.S. Supreme Court chief justice Warren Burger

The average prisoner in the United States at the beginning of the twenty-first century spends about 5 months in jail, 29 months in prison, and 19 months on parole—a total of 4.4 years under correctional supervision. The obvious question to ask is: are those months being used to address any of the problems described in chapter 2? Clearly, the answer is important to understanding how well prepared prisoners are to reenter society.

The data show that U.S. prisons today offer fewer services than they did when inmate problems were less severe, although history shows that we have never invested much in prison rehabilitation. Today, just one-third of all prisoners released will have received vocational or educational training while in prison, despite serious deficiencies in these areas. And despite the fact that three-quarters of all inmates have alcohol or drug abuse problems, just one-fourth of all inmates will participate in a substance abuse program prior to release. Even when they *do* participate, the treatment programs consist mostly of inmate self-help groups rather than the intensive therapeutic communities found to be most effective. It is not that inmates do not want to participate in these programs. On the contrary, virtually all prison programs have long waiting lists. Moreover, while no one argues against the benefits of having inmates transition to a halfway house facility prior to complete release, these programs have all but disappeared in America. Fewer than 10 percent of all prison releasees initially live in a halfway house or other community facility prior to freedom in the community.

Inmate Participation in Prison Programs

Virtually all data on in-prison program participation come from inmate self-reports, as in the national Survey of Inmates in State and Federal Prisons. Individual states cannot usually tell researchers the number of prisoners who have a need for different types of programs, or the extent to which they are participating in programs of various types. Even when we know the counts of inmate participants, we seldom have the details about the nature (e.g., intensity, duration) of the programs. Moreover, most prison education, substance abuse, and treatment programs are never evaluated. It is quite telling that such little data exist about prison education and treatment: we measure what matters most to us.

Table 5.1 summarizes the available information on inmate participation in prison programs. Data on all inmates are presented separately from that on releasees (i.e., inmates to be released within 12 months of the survey), since one presumes participation rates increase as inmates near their release dates.

In most instances, federal inmates have a greater chance of participating in programs than do state prisoners. This is particularly true with work assignments and prison industry jobs (i.e., income-producing businesses operated in prison). A greater percentage of federal than state prisoners also participate in prerelease programs, although by any measure, federal prisoners have fewer treatment needs than do state prisoners. Federal prisoners have more work experience, higher levels of education, and fewer substance abuse issues than do state inmates. And the number of federal prisoners participating in substance abuse programs has increased. The Violent Crime Control and Law Enforcement Act of 1994 required the federal Bureau of Prisons (BOP) to provide substance abuse treatment or drug education to every eligible inmate. There is no similar law that applies to state prisoners.

However, as shown in table 5.1., prison program participation rates are distressingly low. Overall, about one in four federal or state inmates had participated in a drug or alcohol program since their admissions. In 1997, fewer than half of the inmates in either prison sys-

Table 5.1. Inmate participation in prison programs, 1997

Type of program attended	All inmates		Releasees	
	State	Federal	State	Federal
Residential inpatient treatment	33%	28%	36%	33%
Alcohol program	24	20	27	24
Drug program	24	25	29	28
Education classes	38	45	35	43
Vocational training	31	29	27	27
Any work assignment	60	87	56	87
Prison industry jobs	3	17	2	11
Prerelease programs	8	13	12	37
Number of inmates	1,059,607	89,072	400,821	22,583

Note: The percentages show inmate participation since admission to prison for the current offense.

Source: Government Accounting Office 2001.

tem (federal, 45 percent, and state, 38 percent) had been involved in an education program since being admitted. And less than one-third of the inmates received any vocational training. Although 87 percent of federal inmates and 60 percent of state inmates had work assignments, only 17 percent of federal and 3 percent of the state inmates had assignments in prison industry jobs. Finally, only 13 percent of the federal inmates and 8 percent of state inmates had participated in prerelease programs.

As one would expect, participation in prerelease programs increases significantly among inmates scheduled to be released within 12 months, particularly among federal inmates (37 percent). The federal prerelease program is much more comprehensive than that in virtually any state prison system. The BOP prerelease program offers courses in six core areas: health and nutrition, personal growth and development, personal finance and consumer skills, employment, release requirements and procedures, and information on community resources. Beginning 24 months before release, inmates are encouraged to enroll in and complete at least one course in each core area.

By any measure, the figures contained in table 5.1 are extremely low, given the high need for treatment, education, and work training. But, as discussed in chapter 3, public and financial support for correctional treatment waned during the 1980s and 1990s. As the prison population boomed, money to support rehabilitation programs did not keep pace. Recent analysis by Lynch and Sabol (2001) shows that the rate of prison program participation has declined for state inmates since the early 1990s.

As shown in figure 5.1, about one-third of soon-to-be-released inmates in 1997 reported that they participated in vocational programs (27 percent) or educational programs (35 percent), down from 31 percent and 43 percent, respectively, in 1991. As Lynch and Sabol note, these decreases in participation rates are steeper than they appear, because smaller shares of bigger populations are involved, which means that significantly larger numbers of prisoners are being released without vocational or educational training.

A decline in prison program participation levels should not be used to infer that prisoners are less in need of services or less willing to participate in programs. Rather, low participation rates are likely a symptom of program availability. Existing programs simply cannot accommodate all prisoners who are willing to participate. In a recent

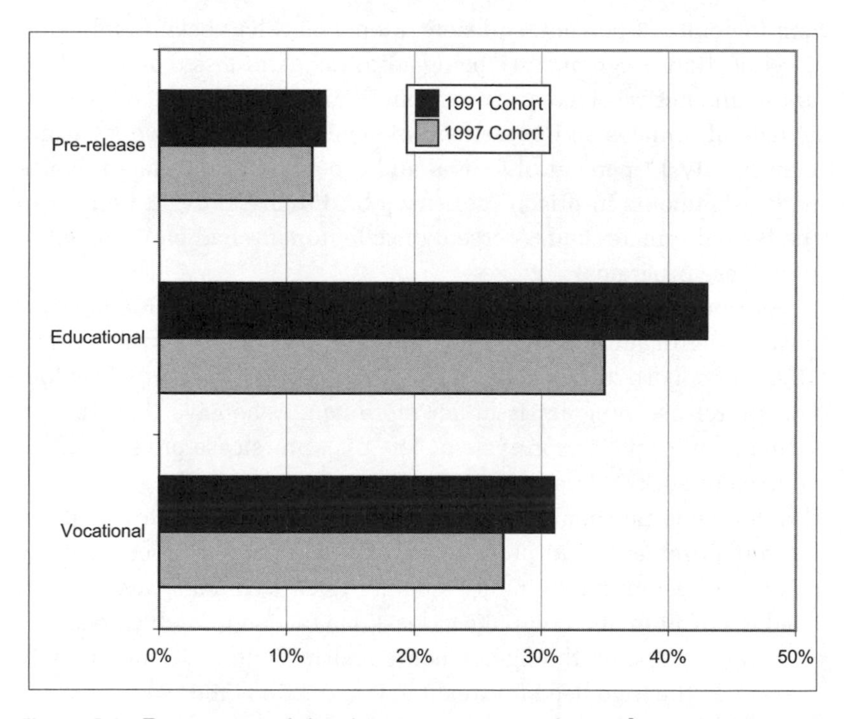

Figure 5.1. Program participation among state prison releasees, 1991 versus 1997. *Source*: Lynch and Sabol 2001.

Ohio study, incoming inmates were asked how likely they would be to participate in prison programs targeting job skills. More than 68 percent of the respondents reported that they would be "very likely" to take part in prison programs aimed at teaching job skills. Less than 10 percent of the inmates expressed unwillingness to participate in such programs (Henderson 2001).

The nation's war on drugs sent tens of thousands of people to prison in the 1990s, and yet until recently there was little attention paid to providing treatment once they were incarcerated. Health and Human Services (HHS) conducted the first national survey of substance abuse treatment in adult correctional facilities in 2000. The survey found that 45 percent of state prisons and 68 percent of jails had *no* substance abuse treatment of any kind. Even when a program existed, the research found that treatment was usually minimal. As Bruce Fry of HHS recently testified: "It is estimated that about 70 percent of persons in state prisons need treatment. Since most are not treated in prison, when they leave prison they are at extremely high risk of relapse, and are likely to commit crimes again and again until they are caught and put back into prison, where the cycle begins all over again" (Government Accounting Office 2001, p. 27).

Despite the fact that the federal government has been funding the expansion of prison substance abuse treatment, it appears that we are unable to keep up with the demand. The National Center on Addiction and Substance Abuse (1998) reports that a slightly lower proportion of those with drug addiction are receiving treatment. In 1993, 22 percent of inmates needing treatment were in treatment; by 1996, only 18 percent of needy inmates were in treatment. This treatment could be as little as short-term drug education, or self-help groups, or longer-term residential treatment. However, residential treatment or long-term counseling is exceedingly rare in prisons. Research has shown that fewer than 5 percent of all prison inmates received residential substance abuse treatment. The vast majority (nearly 75 percent) of drug treatment in prisons consists of inmate self-help groups, specifically Alcoholics Anonymous (AA) and Narcotics Anonymous (NA).

Research has also shown that there are racial differences in prison drug treatment participation. Some studies found that black and Hispanic prisoners, despite their higher drug use and addiction rates, are less likely than whites to participate in prison substance abuse programs (Mumola 1999).

Work Release, Halfway Houses, and Community Reentry Centers

Prisoners should ideally make the transition from prison to the community in a gradual, closely supervised process. The president's crime commission noted years ago: "This process of graduated release permits offenders to cope with their many postrelease problems in manageable steps, rather than trying to develop satisfactory home relationship[s], employment and leisure time activity all at once upon release. It also permits staff to initiate early and continuing assessment of progress under actual stresses of life" (1967, p. 177).

Everyone agrees that public safety would be enhanced if prisoners were provided transitional housing and required to have a test period before gaining freedom in the community. Yet despite this logic, transitional work and housing programs have been cut significantly in recent years. While all states legally permit work and educational furloughs, and most states operate halfway houses or reentry facilities, the vast majority of prisoners (more than 90 percent) now being released do not participate in such programs. In fact, the figure has not increased much in the last 35 years, when data revealed that just 3–4 percent of all inmates released in 1965 participated in such transition programs. Today, just 7 percent of all prison releasees initially live in a halfway house or other community facility (Camp and Camp 2000).

Furloughs, work release, and halfway houses basically are all designed to give the inmate a chance to acclimate to the free world and develop work and social relationships that will assist at release. Furloughs are authorized, unescorted leaves from prison granted for specific purposes and for designated periods, usually 24 or 72 hours, although they can be as long as several weeks or as short as a few hours. Furloughs were used extensively between 1950 and 1975 but were hard hit by the get-tough approach and bad national publicity.

Willie Horton, a Massachusetts prisoner who committed murder while on furlough, became a political issue during the 1988 presidential campaign. Reacting to the adverse publicity given Horton's crime and the tougher furlough policy, the Bureau of Prisons reduced federal furloughs by one-half. In 1998, 31 states and the BOP permitted furloughs, but just 8,681 inmates were allowed to take furloughs (.02 percent of all inmates released that year) (Bartollas 2002). California, for example, granted 14,000 furloughs in the early 1970s but granted none in 1998.

Work release takes the prisoner even further into the community, as its objective is to place offenders in jobs they can retain after their release or, at a minimum, increase their job readiness. Inmates may be housed in a separate community-based facility during work release, or housed within the prison but allowed to leave the prison during the day to work. A large study of work release in the state of Washington by Turner and Petersilia (1996) found that although work release participants did not have lower prison return rates than other inmates (mostly due to high rates of technical violations), the arrest rates for work release inmates were very low, and work release played a role in the successful transition of one-fourth of those released from prisons.

All but a few states have laws permitting work-release programs, but states vary in their commitment to the program. At the end of 2002, only about a one-third of U.S. prisons reported operating such programs, and fewer than 3 percent of U.S. inmates participated in them. The states that placed the most inmates on work release were New York, Illinois, and Florida. The federal BOP placed no inmates on work release during 1998.

Halfway houses, as the very name suggests, are positioned to be "halfway out" residential transition facilities. Prison inmates are permitted to serve the last one to six months of their prison terms in the community, under the restrictions of the halfway house facilities. The notion is that these facilities will provide an environment that helps to ease a parolee's reentry into the community. Halfway houses provide the basic necessities of food, clothing, and health care, while the inmate looks for permanent housing and employment. Most facilities also offer emotional support to deal with the pressures of readjustment.

Halfway houses, which were fairly widespread in the 1970s, have declined in popularity. The American Correctional Association (2000) reports that just 55 halfway houses were being operated by 10 state agencies in 1999. There were fewer than 20,000 inmates served in halfway houses during that year (.04 percent of all inmates released that year). Halfway houses are also called residential centers, work release centers, or community reentry centers.

Halfway houses or community reentry centers (the newer term) have never reached more than a small number of prison releasees, but they represent a promising program. Part of the difficulty is the community's reaction to the concept and finding a suitable location for the facility. A Lou Harris poll, for example, found that although

77 percent of a representative U.S. sample favored the halfway house concept, 50 percent would not want one in *their* neighborhood, and only 22 percent believed that people in *their* neighborhood would favor a halfway house being located there (Abadinsky 1997, p. 398).

A growing irrationality runs through much of sentencing practice today. Local citizens often fear criminals, particularly those recently released from prison. But, in most instances, these criminals are returning to their community in any event. Giving them a place to live and structured assistance at release can provide residents with *more* security than if the inmate were simply on the streets. Virtually all halfway houses and neighborhood reentry centers have community advisory boards, composed of neighbors, local businesses, and law enforcement. This group can be kept advised of parolees' whereabouts and progress, which leads to greater public safety, not less, for community residents. The key, of course, is to assure that the reentry center program incorporates both surveillance and services and that both are intensive enough to make a difference.

An excellent example of such a program is the Illinois Department of Correction's Chicago Day Reporting Center (DRC). The program is operated by BI Incorporated, a private corrections company. The DRC is for high-risk parolees on the Southside of Chicago. Inmates do not live at the facility but initially report to it every day. Inmates with two or more prior incarcerations, a sentence of 10 years or more, or who are under 25 years old and serving time for a violent crime are eligible. Each accepted applicant completes the Level of Service Inventory–Revised (LSI-R, described in chapter 3) and is then assigned a case manager, who develops a supervision and treatment plan.

The DRC offers many programs, including anger management, family reintegration, employment training, cognitive skills, GED and educational courses, and job development. Substance abuse education and treatment are central to the DRC. Center residents normally stay in the program about six months, during which time they gradually progress through three phases, each with more relaxed restrictions on curfew, drug testing, and electronic monitoring. Immediately upon release from prison, inmates report to the center seven days a week, have a curfew from 8 P.M. to 6 A.M., and are subject to required urinalysis. By the time they have progressed to the third phase, they are reporting to the center three days a week, curfew is 12 A.M. to 6 A.M., and urinalysis is random. All parolees must be employed to get out of phase 3. The program also incorporates six months of aftercare services. At any one time, the DRC has about 150 parolees reporting, and during the first three years (1998–2001), 1,503 clients participated in the program.

A recent evaluation of BI's system shows that the average length of stay in the DRC program is 7.2 months, at a cost of about $6,600 per offender (BI Incorporated 2002). Rearrest and reincarceration rates were significantly lower than those of a matched comparison group. Generally, participants in the DRC were returned to prison at about half the rate of the comparison group. At the end of year one, 10 percent of the DRC participants had been returned to prison as compared to 35 percent of the matched comparison group. The favorable results continued through the full three-year follow-up. By year three, 35 percent of the DRC participants had been returned to prison for a new crime, compared with 52 percent of the comparison group. The comparison group was similar in terms of age, race, gender, education, and nature of current and past crimes. BI's evaluation (2002, p. 12) concludes: "Overall, this represents a 40.6% reduction in new criminal convictions over the comparison group (or 263 fewer crimes committed) which translates into an estimated savings of $3.6 million over 3 years to the Illinois taxpayer."

Programs such as BI's Chicago Day Reporting Center make perfect sense. First, they save money. More important, the program seems to have reduced drug use, increased job attainment, and responded to the real needs of residents—as judged by evaluations completed by the DRC participants themselves. These factors should increase the cost effectiveness of the program over time, although this is not yet known. Eighty-four percent of the drug tests were negative on average over the first two-year period, and nearly half of the residents were employed. Written evaluations from parolees showed they experienced a high degree of satisfaction with the quality and type of services received.

Today, halfway houses and other transitional inmate programs face tough political battles. Correctional leaders and local politicians are wary of supporting such facilities since it makes them vulnerable to highly publicized failures, especially when a parolee commits another heinous crime. So, we have stopped funding transitional work and residential programs and now release the vast majority of prisoners without needed housing and social supports. We should not be surprised when two-thirds of all prisoners are rearrested.

Mental Health Treatment

According to the Bureau of Justice Statistics (BJS), U.S. state prisons now house more than 191,000 mentally ill inmates. Inmates with mental illness have a higher probability of receiving some treatment than inmates with substance abuse histories or work or educational deficiencies. Nearly 13 percent—one in every eight state prisoners or 79 percent of those mentally ill—received some mental health therapy or counseling services in 2000. The BJS also found that nearly 10 percent of all state prison inmates in 2000 were receiving psychotropic medications (including antidepressants, stimulants, sedatives, tranquilizers, and antipsychotic drugs). More than 90 percent of the inmates having a diagnosed mental illness were taking such medication.

Few inmates (about 10 percent of all those identified as mentally ill) are confined in specific mental health facilities; the remainder are housed in the general prison population (Beck and Maruschak 2001). Inmates with mental illness are particularly vulnerable to victimization and violent outbursts, and they are disproportionately moved to supermax or maximum-security prisons (see chapter 2).

Most prisoners with mental illness will eventually be released. Unfortunately, the medications and counseling begun in prison are often not continued in the community. A recent survey revealed that just 65 percent of correctional facilities report helping inmates obtain community mental health services at release (Beck and Maruschak 2001). Moreover, fewer than a quarter of parole administrators indicate that they have special programs for parolees with mental illness (Association of Parole Authorities, International 2001b). Prisoners are often left to fend for themselves in navigating the difficult social service delivery system when they return to the community. They often stop taking their medications and return to the kinds of behavior that led to their imprisonment, and the cycle repeats itself.

Conclusions

Prison work and treatment programs have fallen on hard times. There remains an increasingly large mismatch between the need for programs and program availability. This is not just the case with in-prison programs, but is also true for furlough and residential programs designed to ease the transition between prison and the free community. It is safe to conclude that the majority of inmates with serious problems return to the community with those problems unaddressed.

Some states (e.g., Oregon, Washington, Ohio, and Texas) have begun to implement work and education programs that reduce recidivism. These innovative program models are showing that prison programs can reduce recidivism and subsequent justice system costs. It is not easy and it is not inexpensive, but it *is* possible. It requires political leaders who are willing to think differently about prisons and their role in prisoner reentry. Unfortunately, as we will see in the next chapter, the nation has not chosen to invest in reentry programs and instead has erected a growing number of legal and practical barriers to postrelease success.

SIX

How We Hinder

Legal and Practical Barriers to Reintegration

Prisoners return home with most of their treatment and vocational training needs unmet, and they will soon learn that they occupy an in-between status. They are back in society but not free. Under the federal law and the laws of every state, a felony conviction has consequences that continue long after a sentence has been served and parole has ended.

Convicted felons may lose many essential rights of citizenship, such as the right to vote and to hold public office, and are often restricted in their ability to obtain occupational and professional licenses. Their criminal record may also preclude their receiving government benefits and retaining parental rights, be grounds for divorce, prevent their serving on a jury, and nearly always limits firearm ownership. The restrictions on employment and housing create formidable obstacles to law-abidingness. One has to question whether we are jeopardizing public saftey by making it so difficult for prison releasees to succeed.

It is important to note that while the rehabilitation services available to assist inmates both in prison and after release have *decreased* in the past decade, the legal and practical barriers pertaining to their activities after release have *increased*. One survey shows that, after a period when states were becoming less restrictive of convicted felons' rights, the get-tough movement of the 1980s and 1990s had the effect of increasing the statutory restrictions placed on ex-prisoners (Olivares, Burton, and Cullen 1996).

Jeremy Travis refers to these restrictions as "invisible punishments" and notes their increasing importance to reintegration and sentencing policy:

> Over the same period of time that prisons and criminal justice supervision have increased significantly, the laws and regulations that serve to diminish the rights and privileges of those

> convicted of crimes have also expanded. Yet we cannot adequately measure the reach of these expressions of the social inclination to punish. Consequently, we cannot evaluate their effectiveness, impact, or even "implementation" through the myriad of private and public entities that are expected to enforce these new rules. Because these laws operate largely beyond public view, yet have very serious, adverse consequences for the individuals affected, I refer to them, collectively, as "invisible punishment." (2002, p. 16)

A complete state-by-state survey of civil disabilities of convicted felons can be found in *Civil Disabilities of Convicted Felons*, published periodically by the Office of the Pardon Attorney, U.S. Department of Justice (Love and Kuzma 1997). Most restrictions apply to all convicted felons, and not separately to parolees. In addition to the loss of some aspects of general citizenship (e.g., right to serve on a jury, vote, or hold public office), there are a number of other restrictions related to employment, parenting, marriage, and eligibility for housing assistance and welfare.

Some states have tried to mitigate the stigma of a felony conviction, as well as restore one or more of the rights previously denied, by allowing some disabilities to be removed automatically by the passage of time or the occurrence of an event, such as completion of sentence, or through some affirmative executive or judicial act, which may be based on evidence of rehabilitation. However, as a report on the subject concluded: "The laws governing the rights and privileges vary widely from state to state, making something of a national crazy-quilt of disqualifications and restoration procedures" (Love and Kuzma 1997, p. 3). The laws of the different states are complicated, often unknown to the offenders to which they apply, and the restrictions are difficult to get removed once they have been applied to you. Importantly, with growing computerization and greater public access to criminal records, the stigma and legal barriers affecting ex-prisoners are expanding and increasing in their importance.

Publicly Available Criminal Records

Loss of many civil rights is predicated on the existence of a criminal history record, usually one containing a felony rather than a misdemeanor conviction. According to a 1999 survey conducted by

SEARCH for the U.S. Department of Justice, more than 59 million individuals—or 29 percent of the nation's entire adult population—were in state criminal history files (Bureau of Justice Statistics 2001a). These state records may include arrests for misdemeanors or felonies, regardless of whether the arrest resulted in conviction. These records usually do not include minor infractions, such as driving tickets. In comparison, state criminal justice repositories covered just 30.3 million subjects in 1984 (or 17 percent of the U.S. adult population). Thus, the number of criminal history files maintained on U.S. citizens nearly doubled from 1984 to 1999.

The FBI also maintains criminal history information and reports that it had automated, fingerprint-based criminal history information on more than 43 million individuals in 1999 (24 percent of all adult citizens). FBI records pertain to federal offenders but also include records of state offenders voluntarily reported to the FBI by state agencies. FBI records include information about arrests for felonies and serious misdemeanors, not traffic offenses, infractions, or other misdemeanors.

FBI and state criminal record repositories historically did not maintain juvenile record information, except with respect to juveniles tried as adults. However, this nearly century-long practice ended in 1992 when the attorney general adopted a rule authorizing the FBI to accept—and disseminate under the same standards used for adults—state-reported records of serious offenses by juveniles.

Of course, having a criminal record is not nearly as stigmatizing as having been convicted and served time on probation, in jail, or in prison. Uggen and colleagues (2002b) recently used demographic life tables combined with recidivism probabilities to produce national estimates of the number of current and former criminal offenders in the United States in 2000. Their results are striking.

As shown in table 6.1, a growing number of Americans are now considered part of the criminal class, having been convicted and sentenced for a felony crime. This ex-felon lifetime stigma is significant and disproportionately felt among black adult males. Uggen and colleagues estimate that 15–19 percent of U.S. adult black males are current or former prisoners, and 29–37 percent are current or former felons. The authors note: "We realize that these estimates may appear surprisingly large in magnitude . . . yet it is extremely unlikely that our estimates of current prisoners and current felons are biased upward."

Not only are more Americans acquiring a criminal record, but also

Table 6.1. U.S. adult population with criminal records, 2000

		Percentage of Population		
Type of criminal record	Total	All adults	Adult males	Adult black males
Prisoners (includes current or former prisoners and parolees, federal and state)	5 million	2.5	5	15–19*
Felons (includes prison, parole, felony probation, and convicted felony jail populations)	13 million	6.5	11	29–37*

*The lower bound estimates assume a 25% higher recidivism rate for black prisoners, probationers, and parolees.

Source: Uggen et al. 2002b.

the growing use of computerized record-keeping systems means that the information is more easily shared. A major initiative of the U.S. Department of Justice in recent years has been to give financial support—nearly $400 million between 1995 and 2001—to help states improve the quality, completeness, and accessibility of their criminal history records. The National Criminal History Improvement Program's (NCHIP) goal is to enhance and upgrade the nation's criminal history records. These enhanced computerized systems—initially designed to assure that criminals did not buy weapons or hold positions involving children and the elderly—certainly affect the efforts of convicts trying to go straight as well. By the end of 2002, 40 states reported that more than 75 percent of their criminal history records are automated.

Certainly, the public safety benefits of sharing criminal record information are undeniable. But, as in other areas where private information is publicly shared, there are inherent dangers as well. Some of the criminal record information in the FBI and state registries has been shown to be inaccurate, and yet it is shared with landlords, financial institutions, and employers as if it were valid. In fact, in a recent Department of Justice review of the nation's criminal history information systems, data quality emerged as one of the most important issues identified by users. This report also noted that about 60 percent of the arrest entries fail to record final disposition data. Yet, as noted below, 10 states provide members of the general public with this arrest-without-disposition information.

Criminal history information, once available solely to law enforcement and the courts, is now widely available to the public at large, although the degree of openness varies from state to state. Nearly all states make a distinction between arrest records and conviction records. In general, states are less likely to freely disseminate information on arrests, especially arrests for cases that are still open or have occurred within the previous year. States tend to place fewer restrictions on public access to conviction records.

At the end of 2002, 33 states allowed anyone to obtain criminal record, or "rap sheet," information, whereas the other states limited the dissemination of rap sheet information to individuals or organizations specified or authorized by statute (e.g., criminal justice agencies, employers). These results are contained in table 6.2. Just 15 states notify the rap sheet subject when an individual or organization requests information from his record. Of the states that allow anyone to have access, 20 limit the disseminated data to conviction-only information. The remaining states generally provide requesters with all information except sealed or expunged records or most juvenile data (Johnson 2001).

A survey recently completed by the Legal Action Center (see table 6.3) found that criminal records are now widely available to the public via the Internet. They reported that, in 25 states, the public has access to criminal records on the Internet for all individuals in prison. In 6 of those states, information that the public can access pertains only to inmates currently in prison or on parole. In 19 of those states, the publicly accessible information is on currently and formerly imprisoned and paroled offenders (Mukamal and Stevens 2002).

The information available to the public via the Internet includes both criminal record and personal information. For example, the public can search the Illinois Department of Corrections' (DOC) website using an inmate's name, date of birth, or DOC number. A screen will immediately appear with a current picture of the inmate (or parolee), the inmate's current status, residence location (if paroled), date of birth, height, weight, race, color of hair and eyes, scars or tattoos, security classification, county of commitment and release, discharge date, conviction crime, number of counts, sentence imposed, and other personal information. In some other states' Internet sites, information on modus operandi, cars driven, home address, gang affiliation, and substance abuse histories are also included.

Table 6.2. State policies on access to state criminal history records

Available to the general public	Available to criminal justice personnel only	Available to non–criminal justice entities if authorized by statute
Alabama*	Arkansas	Indiana
Alaska	California	Louisiana
Arizona*	Kentucky	New York
Colorado	Maryland	
Connecticut	Massachusetts	
Delaware*	New Jersey	
Florida*	New Mexico	
Georgia	Nevada	
Hawaii	North Carolina	
Idaho	Ohio	
Illinois	Rhode Island	
Iowa*	Tennessee	
Kansas*	Utah	
Maine	Vermont	
Michigan*		
Minnesota		
Mississippi		
Missouri		
Montana		
Nebraska*		
New Hampshire		
North Dakota		
Oklahoma*		
Oregon		
Pennsylvania		
South Carolina		
South Dakota		
Texas		
Virginia		
Washington		
West Virginia		
Wisconsin		
Wyoming*		

Note: Asterisks (*) indicate states that provide the public with "everything on record," including arrests without final dispositions.

Source: Johnson 2001, with additional updates provided by Johnson 2002.

Table 6.3. State policies on making prisoner records publicly available on the Internet

Records available for current and former prisoners and parolees	Records available for current prisoners and parolees only	Prisoner records not publicly available
Arizona	Alabama	Alaska
Arkansas	Iowa	California
Florida	Kentucky	Colorado
Georgia	Nevada	Connecticut
Illinois	Pennsylvania	Delaware
Kansas	Vermont	Hawaii
Louisiana		Idaho
Michigan		Indiana
Mississippi		Maine
Montana		Maryland
Nebraska		Massachusetts
New York		Minnesota
North Carolina		Missouri
Ohio		New Hampshire
Oklahoma		New Jersey
South Carolina		New Mixico
Texas		North Dakota
Washington		Oregon
Wisconsin		Rhode Island
		South Dakota
		Tennessee
		Utah
		Virginia
		West Virginia
		Wyoming

Source: Mukamal and Stevens 2002.

The Florida DOC, for example, supports public access to its state criminal record system, and it is more inclusive both in the kinds of people it covers and the information it contains. Florida's DOC Internet website allows the public to search for current and former prisoners, current and former parolees, current and former felony probationers, and absconders or fugitives. For each of those databases, detailed personal and crime information is available, including aliases, fingerprint classification, driver's license number, prior criminal record, and for those in the community, the address of the ex-prisoner's stated residence upon release.

In addition to the greater openness and completeness of state repositories, several services have emerged that perform nationwide criminal history record reviews for small fees. An Internet search of the term "criminal history record" will turn up several companies that will perform multistate criminal background checks for as little as $15 to $30 per state. An example of a widely used service is www.backgroundferret.com. This organization advertises that it can conduct a background check in any one of 34 states within four hours, and it will also do searches of county-level records.

Of course, such open access to criminal records is tremendously useful in protecting victims, community members, and employers. This value cannot be overstated. But we also need to think seriously about the detrimental effects on returning inmates, given that these records—some of them inaccurate—will be used to make decisions about them for the rest of their lives. A compromise policy seems reasonable. For example, perhaps only offenders with particularly serious crimes, or those whose crimes were recent (e.g., within the past five years) would have their records publicly shared. It would also make sense to limit what is shared with persons requesting information, for example, sharing only arrests followed by convictions or the mere existence of a prison record.

Employment Barriers and Workplace Restrictions

Most experts, as well as prisoners themselves, believe that finding a job is critical to successful reintegration. Employment helps ex-prisoners be productive, take care of their families, develop valuable life skills, and strengthen their self-esteem and social connectedness. Research has empirically established a positive link between job stability and reduced criminal offending. Lipsey's (1995) meta-analysis of nearly 400 studies from 1950 to 1990 found that the single most effective factor in reducing reoffending rates was employment. For recent reviews of the relationship between employment and crime, see Uggen (2000), and Bushway and Reuter (2002).

Parole boards always require parolees to "look for work" or "obtain a job" as a condition of release. However, it is important to recall that 18–21 percent of prison inmates report having a mental or physical condition that limits their ability to work (see table 2.6). A survey by the Association of Parole Authorities, International (APAI) found that 14 states say they would revoke for "failing to secure or hold a job," even if no crime were committed, while 31 states say they would not revoke if the person were attempting to locate work. Among parole violators in state prison in 1997, 1.2 percent (about 28,000 persons) reported that their parole had been revoked for "failure to maintain employment."

Holzer, Raphael, and Stoll (2002) note that, aside from their offender status, ex-prisoners have a number of other significant barriers to employment, including:

- very low levels of education and of previous work experience
- substance abuse or other mental health issues
- residing in poor inner-city neighborhoods that have weak connections to stable employment opportunities and are relatively removed from centers of job growth
- a lack of motivation for and attitudes of distrust and alienation from traditional work

In addition, ex-offenders are legally barred from a growing number of jobs, and they face an explicit unwillingness of many employers to hire them for the jobs from which they are not legally barred.

Formal Restrictions on Jobs, Bonding, and Licensing of Ex-Convicts

It is generally illegal for an employer to impose a flat ban on hiring ex-offenders. However, employers are increasingly forbidden from hiring them for certain jobs and are mandated to perform background checks before hiring an applicant for many others. The most common types of jobs with legal prohibitions against ex-offenders are in the fields of child care, education, security, nursing, and home health care, particularly where vulnerable populations (e.g., the elderly or disabled) are involved. Since 1985, the number of barred occupations has increased dramatically.

In California, for example, parolees are legally barred from working in the professions of law, real estate, medicine, nursing, physical therapy, and education. In Colorado, the jobs of dentist, engineer, nurse, pharmacist, physician, and real estate agent are closed to convicted felons. All states restrict former offenders from employment as barbers (even though many prisons provide training programs in barbering), beauticians, and nurses. In some instances, newly released offenders may find themselves legally barred from jobs they held before they were incarcerated. Even a prior arrest as a juvenile is an absolute bar to employment in a criminal justice occupation in many states, despite the fact that criminal justice agencies that have hired former convicts rate their job performance equal to or better than that of the average employee (Clear and Cole 2000).

Even when employers are willing to employ former inmates in entry-level jobs, they are sometimes unwilling to advance them to positions of responsibility. In addition to restrictions imposed by employers, some unions flatly exclude all ex-convicts. Ex-offenders also have difficulty in meeting employers' requirements of bonding against theft, a common practice in many service businesses. *Bonding* is a type of insurance that protects an employer against negligent or criminal activities committed by its employees. The courts ruled in *Hawker v. New York* (1968) that employers are legally allowed to refuse bonding to felons, stating, "Employers may make the record of a conviction conclusive evidence of the fact of the violation of the criminal law and the absence of the requisite good character." Prospective employers sometimes insist on bonds from people with criminal records that they would not require from other employees, and many bonding companies flatly refuse to underwrite bonds for ex-prisoners.

Moreover, the licensing requirements applicable to many jobs present still further obstacles to the employment of ex-offenders. Nearly 6,000 occupations are licensed in one or more states in the United States, many of which would be otherwise within reach of the ex-offender populations (Clear and Cole 2000). Licensing regulations, which apply to occupations ranging from law and medicine to collecting garbage and cutting hair, frequently contain broad enough standards of competency and honesty to result in flat proscriptions against all offenders. Often, there is no rational connection between the restriction placed on an ex-offender's occupation and the crime she committed.

Ironically, it is sometimes the jobs on which prison job programs focus that require licensing for which the ex-convict is ineligible. For example, one of the most popular vocational training courses in the New York City Reformatory is the barber school, but New York state usually denies applications for barber's licenses when the applicant has a prison record. It is important to remember all of these barriers when we question the relationship between in-prison work-training programs and postprison employment and ask, "Why don't they work better?"

Public employment (e.g., working for the county, state, or federal government), usually the largest employer in most states, is permanently denied to felons in six states: Alabama, Delaware, Iowa, Mississippi, Rhode Island, and South Carolina (Kuzma 1998). The remaining jurisdictions permit public employment in varying degrees. Of these states, 10 leave the decision to hire to the discretion of the employer, while 12 jurisdictions apply a "direct relationship test" to determine whether the conviction offense bears directly on the job in question. But the courts have interpreted the direct relationship standard liberally. For example, a California case (*Golde v. Fox*) found that the conviction for possession of marijuana for sale was substantially related to the business of real estate broker as it shows lack of honesty and integrity.

There are practical problems as well. Even for jobs that are legally accessible, ex-convicts are often precluded from applying because they do not possess the necessary documentation. Ex-convicts often need assistance in applying for various forms of identification and other important documents, such as drivers' licenses, Social Security cards, and birth certificates. These documents are vital for obtaining employment. Applying for and getting these documents can be particularly confusing and frustrating for a former prisoner, and the individual often needs one piece of identification in order to get another. Also, since the terrorism events of 11 September 2001, securing government-issued identification is more difficult.

A driver's license is often a prerequisite to establishing one's identity or obtaining many jobs, and some states are working with the Department of Motor Vehicles to renew inmates' drivers' licenses (if eligible) before release. However, Congress passed a law in 1992 requiring states to revoke or suspend the drivers' licenses of people convicted of drug felonies or lose 10 percent of the state's federal highway funds. This federal law requires states to revoke mandatorily or suspend individuals' drivers' licenses for at least six months upon conviction of a drug-related felony, and drug-related felonies are defined within the law as including DUIs (driving under the influence). As of 2002, 19 states and the District of Columbia had enacted conforming legislation (Travis 2002). The states that revoke drivers' licenses to conform with this federal law are Alabama, Arkansas, Colorado, Delaware, Florida, Georgia, Indiana, Iowa, Massachusetts, Michigan, Missouri, New Jersey, New York, Ohio, Pennsylvania, South Carolina, Utah, Virginia, and Wisconsin.

Employer Use of Criminal History Records in Hiring Decisions

Whether or not the felon is *legally* eligible for the job or not, research suggests that most employers will ask about the applicant's criminal record, and once it is revealed, the applicant's chances of being hired are significantly reduced. Western, Kling, and Weiman (2001) found that employers are less likely to hire ex-convicts than those who provide *no* information about past convictions (i.e., leave the item blank) on employment applications.

Employers may legally consider an applicant's conviction(s) in making hiring decisions. If an applicant fails to disclose such information or misrepresents the information, and the employer discovers the deception, the individual can be legally fired. However, employers cannot legally use arrest records to exclude persons from employment unless there is a business justification. If it can be demonstrated that the applicant actually engaged in the conduct for which she was arrested and that the conduct is job-related and relatively recent, exclusion would be justified (U.S. Department of Labor 2001).

Evidence suggests that employers primarily use a criminal history record to make judgments about the general or essential character of an applicant. Employers who indicate they are not willing to hire ex-offenders say they are most concerned about their general "trustworthiness" rather than anything specifically related to the offense or the job in question. Because ex-offenders are seen as less trustworthy, they are limited to the "spot market," where employers offer only temporary or seasonal employment and thus trustworthiness is perceived to be less important.

Harry Holzer and his colleagues conducted surveys of employers in Atlanta, Boston, Detroit, and Los Angeles. The surveys inquired about the likelihood that the employer would be willing to hire an applicant with a criminal record. More than 60 percent of 3,000 employers surveyed indicated that they would "probably not" or "definitely not" be willing to hire an applicant with a criminal record, with "probably not" being the modal response. The responses were similar across the four metropolitan areas. The survey specifically questioned employers who had recently hired low-skilled workers, since they perhaps would be the most likely to hire ex-offenders. These results confirm that a large majority of employers are unwilling to hire ex-offenders (Holzer 1996).

The Holzer surveys also asked employers about their willingness to hire other categories of applicants. The results showed that 82 percent of those interviewed said they would hire a welfare recipient; 82 percent said they would hire a GED/government trainee; and 68 percent said they would hire someone who had been unemployed for at least one year. These results led Holzer and colleagues to conclude, "Employers are much more reluctant to hire ex-offenders than *any* other group of disadvantaged workers. Employers fear the legal liabilities that could potentially be created by hiring offenders, and they view their offender status as a signal of lack of reliability and trustworthiness" (2002, p. 10).

These results were confirmed recently in a national survey by Wirthlin Worldwide of 600 businesses participating in the Welfare to Work Partnership, a nonpartisan effort to assist businesses with hiring people on public assistance (Wirthlin Worldwide 2000). The Wirthlin survey reported that persons with a past criminal conviction were the "hardest to serve," and 40 percent of the respondents reported that they would "never hire anyone with a felony drug conviction" (see figure 6.1).

Both the Holzer and Wirthlin surveys revealed that employers are reluctant to hire ex-convicts partly because they fear that they will incur liability if that person commits a new crime. This is known as *negligent hiring* and refers to instances where employers who knew, or should have known, that an employee had a history of criminal behavior may be liable for the employee's criminal acts. Under the theory of negligent hiring, employers may be exposed to punitive damages as well as liability for loss, pain, and suffering. The Wirthlin survey found that employers would be more likely to consider hiring an ex-convict if the government would insure them against any financial loss or legal liability should something go wrong. Indeed, a number of state and federal bonding programs now exist.

In most cases, however, an employer will not face legal liability if she hires an ex-offender. While state standards differ, the key to determining liability is usually whether the employer could have foreseen the crime, specifically, whether the employee had a history or propensity for harmful behavior and, most important, whether the employer knew or should have known of the employee's propensity. Generally, an employer's reasonable efforts to check and consider a prospective employee's background will satisfy the legal requirement and eliminate the risk of liability for the employer (U.S. Department of Labor 2001).

Despite these legal protections, most employers simply will not

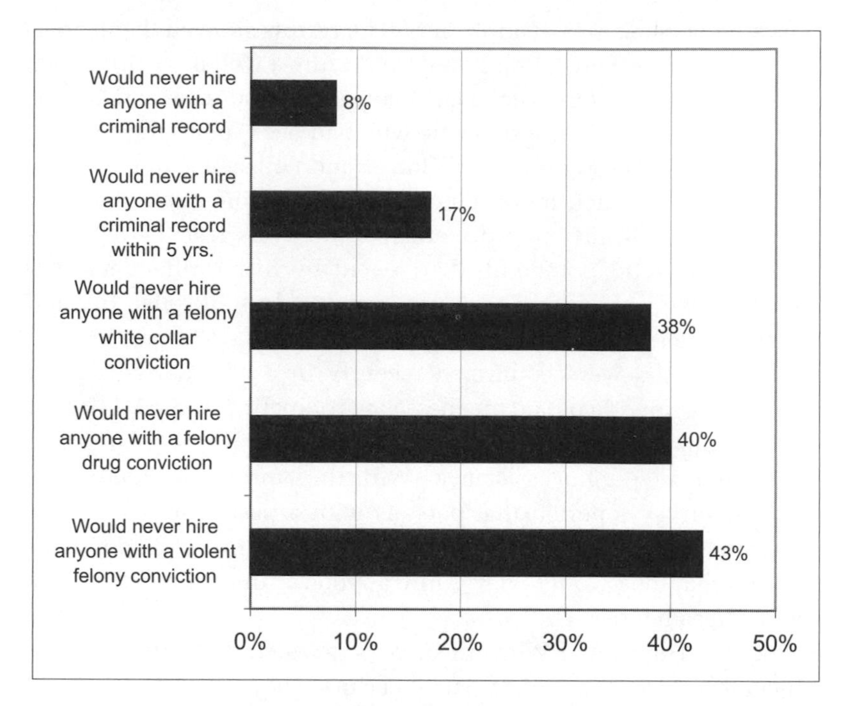

Figure 6.1. Employers' reported levels of comfort with those with criminal records. *Source*: Wirthlin Worldwide 2000.

take the chance when the job entails working directly with customers or handling property that belongs to others. Holzer and colleagues found employers relatively more willing to hire ex-offenders in construction and manufacturing than in retail trade or the services. Unfortunately, the kinds of jobs into which employers are willing to hire those with criminal records are those that are diminishing over time as a fraction of the workforce (i.e., blue collar jobs and those in manufacturing), while those in which employers are most reluctant (i.e., involving customer contact, child care, or elder care) are increasing.

Holzer's research found that, in 2001, about 63 percent of employers always or sometimes checked the criminal backgrounds of applicants, compared to 48 percent in 1994. His team also found that employer uncertainty about the exact identity of ex-offenders also generates the prospect that they might avoid an entire class of workers (i.e., less-educated young black men) whom they suspect of being offenders. Holzer and colleagues found that "employers who are unwilling to hire ex-offenders but who also do not check criminal records—such as small establishments without human resource departments and with relatively informal screening activities—tend to hire fewer young black men than do establishments that check records." They conclude: "If it is true that the use of record checks is growing over time, our results imply that this will improve the job prospects of young men who might be wrongfully suspected of having had problems with the law, but could further impede the prospects of those who really are ex-offenders" (2002, p. 5).

No state or federal prison tracks the number of inmates employed after release, but the few available statistics continue to reveal high rates of joblessness among this group. Unemployment among ex-offenders has been estimated at between 25 and 40 percent (Finn 1998b). In California, for example, it is estimated that as many as 80 percent of ex-offenders remain jobless a year after being released from prison (Petersilia 2000). Again, however, it is worth pointing out how woefully inadequate our state of knowledge is regarding prisoner reentry. Employment has been shown to be a key factor in reintegration, and yet we make no effort to routinely collect job-related information.

Western and Beckett (1999) have shown that the unemployment of a large number of felons also has broad economic implications. They argue that one of the reasons America's unemployment statistics look so good in comparison to those of Western European nations is that 1.4 million mainly low-skilled workers—precisely the group unlikely to find work in a high-tech economy—are in prison and are thus not considered part of the labor force. If they were included, the researchers note, unemployment statistics would be 2 percent higher than the unemployment level now reported. They caution that the diminished employability of a growing number of ex-convicts points to higher rates of unemployment in the future.

Western and colleagues also find that conviction status imposes a significant, immediate "wage penalty" on criminal offenders and alters long-term earnings trajectories by restricting access to career jobs (Western, Kling, and Weiman 2001). They estimate that when offenders do secure jobs, they earn 10–30 percent less than individuals with the same characteristics who were not incarcerated. Evidence suggests that the effects of arrest and incarceration on finding a job likely decrease over time, however, the effects of incarceration on earnings appear to be sustained. Moreover, Nagin and Waldfogel (1998) find that the effect of imprisonment on employment and future earnings is particularly pronounced for inmates over age 30, suggesting that as the prison and parole population ages, their employment prospects become bleaker.

Finding employment today is much more difficult for the ex-prisoner. Data from the BJS Survey of Prison Inmates shows that in 1974, 62 percent of prisoners reported being employed full time prior to incarceration; this number had fallen to 56 percent by 1997. When the unemployment rate was lower, in 1998–1999, ex-convicts were being hired for some jobs that had been closed to them in the past. But as the economy has slowed, the job prospects for returning prisoners are quite bleak. Not only are low-skill jobs declining overall in the United States, but also there is greater competition for those that remain due to welfare reform legislation.

The 1996 welfare reform law, the Personal Responsibility and Work Opportunity Reconciliation Act, imposed a five-year lifetime limit on welfare benefits and required welfare recipients to work to receive benefits. Since then, welfare caseloads have dropped nearly 50 percent. These stringent welfare rules made work a more urgent priority, since recipients lose a large portion of their already meager incomes unless they find jobs. As welfare recipients move into the workforce, they compete for the exact same jobs as ex-offenders.

Clearly, the bias and stigma arising from having a criminal record limit the job prospects of ex-inmates. Civil disabilities and other legal restrictions limit the jobs for which they can apply, and in jobs for which they are legally eligible, there is stiff competition for a declining number of them. If parolees are truthful about their backgrounds, many employers will not hire them. If they are not truthful, they can be fired for lying if the employer learns about their conviction.

Housing and Homelessness

Parole officials say that finding housing for parolees is by far their biggest challenge, even more difficult and more important than finding a job. In some states, parolees are given two- to four-week vouchers to pay for an inexpensive room in a hotel or local boarding facility. But that time passes quickly, and without a stable home base, few services can be effectively delivered. As a Massachusetts report on the subject put it:

> For the returning prisoner, the search for permanent, sustainable housing is more than simply a disagreeable experience. It is a daunting challenge—one that portends success or failure for the entire reintegration process. . . . Housing is the linchpin that holds the reintegration process together. Without a stable residence, continuity in substance abuse and mental health treatment is compromised. Employment is often contingent upon a fixed living arrangement. And, in the end, a polity that does not concern itself with the housing needs of returning prisoners finds that it has done so at the expense of its own public safety. (Bradley et al. 2001, p. 7)

State prisoners are often incarcerated in facilities far away from their return destination and have no opportunity to secure housing prior to discharge. Parole conditions can also prevent parolees from living or associating with others who are criminally involved. This restriction includes family and friends who may be willing to take this person in, further limiting housing options. Since ex-inmates are usually unable to amass the funds required to move into an apartment (first and last months' rent, security deposit), the private housing market—which represents 97 percent of the total housing stock in the United States—is usually cost prohibitive. Even if the ex-prisoner can afford it, landlords conducting background checks or requiring credible work histories usually pass over an applicant with a prison record.

So, ex-prisoners attempt to locate suitable public housing—and yet some laws now *require* public housing agencies and providers to deny housing to certain felons (e.g., drug and sex offenders). Even if they qualify, waiting lists can be as long as two to three years for subsidized housing. Convicts therefore show up at over-crowded shelters with long waiting lists and limits on the number of days they can remain in residence.

Despite its importance, we know almost nothing about the exact housing arrangements of former prisoners, and estimates vary widely. The Bureau of Justice Statistics reports that 12 percent of U.S. prisoners were homeless immediately prior to their incarceration. *Time* magazine reported, "30% to 50% of big-city parolees are homeless" (Ripley 2002, p. 60). Massachusetts reports that nearly a quarter of all released prisoners experience homelessness within a year of release (Bradley et al. 2001). California Department of Corrections officials report that overall 10 percent of the state's parolees are homeless, but in large urban areas (e.g., San Francisco, Los Angeles), the rate of homelessness among parolees is estimated to be 50 percent.

Public housing represents a last resort for the returning prisoner to avoid a shelter or the streets. Yet, subsidized public housing began disappearing as a viable option for many ex-prisoners due to tighter restrictions about who could qualify for the subsidies and who could live in the residences.

Prisoners returning to their families in subsidized public housing complexes are often no longer welcome. Due to the U.S. Department of Housing and Urban Development's "one strike and you're out" policy, the public housing authority may evict all members of the household for criminal activities committed by any one member of a household. These policies were designed to protect law-abiding members of public housing communities from the criminal behavior of other residents. Some courts have upheld these evictions, even if the activities were unknown to the head of the household. Obviously, the fear of being evicted for the future criminal acts of the returning family member is a legitimate concern for the relatives in public housing.

Congress also authorized the exclusion of certain offenders from receiving federally supported public housing. According to the Legal Action Center (2001), public housing law currently requires public housing agencies and providers of Section 8 vouchers and other federally assisted housing to deny housing to

- individuals who have been evicted from public, federally assisted, or Section 8 housing because of drug-related criminal activity (ineligible for public or federally assisted housing for three years)
- any household with a member who is subject to a lifetime registration requirement under a state sex-offender registration program
- any household with a member who is currently abusing alcohol or is illegally using drugs. Current tenants must be evicted on the same basis. The housing provider may permit these individuals to be admitted or remain in such housing if the person demonstrates that he is not currently abusing alcohol or illegally using drugs and has been rehabilitated.

In addition, federal regulations grant the Public Housing Authority the discretion to prohibit admission of all other criminally involved individuals. These restrictions, combined with the fact that the inventory of U.S. public housing continues to shrink, means that parolees are seldom allowed to live in public housing.

The dire housing situation of parolees has led Representative Danny Davis, 7th District of Illinois, to introduce the Public Safety Ex-Offender Self-Sufficiency Act, H.R. 3701, on 2 February 2002. It proposes amending the IRS Code of 1986 to provide landlords with tax credits for renting to ex-prisoners. As of September 2002, it was under review by the House Committee on Ways and Means.

Housing and homelessness certainly affect recidivism, but analysts say there are broader implications, and parolees' homelessness influences overall crime rates in the community. Large numbers of transients/vagrants and panhandling increase citizen fear, and that fear ultimately contributes to increased crime and violence. Wilson and Kelling originally discussed this phenomenon in 1982, labeling their theory "broken windows." Basically, the broken windows theory suggests that neighborhood crime is often caused by the fact that law-abiding citizens are afraid to go onto streets filled with graffiti, panhandlers, and loitering youth. Fearful citizens eventually yield control of these streets to people who are not frightened by these signs of urban decay. Those not frightened turn out to be the same people who created the problem in the first place. A vicious cycle begins where fear-induced behavior increases the sources of that fear. They illustrate this by describing how a broken window can influence crime rates. If the first broken window in a building is not repaired, then people who like breaking windows will assume that no one cares about the building, and more windows will be broken. Soon, the building will have no windows (Wilson and Kelling 1982). As "broken windows" spread—homelessness, graffiti, panhandling—businesses and law-abiding citizens move from the area, and disorder escalates, possibly leading to serious crime.

The broken windows thesis has led to changes in policing that give greater emphasis to enforcement against minor offenses, including the so-called quality-of-life crimes (e.g., homelessness, panhandling). While many find such practices offensive, a study by Fagan, Zimring, and Kim (1998) found that such practices likely contributed to New York City's declining violent crime rate. Unfortunately, many of those picked up by the police and jailed for these offenses are homeless parolees who had few options for housing and work due to the often insurmountable barriers they faced during reentry.

Public Assistance and Welfare

Just as access to jobs and public housing has significantly been curtailed for ex-convicts, so too has general financial assistance. When President Bill Clinton signed the Personal Responsibility and Work Opportunity Reconciliation Act, it dramatically changed the nature of the American welfare system. The law ended individual entitlement to welfare and replaced it with a block grant to states called Temporary Assistance for Needy Families (TANF). TANF imposed a five-year lifetime limit on benefits, required welfare recipients to work to receive benefits, and strengthened child support enforcement requirements for noncustodial parents. As Jeremy Travis wrote, "When Congress dismantled the six decades old entitlement to a safety net for the poor, the poor with criminal histories were less deserving than others. Congress essentially cut offenders off from the remnants of the welfare state" (Travis 2002, p. 19).

One provision of the law requires that states *permanently* bar individuals with drug-related felony convictions from receiving federally funded public assistance and food stamps during their lifetimes. This provision applies to all individuals convicted of a drug felony after 22 August 1996. Patricia Allard (2002) notes that this provision applies *only* to those convicted of drug offenses. Thus, offenders released from prison after serving a sentence for murder, for example, are eligible for welfare benefits and food stamps, but not those who have a conviction for possessing or selling a small quantity of drugs. Congressional records indicate that this drug provision was introduced and ratified with bipartisan support after just two minutes of debate.

The law also gives states the option of testing current welfare recipients for illegal drugs and imposing sanctions against those who test positive. While states can exempt some recipients from work requirements and provide some with assistance beyond the five-year limit, many states are implementing work rules and time limits *more* stringent than required under federal law (Rubinstein 2001). As shown in table 6.4, in 22 states, the ban on welfare and food stamps is permanent *for life* for individuals convicted of drug felonies—regardless of whether that person is only a minor or a first offender—and continues despite an individual's successful job history, participation in drug treatment, abstinence from drug use, or avoidance of recidivism.

An offender's eligibility to receive public assistance is critical to

Table 6.4. State policies on implementing lifetime welfare ban for people convicted of drug felonies

Denies welfare benefits entirely, for life	Partial denial/ term denial	Benefits dependent on drug treatment participation	Opted out of federal welfare ban for people convicted of drug felonies
Alabama	Arkansas	Hawaii	Connecticut
Alaska	Colorado	Kentucky	District of Columbia
Arizona	Florida	Maryland	Michigan
California	Illinois	Minnesota	New Hampshire
Delaware	Iowa	Nevada	New York
Georgia	Louisiana	New Jersey	Ohio
Idaho	Massachusetts	South Carolina	Oklahoma
Indiana	North Carolina	Utah	Oregon
Kansas	Rhode Island	Washington	Vermont
Maine	Texas	Wisconsin	
Mississippi			
Missouri			
Montana			
Nebraska			
New Mexico			
North Dakota			
Pennsylvania			
South Dakota			
Tennessee			
Virginia			
West Virginia			
Wyoming			

Source: Allard 2002.

successful reintegration, since many people with criminal records are not immediately "job ready" and require services, such as substance abuse treatment, job training, or education, before they can enter the job market. During this process of becoming job ready, ex-offenders have historically relied on public assistance to pay for food and housing. Since welfare and food stamps often helped fund room and board in alcohol and drug treatment programs, ex-offenders now find it increasingly difficult to pay for their treatment programs. The Legal Action Center recommends that states narrow the ban and exempt individuals who have completed or are in treatment, which gives the individual an incentive to enter and stay in treatment.

The welfare reform law also stipulates that individuals who are violating their probation and parole conditions are "temporarily" ineligible for TANF, food stamps, Social Security Income (SSI) benefits, and public housing. These violations may include absconding or not reporting to a parole officer, not attending treatment, or testing positive for drug use. For example, not attending a drug treatment program can result in the loss of welfare support (but attending programs can conflict with the welfare-to-work requirement of working a certain number of hours per day).

These policies affect not only the felon but also her children. As noted earlier, women constitute the most rapidly growing segment of the U.S. prison population; the majority (34 percent) are serving a sentence for a drug crime; and 65 percent of them have children. Before being incarcerated, one-quarter to one-third of parents were unemployed, with significantly more mothers in both systems reporting unemployment (50 percent of women in state prison and 38 percent of women in federal prison). In addition, about 35 percent of mothers (and 11 percent of fathers) in prisons received welfare benefits before being incarcerated (Rubinstein 2001).

Allard (2002) estimates that since the ban went into effect in 1996, more than 92,000 women have been convicted of drug offenses in the states enforcing it, most of them low-income black and Hispanic women. Of these, about two-thirds are mothers, with 135,000 children among them. A *New York Times* article urging states to reconsider this provision of the welfare reform law concluded, "Obviously the only people hurt by this denial of benefits are the poor, which usually means a minor offender who is an addict and out of jail trying to make it. The big operators, the manufacturers and distributors of illegal drugs, don't need government benefits. And offenders in prison are being supported by the state" (Schwartz 2002).

One wonders how the children in these fragile family units are to survive when their parents return home. They will no longer be able to receive financial subsidies for housing and food, and the parent's criminal record will make it very difficult to get a job. Without access to welfare benefits, these vulnerable families are left with virtually no safety net.

Parental Rights and Marriage

Congress passed another piece of legislation that dramatically affected the families of prisoners, the Adoption and Safe Families Act of 1997 (ASFA). ASFA was intended to move children into permanent placements within mandated time frames, so that foster children did not languish in foster care, unable to be adopted. But some of its provisions have significantly affected women and men in prison and their parental rights.

ASFA prohibits individuals with certain criminal convictions from being approved as foster or adoptive parents and requires states to terminate parental rights in cases where the parents have been found to have committed murder, voluntary manslaughter, or acts of serious violence against their children. Permanently separating children from their violent parents has merit. But ASFA also accelerates the termination of parental rights for children who have been in foster care for 15 of the most recent 22 months.

An evaluation of ASFA by the Government Accounting Office (GAO) showed that several states have shortened the time frame for initiating the process of terminating parental rights for foster children from the 15-month limit established by ASFA to 12 months. (Government Accounting Office 1999). Although the number of children affected by ASFA is presently unknown, foster care placements have increased dramatically in the last several years. And, since the average prison term served is now 29 months, a growing number of parents in prison will have their parental rights terminated, and clearly, more children will be formally adopted as a result of this act. It is unclear whether this will be beneficial or damaging to the children involved, but the GAO called this a "good piece of legislation."

Criminal Registration and Sex-Offender Community Notification

The rape and murder of seven-year old Megan Kanka in New Jersey by a paroled sex offender led to a series of sex-offender notification laws, called Megan's Laws after the victim. In 1986, only eight states required released offenders to register with local police. By 2002, every state had enacted legislation requiring convicted sex-offenders to register with law enforcement upon release from prison. In 30 states, DNA is also now collected from prisoners convicted of sex crimes. The duration of sex-offender registration requirements range from 10 years to life. Twelve states mandate lifetime registration for sex offenders.

More than 386,000 convicted sex offenders were registered with local law enforcement in 2001—88,000 of them in California alone. The number of registered sex offenders in the United States increased by more than 30 percent since 1998. In 29 states and the District of Columbia, sex-offender information is publicly accessible on a searchable website. A recent publication by the BJS lists the Internet website addresses for each of these states (Adams 2002). On most of these sites, after entering the person's name, a screen will appear showing a photo of the individual, gender, height, weight, color of eyes and hair, ethnicity, date of birth, and conviction offense. Some sites also include the current address, aliases, current vehicles, and target population (for example, see Utah's site at http://www.udc.state.ut.us).

Few would argue with the need to notify communities when dangerous sex offenders are released from prison. Without notification, citizens and victims are denied an opportunity to take precautions to ensure their own safety. With notification, the anonymity of the offender in the community is reduced, thereby increasing public safety.

The more difficult issue is exactly what offenses should require registration and the duration of the registration requirement. "Sex crimes" cover a broad array of criminal behavior, including attempted solicitation of a prostitute, promoting prostitution, oral copulation, kidnapping of a child, rape, sexual abuse if the victim is 16 or 17 years of age and at least 3 years younger than the offender, indecent exposure, and so on. In California and several other states, some of the covered crimes are misdemeanors. In many states, offenders convicted of any of the above crimes are required to register for life.

During the 1990s, the offense categories that trigger the registration mandate have increased. Illinois, for example, now requires sex offenders and those convicted of first-degree murder of a victim under 18 to register. Some states also require all drug addicts, persons convicted of arson or domestic violence, and those designated mentally ill to register.

Increased victim protection and community safety are seen as the positive effects. The negative effect is that registration and public notification are sometimes used to threaten, intimidate, or harass registered offenders. Sex offenders elicit a uniform and united response of revulsion from all of society. Ultimately, this makes it harder for parolees to succeed. They are further alienated from society and excluded from the very social support factors that might help them succeed. While such laws expressly forbid harassment by private citizens, there have been many instances of this occurring. Some argue that public notification drives parolees underground, encouraging them to abscond supervision. Without formal supervision, parolees become less visible than they would have been under the watchful eye of a parole officer. Of course, if they do not abscond, registration increases their public visibility and reduces their anonymity within the community.

Despite the public attention and concern over sex offenders reentering the communities, we have little solid research to weigh the pros and cons of community notification, sex-offender registries, or different treatment programs on their recidivism. Persons convicted of sex crimes generally have slightly lower rates of recidivism than other offenders, but it is not clear what accounts for those differences. It may be that sex offenders have higher rates of absconding, more effective treatments, or other preexisting characteristics that predict lower recidivism.

Several reviews note the paucity of research in this area. As one review put it: "There is almost no literature on the ability of either supervision or community notification (either as added components of treatment or separately) to reduce recidivism of sex offenders" (Quinsey et al. 1998). Even in studies that examine the issue, details of the crime, treatment, conditions of supervision, or community notification are not systematically included, leading Gaes and colleagues (1999) to conclude that sex-offender treatment and supervision is the most difficult to summarize simply because the data are so inadequate.

The tough-on-crime mood of the public during the 1980s and 1990s was concentrated primarily on drug offenders and those convicted of sex crimes. Police arrested more persons for those crimes; a greater proportion of arrestees were sentenced to prison; and now nearly all of them are returning home. A greater number of sex offenders are being mandatorily sent to prison, released automatically at the end of their term, and sometimes subjected to community notification procedures that backfire in terms of reintegration. Many of these offenders are among society's most serious criminals, while others are minor offenders caught up in a broad label of "sex offender." Policies affecting sex offenders seem poorly thought through.

Voting Rights and Democratic Participation

At the end of 2002, every state but two had disfranchisement laws that deprived felons of the right to vote while serving a prison or jail sentence for a felony offense. Uggen (2002) reports that 34 states also prevent felons from voting while they are on parole or probation or both. These laws are a growing impediment to political participation. It is interesting to note the gradient of restrictiveness: Maine and Vermont currently impose no restrictions, yet 10 states *permanently* deny convicted felons the right to vote after a single felony conviction (see table 6.5). Disfranchising felons for life is a custom unheard of in other democratic countries.

Those voting restrictions have resulted in some 4.7 million Americans currently being unable to vote because of their status as felons or ex-felons. Manza and colleagues estimate that disfranchised felons and ex-felons currently make up 2.09 percent of the voting age population (see table 6.6.), a figure that they project will increase to 3 percent within 10 years (Manza, Uggen, and Britton 2001). They also found that more than one-third (37 percent) of those unable to vote had already completed their criminal sentences: 28 percent are probationers, 9 percent are parolees, and just 27 percent are in prison and jail.

Felony disfranchisement laws most severely affect the African-American electorate, given that they disproportionately experience criminal convictions. Nearly 7 percent of *all* black Americans cannot participate in the electoral process because of a felony conviction (see table 6.6). Of these, 1.4 million are African-American males, representing 13 percent of all black men. Certainly such exclusions are fundamentally contrary to our conceptions of democracy and citizenship.

Fellner and Mauer (1998) report that Florida and Texas each disfranchise more than 600,000 people. In Alabama and Florida, almost one-third of black men are disfranchised for life. In Iowa, Mississippi, Virginia, and Wyoming, one in four African-American men is disfranchised for life. In Minnesota, almost 22 percent of African-American men and 5 percent of African-American women are currently denied the right to vote.

Important new analyses by Uggen and Manza (2001) show that the Republican presidential victory of 2000, in which George W. Bush defeated Albert Gore, would have been reversed had felons been allowed to vote. They statistically modeled the expected voter turnout

Table 6.5. State policies on felon voting rights

Current and former prisoners, parolees, felony probationers cannot vote	Current prisoners, parolees, felony probationers cannot vote	Current prisoners and parolees cannot vote	Only current prisoners cannot vote	No felony disfranchisement; everyone can vote
Alabama*	Alaska	California	Hawaii	Maine
Arizona	Arkansas	Colorado	Illinois	Vermont
Delaware	Georgia	Connecticut	Indiana	
Florida*	Idaho	Kansas	Louisiana	
Iowa*	Minnesota	New York	Massachusetts	
Kentucky*	Missouri		Michigan	
Maryland	Nebraska		Montana	
Mississippi*	New Jersey		New Hampshire	
Nevada*	New Mexico		North Dakota	
Tennessee*	North Carolina		Ohio	
Virginia*	Oklahoma		Oregon	
Washington*	Rhode Island		Pennsylvania	
Wyoming*	South Carolina		South Dakota	
	Texas		Utah	
	West Virginia			
	Wisconsin			

Note: Asterisks (*) indicate states that bar felons from voting after a single felony conviction.

Source: Uggen 2002.

Table 6.6. Percentage of citizens affected by felony disfranchisement provisions

Race	Percentage of voting-age population
Black	6.57
White, Hispanic, and other	1.49
All	2.09

Source: Manza, Uggen, and Britton 2001; Uggen 2002.

and vote choice of disfranchised felons and found that they would have had a sizable impact on this and several other recent elections. They concluded:

> Had disfranchised felons been permitted to vote, we estimate that the Democrat Gore's margin of victory in the popular vote would have risen to approximately one million votes. Regardless of the popular vote, however, one state—Florida—held the balance of power. Florida has more disfranchised felons, 887,000, than any other state. If they participated in the election at the estimated rate of turnout (21.6%) and Democratic preference (74.5 percent), Gore would have prevailed in Florida by more than 90,000 votes. If disfranchised felons in Florida had been able to vote, the Democrat Gore would almost certainly have carried the state and the election. (Uggen and Manza 2001, p. 32)

Because felons are drawn disproportionately from the ranks of racial minorities and the poor, disfranchisement laws tend to take votes from Democratic candidates. The Uggen and Manza analyses predict that, overall, about 31 percent of disfranchised felons would have voted in senatorial and presidential elections, and Democrats would have received seven of the ten votes cast. (Ninety percent of African Americans supported Gore in 2000.) They conclude: "By removing those with Democratic preferences from the pool of eligible voters, disfranchisement laws have thus provided a small but clear advantage to Republican candidates in every presidential and senatorial election from 1972 to 2000" (Uggen and Manza 2001, p. 4).

Uggen and Manza note that this is particularly interesting since Republicans sponsored most of the punitive crime legislation from the 1960s to the 1980s, and that legislation has resulted in greater imprisonment. The result of greater imprisonment has been to remove more and more Democratic voters from the pool of those eligible to vote, ensuring that Republicans have a competitive advantage in the voter base and assuring the continuation of more punitive crime policies.

Of course, losing the right to vote is not the most pressing concern for most convicted felons, and few criminologists have considered its broader implications. But in interviews with 33 felons who had lost the right to vote, Uggen and colleagues found evidence that disfranchisement "carried a sting," "was like salt in the wound," and "part of a larger package of restrictions that confounded efforts to become 'normal citizens'" (Uggen, Manza, and Behrens 2002). Not allowing felons to vote causes some offenders to feel alienated from their communities and the political process, and perhaps restoring their voting rights and other civil disabilities is one way to reengage them in community life. Uggen and colleagues suggest that the process of restoring the felon's civil disabilities not only allows the offender to move beyond the stigma, but if formalized in some type of reintegration ceremony can be part of the "delabeling" or "decertification" process that Maruna (2001) and others say is key to allowing some felons to move on with their lives.

Uggen notes that these civil disabilities also prevent felons from participating in community life more generally. Many convicted felons would like to volunteer, coach youth sports, work in food banks, assist the elderly, or engage in some other form of civic service. Yet many are prevented from doing so as a result of their criminal records. He notes that the impact of such volunteerism on criminal behavior has yet to be established, although some studies suggest that volunteer activities may reduce offending.

Seven states have recently undertaken initiatives to restore or preserve felons' and ex-felons' voting rights. In Alabama, Florida, Pennsylvania, and Nevada, members of the legislature have proposed the automatic restoration of ex-felons' voting rights once their sentence has been completed, and in Connecticut, the legislature is considering restoring the voting rights for probationers and parolees (Allard and Mauer 2000).

Ranking the States in Felon Exclusion Policies

Tables 6.2, 6.3, 6.4, and 6.5 reveal widely varying state policies regarding the public sharing of criminal records and the exclusionary policies imposed on felons. Some states allow the general public to have full access to the criminal records of everyone else in the state, whereas others permit only criminal justice personnel to access them. Some states disfranchise for life persons convicted of a single felony, whereas Vermont and Maine let those in prison and jail vote. Similarly, some states exclude first-time drug offenders from receiving food stamps and living in public housing, whereas other states have opted out of this federal ban, knowing that they sacrifice federal funds by doing so.

In figure 6.2, the author has combined the information in these four tables to create a summary "felon exclusion" index in the hopes of discerning geographical patterns. The index simply assigned a score of 1 to 3 to each state's response in tables 6.2 and 6.3, a score of 1 to 4 for each response in table 6.4, and a score of 1 to 5 for each response in table 6.5. These individual scores were added, and the states were arrayed from lowest (most exclusionary policies) to highest (most inclusive policies). The states were then grouped into equal quartiles, and the results appear in figure 6.2. States in black have the most exclusionary policies; those in white have the most inclusionary policies.

Information in the four tables appears interconnected. In other words, states that disfranchise all convicted persons and impose lifetime welfare bans on drug offenders also tend to be those that post criminal records on the Internet and allow open public access to them. Differences among the states were substantial as well, with ratios of roughly 3:1 between high- and low-ranking states. For example, Mississippi had the most exclusionary policies, with a summary score of 4, whereas Vermont had the most inclusive, with a summary score of 12.

Geographically speaking, the national map is fairly straightforward. Felons face the most exclusionary policies in the South and in Texas, although Arizona, Nebraska, and Kansas also scored in the highest categories of exclusion. States that were more inclusive, in that they continued to provide welfare and housing subsidies to convicted felons and did not post criminal records on the Internet, were in the Northeast section of the nation, but Oregon, Ohio, Indiana, and Utah were also included in this category. California lies near the national average.

It is not clear what causes states in the Northeast to have such different policies, but social historians found higher levels of civic engagement, social capital, and social trust in these states as well and

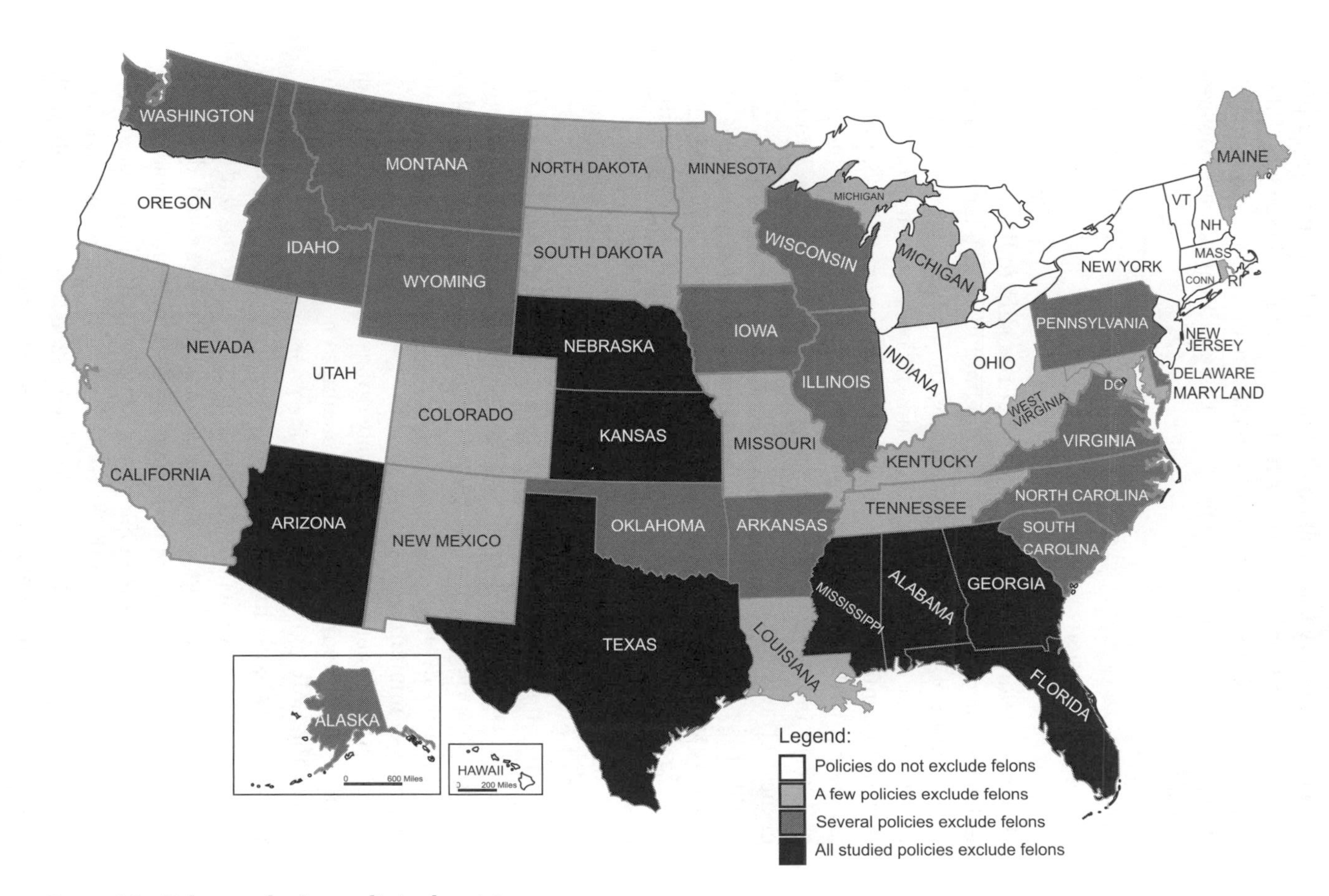

Figure 6.2. Felon exclusion policies by state.

have attributed the differences to paths of migration and patterns of nineteenth-century immigration (Putnam 2000). What is more important for our interests in prisoner reentry is: what difference do these policies make, and how do they enhance or impede an inmate's chances of remaining crime-free? That is a critical but unanswered question.

Conclusions

Denying certain rights and benefits of citizenship to those who commit crimes is certainly not new. Throughout history, felons have suffered a kind of civil death. Historically, they have been barred from certain trades and lost the right to inherit or bequeath property or enter into contracts. The Fourteenth Amendment to the U.S. Constitution explicitly recognizes the power of the states to deny the right to vote to individuals guilty of "participation in rebellion or other crimes" (Travis 2002).

What is new is that these invisible punishments and legal restrictions are growing in number and kind, being applied to a larger percentage of the U.S. population and for longer periods of time than at any point in U.S. history. Given that 59 million Americans (29 percent of all adults) have a criminal record on file with state authorities, and 5 million (6.5 percent of all adults) have served a prison term, the effect of these restrictions has a profound effect on American democracy. And the fact that blacks are overrepresented in all major categories of criminal justice populations means inevitably that these legal restrictions have taken an especially heavy toll on minority communities.

Recent enactments are qualitatively different as well. The denial of welfare, food stamps, and public housing to convicted offenders removes the only existing safety net for poor people in this country. Such policies explicitly reduce the chances that large numbers of citizens will ever enjoy legitimate work, housing, or drug- and alcohol-free lives, since the financial supports that might have enabled them to get back on their feet after prison have been eliminated. Moreover, the growing legal barriers to employment coupled with the growing public and Internet access to their criminal records reduce ex-offenders' legitimate chances further. Jeremy Travis (2002) sees parallels with practices from another era when convicts were sent to faraway lands, and punishments became instruments of social exclusion.

Of course, these laws and restrictions also serve an important public safety benefit. For instance, denying drug offenders access to public housing is designed to create safer housing conditions for other residents, many of whom are elderly or disabled. Not allowing ex-convicts to work with vulnerable populations is also designed to protect innocent victims. Requiring violent and sex offenders to register with local law enforcement helps police notify citizens and victims of their release. It also assists the police in solving crimes.

So, laws imposing restrictions on felons struggle between the need to protect the community versus the need to foster offender reintegration. If we prioritize the personal freedoms of returning offenders, we might oppose the growing number of restrictions. On the other hand, if we believe that protecting the public should take precedence over individual rights, we might applaud them. It is these tensions between individual-rights advocates and public-order advocates that create most of the crime policy debates in the United States.

How these civil disabilities benefit communities and disadvantage returning convicts is of critical importance and a question for which no empirical data exist. Of course, it does not have to be an all-or-nothing proposition. As Travis (2002) notes, a more fruitful approach would be to narrow the range of crimes or offenders subject to various restrictions, or limit the time frame for which they apply. Currently, a felon convicted of the lowest felony in Florida loses his right to vote for life, as does a serial murderer. Similarly, a minor drug user can be evicted from public housing as easily as a major drug dealer can. A teenager convicted of statutory rape for consensual intercourse with his underage girlfriend may be subject to lifetime registration along with a repeated child molester—and both will be identified as sex offenders on publicly accessible Internet websites (Travis 2002). Clearly, such policies need review. We will likely discover that some of these broad policies are crime enhancing rather than crime reducing over the long run.

SEVEN

Revolving Door Justice

Inmate Release and Recidivism

It is not surprising that most inmates who leave prison become reinvolved in crime. After all, they had serious needs prior to imprisonment; most of them went untreated in prison; and now they face a staggering number of personal and financial problems at release. As *USA Today* entitled its cover story on the topic of prisoner reentry, they are "Unready, Unrehabilitated, and Up for Release" (Johnson 2000). The public fears newly released offenders, remembering the horrendous crimes committed by Willie Horton, Richard Allen Davis, and other notorious parolees. In fact, much of the recent interest in prisoner reentry has been grounded in the assumption that those being released each year pose a substantial risk to public safety.

But how accurate are these public perceptions? How many of those released from prison will be subsequently arrested, convicted, and incarcerated? What is the contribution of parolees to the overall level of crime in the community? Of all persons arrested, convicted, incarcerated, and sentenced to death, how many of them were on parole at the time they committed their crimes? Some of these measures focus on the individual offender's probability of recidivism, while the others use various criminal justice populations (e.g., arrestees, inmates) to estimate the contribution of parolees to crime.

By any measure, we are doing poorly. Recent data tracking inmates released from prison in 1994 show that two-thirds are rearrested, and nearly one-quarter are returned to prison for a new crime within three years of their release. These rearrest rates are 5 percent higher than among inmates released in 1983. Inmates originally convicted of property crimes had the highest recidivism rates, followed by drugs, public order, and violent crimes. Younger prisoners and those with longer criminal records were more likely to be rearrested, as were men and those who were black. Risk of recidivism was highest during the year after release. Analysts estimated that this 1994 parole release cohort was responsible for about 5 percent of all serious crime arrests that occurred during the three-year follow-up period.

Of course, it is important to remember that more than 85 percent of all parolees are on caseloads where they are seen less than twice a month, and the budget available to support their supervision and services is generally about $1,800 per offender—even though effective treatment programs cost much more than that. It is no wonder that recidivism rates are so high. In a sense, we get what we pay for, and as yet, we have never chosen to invest sufficiently in parole or reentry programs. Nevertheless, most view these data as showing that the parole system is neither helping offenders nor protecting the public and that major reform is needed.

How Many Prisoners Succeed?

Prisoner Recidivism Rates and Parolee Contribution to Crime Levels

The Bureau of Justice Statistics recently released the results of the largest recidivism study ever conducted in the United States. The report, *Recidivism of Prisoners Released in 1994,* was written by Langan and Levin (2002) and is the first major recidivism study in more than a decade. The study tracked 272,111 prisoners discharged in 15 states, which represented two-thirds of all state prisoners released in 1994. By linking state and FBI criminal-history records, the researchers assembled information on rearrests both within and outside the states in which the prisoners were released. Recidivism information was collected only on felonies and serious misdemeanors, and the authors acknowledge that their study understates the actual levels of recidivism.

Langan and Levin found that 67 percent of former inmates were rearrested for at least one serious new crime within three years after their release in 1994: 47 percent were convicted of a new crime; 52 percent were returned to prison for either a new crime or a technical violation (e.g., failing a drug test). The 272,111 offenders accumulated 744,000 serious criminal charges within the three years after release. Fully one-quarter of all released prisoners (25.4 percent) were resentenced to prison for a new crime they committed in the follow-up period.

State prisoners with the highest rearrest rates were those who had been incarcerated for stealing motor vehicles (79 percent), possessing or selling stolen property (77 percent), burglary (74 percent), robbery (70 percent), or using, possessing, or trafficking in illegal weapons (70 percent). The overall recidivism rate for inmates originally convicted of property crimes was 73.8 percent. Drug offenders, who represented 32 percent of the inmate release cohort, had a rearrest rate of 66.7 percent.

Those with the lowest rearrest rates had been in prison for homicide (41 percent), sexual assault (41 percent), rape (46 percent), or driving under the influence of drugs or alcohol (51 percent). Generally speaking, highest rearrest rates were experienced by those who were originally in prison for what are generally thought of as crimes for money. By contrast, many of those with the lowest rearrest rates were in prison for crimes not generally motivated by desire for material gain (e.g., homicide).

The study also clearly documented that the first year after release from prison is the period when most recidivism occurs, accounting for nearly two-thirds of *all* the recidivism events in the first three years. Langan and Levin reported that nearly 30 percent of all released inmates were rearrested for a serious crime in the first six months, and 44.1 percent were rearrested within the first year. These results are contained in table 7.1.

It is interesting that the "two-thirds rearrest rate" at three years has been documented for about 35 years, since Daniel Glaser (1969) conducted his classic follow-up study of prisoners in *The Effectiveness of a Prison and Parole System.* Since that time, several other national recidivism studies have been conducted, all reporting approximately the same recidivism rates. For examples, see Bureau of

Table 7.1. Percentage recidivism of offenders released from state prisons

Time after release	Rearrested	Reconvicted	Returned to prison with new sentence
6 months	29.9	10.6	5.0
1 years	44.1	21.5	10.4
2 years	59.2	36.4	18.8
3 years	67.5	46.9	25.4

Source: Langan and Levin 2002.

Justice Statistics (1984), Greenfeld (1985), Beck and Shipley (1987), and Gottfredson and Gottfredson (1994). Greenfeld used BJS recidivism data to construct 20-year estimates for returning to state prison. He and others have shown that the risk of recidivism declines dramatically after three years, and after five years of arrest-free behavior, recidivism is extremely low.

Other Langan and Levin (2002) study findings include:

- Recidivism was inversely related to the age of the prisoner at the time of release: the younger the prisoner was when first arrested, the higher the rate of recidivism—more than 80 percent of those under 18 were rearrested, compared to 43 percent of those 45 or older.
- Men were more likely to be rearrested (68 percent) than women (57 percent). Blacks (73 percent) were more likely to be rearrested than whites (63 percent).
- Significantly, the prisoner's length of time served in prison was not related to recidivism.
- Nearly 8 percent of all released prisoners crossed state lines and were rearrested. New York, Arizona, and California had the most arrests of out-of-state offenders in the study.

Prior arrest record was a good predictor of both whether or not an inmate would be rearrested and how quickly. Prisoners who had one prior arrest had a 41 percent rearrest rate within three years. With two prior arrests, the rearrest rate within three years increased to 48 percent. With three priors, it increased to 55 percent. With each additional prior arrest, the recidivism rate rose, reaching a rearrest rate of 82 percent for inmates with more than 15 prior arrests. Inmates with 16 or more prior arrests had a 61 percent recidivism rate within the first year after release.

Langan and Levin estimated the fraction of all serious crime arrests (murder, rape, robbery, aggravated assault, burglary, larceny, and motor vehicle theft) for which these former prisoners were responsible during the three years following their release. They found that the arrests of the released prisoners accounted for 4.7 percent of all arrests for serious crime between 1994 and 1997. When examined by specific crime type, the released prisoners accounted for 8.4 percent of all the homicides, 5.4 percent of all the rapes, and 9 percent of all the robberies. As Allen Beck, chief of the Corrections Statistics Program at the BJS, told the author:

> This is not inconsequential, when we consider one release cohort being responsible for nearly 9 percent of arrests for robbery and homicide in a single year. Their contribution to crime in the community is also reduced over time as the proportion of the cohort still free is reduced by reincarceration. And, these arrests were based on a single release cohort. Obviously, if one took into account arrests of prison releasees from other release cohorts (e.g., those released in [the] following year), the numbers would rise appreciably. My guess is that the percentage may easily double. So, an informed estimate of what proportion of *all* index arrests that parolees may be responsible for in the United States for any given year might be 10 to 12 percent.

Langan and Levin's *Recidivism of Prisoners Released in 1994* is the BJS's second major study of prisoner recidivism. The previous study, by Beck and Shipley (1989), *Recidivism of Prisoners Released in 1983*, tracked prisoners released 10 years earlier. It is instructive to compare the two studies, since over this time period the nation abandoned rehabilitation as its central prison goal and began the prison-building binge that was designed to reduce crime through incapacitation and deterrence. If harsh and more frequent prison terms were achieving deterrence, recidivism rates should have declined over this time period as prisoners released tried to avoid future incarcerations. But the data show this has not happened, and just the opposite has occurred.

The general recidivism findings between the two studies are similar, although there are disturbing trends. Both studies find that roughly two-thirds of inmates are rearrested, and that males, those with significant prior criminal histories, minorities, the young, and those convicted of property crimes have higher recidivism rates. But the overall rearrest rate for those released in 1994 is 5 percent higher than among prisoners released during 1983. There is also evidence that more were arrested quickly. In the 1983 study, one of four released prisoners was rearrested in the first six months; by 1994, that number was about one in three. Drug offenders' rearrest rates also increased significantly during this decade: in 1983, 50 percent of those convicted of drug crimes were rearrested, but by 1994, that rate had increased to 67 percent.

Most important, however, is the increased percentage of serious crimes attributable to persons released from prison. The 1983 prisoner cohort accounted for 2.8 percent of all serious crimes arrests recorded in the subsequent three years. But the 1994 prisoner cohort was responsible for 4.7 percent of all serious crime arrests in the three-year follow-up. If one examines these figures by crime type, the difference is even more dramatic. The percentage of Uniform Crime Reports (UCR) arrests attributable to the 1983 prison release cohort for murder or nonnegligent manslaughter was 2.3 percent, but for the 1994 cohort was 7.7 percent. Similar increases are noted for other violent crimes (e.g., for rape, 1.8 percent of arrests were attributable to the 1983 prisoner cohort versus 4.4 percent for the 1994 cohort).

It is impossible to know whether these recidivism indicators reflect more criminality on the part of released prisoners or greater diligence on the part of the police (e.g., more arrests relative to crimes committed). But there is reason to suspect it is the former, since the percentage of crimes known to police that had been solved by arrest (the clearance rate) actually declined over this time period. There is no indication that this measure of police productivity has increased.

It appears from the available evidence that persons being released from prison today are doing less well than their counterparts released a decade ago in successfully reintegrating into their communities. More of them are being rearrested; these arrests are occurring more quickly; and as a group, ex-convicts are accounting for a growing share of all serious crimes experienced in the United States.

State Variation in Prisoner Recidivism

Recidivism rates, like other aspects of corrections, vary greatly among states, and national averages are disproportionately influenced by the rates in a few large states. California, for example, has one of the largest parolee populations (nearly 20 percent of all U.S. parolees), and it reports one of the highest prison return rates—66 percent—in the nation (Petersilia 2000). However, California officials say that their prison return rate includes inmates who are returned to jail pending a parole hearing, even if they are subsequently continued on parole in the community. In other words, California officials believe they record as "recidivism" a number of events that other states do not include. If one counts "returned to prison" only, California has a lower recidivism rate: 43 percent returned to prison within one year, 55 percent within two years (Berecochea 2002). This is still one of the highest prison return rates in the nation.

Comparing recidivism rates across states is very misleading, however, because states use their prisons differently. For example, Hawaii operates an integrated prison and jail system, so its "prisoners" (as a group) contain persons who would be serving time in local jails in other states. Jail inmates have less serious convictions and prior criminal records, factors known to be associated with recidivism. So, when one compares Hawaii's prison recidivism rates with those of other states, its average will be lower simply because it houses (on average) a lower-risk population. Pennsylvania, on the other hand, uses its prisons only to house people sentenced to more than two years; other convicts are housed in local jails. In most states, prisons house anyone having a sentence of greater than one year. Thus, Pennsylvania prisons generally house a more serious inmate population.

The age at which offenders are considered "adult" (and hence, subject to adult prisons) is also critical when comparing prison recidivism rates. In most states, youth below the age of 18 at the time of the offense are handled in juvenile court. However, in New York, Connecticut, and North Carolina, persons aged 16 years and older are considered adults for most criminal matters. As such, the prison population in these states houses a greater number of young people, a factor related to higher recidivism, all other things being equal.

A state's parole revocation policy can dramatically affect recidivism rates. A strict revocation policy can quickly increase parolee recidivism rates even if there have been no changes in the underlying criminality of the parolees. Parolees can "fail" in one of two ways: either by being arrested for another crime or by violating one of the conditions of parole release (using drugs, possessing a weapon, and so on). In either case, parole authorities can revoke parole and send the person back to prison. The decision to revoke is quite discretionary with parole authorities: they may choose to overlook a violation and not send the person back to prison. This discretionary power is "nearly equivalent to the judge's power to sentence an offender in the first place, because it can mean that the offender will return to prison" (Walker, Spohn, and DeLone 2002, p. 18). Given that parole board members are usually politically appointed, their policies often reflect the political wills of their state governors.

Perhaps most important is the fact that the probability of being sent to prison in the first place, given conviction, differs significantly across the states. For example, Rand researchers found that, on average, prison inmates in California had more serious and lengthy criminal records than inmates in either Texas or Michigan (Chaiken and Chaiken 1982). Prior criminal record is the strongest predictor of recidivism; California inmates, therefore, would be expected to have higher recidivism rates when compared with other states, which imprison persons earlier in their criminal careers. Finally, the extent and intensity of postprison parole supervision and services certainly affects recidivism. These and other factors determine a state's recidivism rate, and comparing recidivism across states is grossly misleading, although it is commonly done.

Importantly, a number of states are reporting *decreases* in their prison return rates, after years of trends in the opposite direction. Texas has reported that its three-year reincarceration rate has dropped from nearly 50 percent for 1992 releasees to 31 percent for 1997 releasees. Similarly, Pennsylvania has reported that its three-year incarceration rate has also declined from 50 percent for 1994 releasees to 42 percent in 1997.

The reason that prison return rates are declining in certain states is subject to several possible explanations. Some believe it is attributable to longer lengths of stay and the associated aging of the prisoner release cohorts. It could also be due to widely divergent approaches to measuring recidivism or to the fact that some states use community-based intermediate sanctions rather than prison for less-serious technical violations. Some states, such as Washington, cannot legally return an offender to prison for a technical violation. That offender must be handled in the community.

Most believe that prison return rates are declining as a matter of policy, rather than due to changes in offender behavior. Public opinion polls put prison spending at the top of their budget-cutting lists, and legislators are increasingly mandating that corrections find other-than-prison alternatives for nonviolent offenders who violate parole conditions. For example, Proposition 36, passed by California voters in 2000, diverts lower-level drug offenders to treatment rather than to prison. Such a policy should reduce the prison reincarceration rates of parolees in that state.

So, while prisoner recidivism rates are commonly used to measure the effectiveness (or ineffectiveness) of parole and prisons or the continued public safety risk posed by parolees, they are inadequate. They often reflect the number of laws being actively enforced and legal and policy differences in the states, rather than differences in offenders' underlying criminal behavior. As Lao-Tze (c. 604–531 B.C.) wrote, "The greater the number of laws and enactments, the more thieves and robbers there will be."

Percentage of Parolees in Arrest, Conviction, and Imprisonment Cohorts

Another way to examine the risks posed by those on parole is to examine their presence among cohorts of all persons arrested for felonies, convicted, incarcerated, and sentenced to death. Various BJS data sources can be used to compile such information, as shown in figure 7.1.

Importantly, it shows that of all persons arrested for felony crimes in 1999, 8 percent were on parole at the time of their arrest. Moreover, the BJS data reveal that 22 percent of those in state prisons in 1999 report being on parole at the time of the crime that landed them in prison. Eighteen percent of all prisoners serving death sentences were on parole at the time of their crime. Clearly, leaving parolees

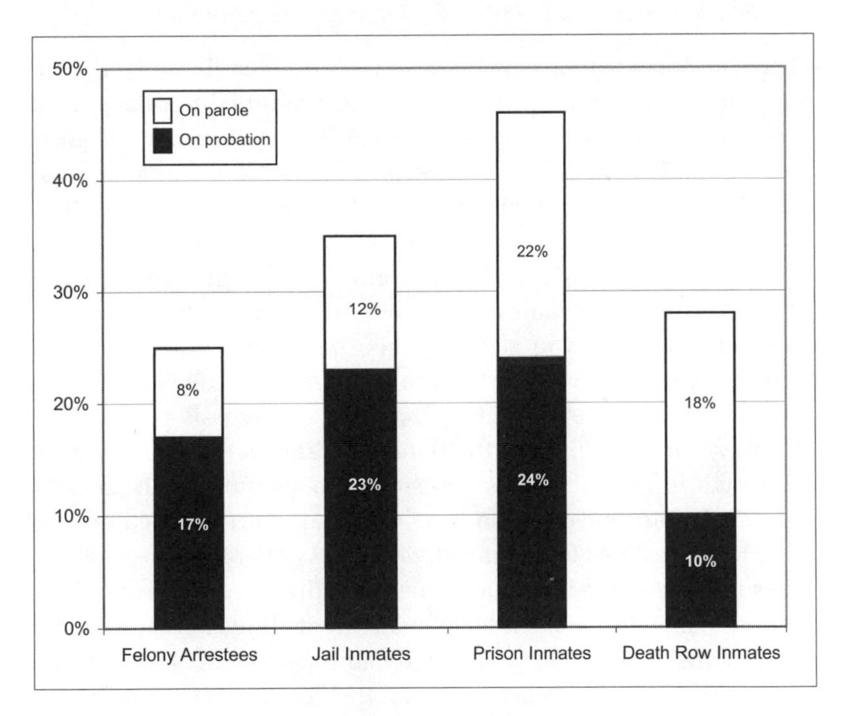

Figure 7.1. Percentage of offenders on probation or parole at the time of their offense, 1999. *Note*: The prison and death row information pertains to state prison inmates. *Source*: Petersilia 2002.

unattended and without services not only is bad policy: it leaves many victims in its wake.

These figures, however, are an inadequate measure of the contribution of parolees to crime. Once under the watchful eyes of parole officers and police, the probability of arrest and incarceration may be higher for parolees than for other people, all other things being equal. In fact, having a prior criminal record is a strong predictor of whether or not a convicted offender will be sentenced to prison versus probation. Also, the police sometimes "round up the usual suspects" for questioning, so the probability of being included in one of the groups shown in figure 7.1 is probably related to being on parole in the first place. Nevertheless, these are the best measures we have. The only completely accurate way to gauge parolees' contributions to crime would be to collect valid self-reports from parolees, which is not feasible.

Parolees Returned to Prison for Technical Violations

When parolees commit new crimes or fail to comply with their release conditions, they may be revoked and returned to prison. High parole revocation rates is one of the major factors linked to the growing U.S. prison population. As shown in figure 7.2, the number of offenders reincarcerated for violating parole or other release conditions increased more than sevenfold from 1980 through 1998.

Since 1980, the number of parole violators returned to state prisons has increased dramatically. As shown in figure 7.3, as a percentage of all admissions to state prisons, parole violators more than doubled from 17 percent in 1980 to 35 percent in 1999. New court commitments declined from 81 percent of all admissions in 1980 to 60 percent in 1999. Beck's (1999) analysis shows that 42 percent of the growth in total admissions to state prisons during this time period can be attributed not to new criminal court convictions, but rather to revocations for technical violations of parole.

In some states, the figures are even more dramatic. For example, in California, in 1999, two-thirds (66 percent) of all persons admitted to state prisons were parole violators. By comparison, in New York, the figure was just over 30 percent, and in Florida, just 7 percent. In Texas, the state most comparable in the size of its prison population to California, the figure is about 20 percent (Hughes, Wilson, and Beck 2001). There is no question that California has the highest rate

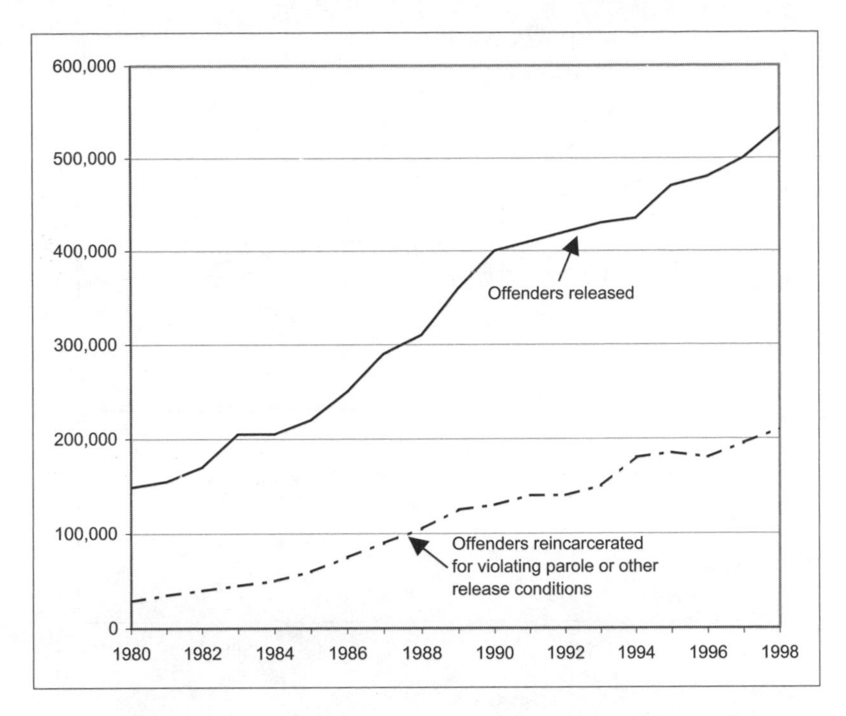

Figure 7.2. Releases from federal prison and state prisons and returns for violating parole, 1980–1998. *Source*: Beck et al. 2002; Government Accounting Office 2001.

of parole violations in the nation. In terms of total numbers, California accounts for nearly 40 percent of all known parole violations that occur in the nation, although it has less than 15 percent of the nation's parole population.

The United States spends a great deal of money to incarcerate nearly 300,000 parole violators nationwide. It is important to understand the reasons for revocation. As shown in table 7.2, about 70 percent of inmates self-report that their parole was revoked because of an arrest or conviction for a new offense; 22 percent said they had absconded or otherwise failed to report to a parole officer; 16 percent said they had a drug-related violation; and 18 percent reported other reasons, such as failure to maintain employment or to meet financial obligations. We should interpret these figures while cognizant of the growing use of technology to test for drugs and the financial difficulties faced by felons upon release.

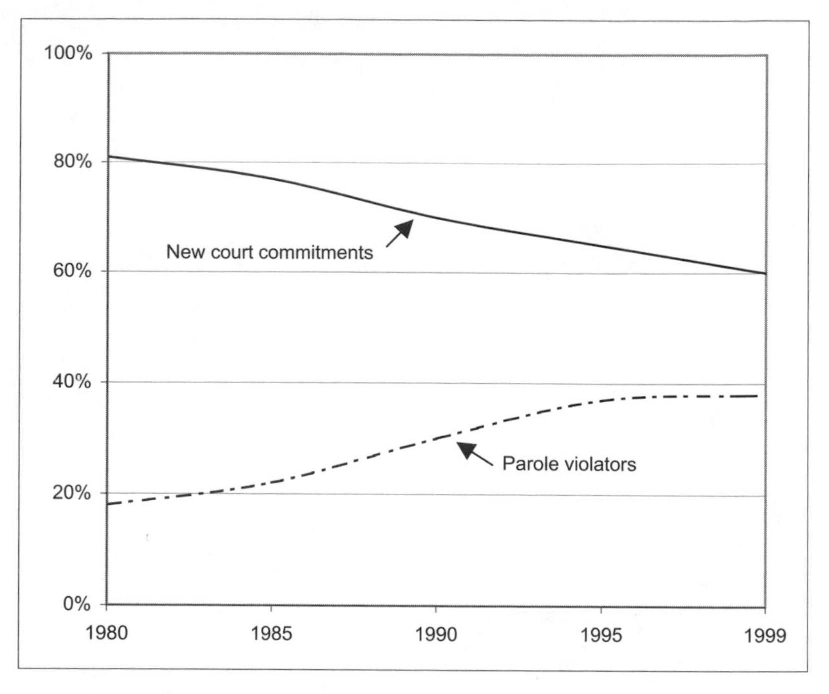

Figure 7.3. Admission to state prison by type of admission, 1980–1999. *Source*: Hughes et al. 2001.

Predictors of Recidivism

With few services and high needs, it is not surprising that so many parolees fail. It would be useful if we could predict which parolees have the highest probability of failure and target our scarce resources to those persons. Recidivism prediction has probably been the focus of more criminological research than any other topic.

Gendreau, Little, and Goggin (1996) used meta-analytic techniques to determine which inmate characteristics best predict adult recidivism. They utilized 131 studies to produce 1,141 correlations with recidivism. They further categorized these "risk of recidivism" correlations as either static or dynamic. *Static factors*, such as age, gender, or prior criminal record, are aspects that are predictive of recidivism but cannot be changed. *Dynamic risk factors*, commonly referred to as criminogenic needs, are values and behaviors that are mutable and thus can be used to design effective treatment programs. These Canadian researchers believe that the design of effective offender treatment

Table 7.2. Reasons for revocation among parole violators in state prison, 1997

Reason for revocation	All states	California	New York	Texas
Arrest or conviction for new offense	69.9%	60.3%	87.1%	78.8%
Drug-related violations	16.1%	23.1%	11.4%	10.7%
Positive test for drug use	7.9	12.2	5.6	4.3
Possession of drugs	6.6	8.9	5.6	5.6
Failure to report for drug testing	2.3	4.6	1.3	1.3
Failure to report for alcohol or drug treatment	1.7	1.1	1.9	1.2
Absconders	22.3%	26.6%	18.4%	19.7%
Failure to report	18.6	24.7	17.2	17.2
Left jurisdiction without permission	5.6	3.9	2.5	4.0
Other	17.8%	20.7%	10.6%	13.8%
Failure to report for counseling	2.8	1.2	2.0	1.9
Failure to maintain employment	1.2	0.7	0.6	0.9
Failure to meet financial obligations	2.3	0.2	0.0	2.7
Maintained contact with known offenders	1.2	1.6	0.4	0.8
Possession of gun(s)	3.5	3.8	1.9	2.3

Source: Hughes et al. 2001.

programs is highly dependent on knowledge of the predictors of recidivism.

Table 7.3 presents the findings. All of the predictors included in this table are statistically significant predictors of recidivism. The value of *r* can theoretically vary from 0 to 1, and the higher the correlation, the stronger the predictive contribution.

Most of the relationships depicted in table 7.3 are modest. The largest *r* values were found for adult criminal history, race, antisocial personality, and companions. When the static and dynamic factors were considered as groups, the dynamic factors were more predictive of recidivism. The fact that dynamic factors (e.g., companions) predict recidivism more than factors known at sentencing or release is why objective instruments fail to predict recidivism completely. Research and common sense suggest that we can not perfectly predict recidivism—after all, we do not write biographies in advance.

Gendreau and colleagues also tested a number of risk prediction instruments. Among the risk scales tested, the Level of Service

Table 7.3. Predictors of adult recidivism

Variables	Effect sizes correlations (*r*)
Static factors	
Adult criminal history	.17
Race	.17
Juvenile antisocial behavior	.16
Family rearing practices	.14
Current age	.11
Intellectual functioning	.07
Family/parent criminality	.07
Gender	.06
Socioeconomic status	.05
Dynamic factors	
Companions	.21
Antisocial personality	.18
Social achievement	.13
Interpersonal conflict	.12
Substance abuse	.10
Personal distress	.05

Source: Gendreau et al. 1996.

Inventory–Revised (LSI-R) produced the highest correlation with recidivism ($r = .35$). This instrument measures both static and dynamic factors and was discussed in chapter 3. Most risk prediction instruments (such as the salient factors score used by the federal Bureau of Prisons) consist almost entirely of static rather than dynamic factors.

Conclusions

We know that more than two-thirds of those released from prison will be rearrested; nearly half will be returned to jail or prison for a new crime or technical violation; and about a quarter will be returned to prison for a new crime conviction in the three years following their release. These recidivism statistics have remained relatively stable since the mid-1960s, although recent data show they have risen. The latest estimates show that ex-convicts accounted for about 5 percent of all serious crime arrests between 1994 and 1997 (and 8–9 percent of homicides and robberies). The evidence also shows that the first year after release from prison is the period when most recidivism occurs, accounting for nearly two-thirds of *all* the recidivism events in the first three years. After five years of arrest-free living, the probability of returning to crime is quite low.

These results have important implications for the kinds of support we need to provide. Reductions in prison programs clearly have not served to deter inmates from returning to prison but rather have made them less able to refrain from crime. The particularly high recidivism rate for property and drug crimes suggests that much crime is committed for money or because of an addiction. The fact that nearly half of all prisoners will be reincarcerated within the three years following release means that we continue to pay for their incarceration. We need to invest in proven treatment and work programs that are cost beneficial in the long run.

The results also suggest that the most intensive services and surveillance should begin immediately upon release and be front-loaded in the first six months to the first year. These recidivism results also have important implications for reconsidering how long parole should last and how long the restrictions we place on ex-felons (e.g., job, voting, housing) should continue. If there is a miniscule risk that an offender who has remained arrest-free for five years will return to crime after that, then what social or utilitarian purpose is served by further restricting his liberty? This issue is considered further in chapter 9.

Of course, we would like to be able to predict which offenders have the highest probability of committing new crimes, as we could then target scarce rehabilitation and monitoring resources on them. Objective recidivism prediction instruments have improved over time, and we now can predict recidivism with about 70 percent accuracy. The best prediction instruments include both static and dynamic factors, with dynamic factors (e.g., substance abuse) being the most important.

Ironically, as our scientific ability to identify the factors that, if changed, could lower recidivism has evolved, resources to implement these programs have decreased. Even if we can not implement needed programs, we should use formal risk prediction instruments to guide parole decision making, as they can reduce both costs and victimization. Failure to do so threatens former and potential victims, the subject to which we now turn.

EIGHT

The Victim's Role in Prisoner Reentry

Corrections needs a culture change. The word is not out there yet that victims need to be considered at the time of offender release. Most victim services focus on the front end of the justice system, and down the road 20 years, no one is paying attention to the victim's needs when the offender is released. The information is available, but no one acts on it.

—Reginald Wilkinson, director, Ohio Department of Rehabilitation and Corrections

The victim's movement was a critical factor in the abolition of discretionary parole and the implementation of mandatory sentencing schemes across the United States. Ironically, however, the abolition of discretionary parole resulted in diminished, not enhanced, victim protection. Parole boards are in a unique position to listen to and address the needs and concerns of crime victims. When discretionary parole is abolished, virtually all offenders are released, rather than only those who can be best managed under community supervision. Moreover, abolishing discretionary parole removed an incentive system for inmates to participate in prison programs that build competency skills. Ultimately, such programs result in reduced recidivism and fewer victims. In fact, from a victim's standpoint, there is *no* benefit from determinate sentencing or automatic prison release schemes, and advocates should revisit their support of it.

What about the Victim?

Virtually all of the national discussion concerning offender reentry has focused on the needs and risks posed by returning offenders, with little thought given to their victims. Victim needs have remained largely ignored. Arguably, crime victims are the people who are most affected by the return of more than 600,000 inmates each year, and we must consider their salient needs and concerns. Victims' rights advocates have spent the last 30 years working to develop greater sensitivity toward crime victims; we must not now forget their voice in the prisoner reentry discussions and initiatives.

It is important to recall that crime produces both an offender *and* a victim. Forty-seven percent of prison inmates are there because they were convicted of a violent crime, where someone was raped, robbed, assaulted, or killed (Beck and Harrison 2001). But violent offenders are not the only ones whose crimes cause victim harm and trauma. An additional 21 percent of the current prison population was convicted of a property crime, most frequently burglary, auto theft, and fraud. Financial crimes also have real victims, who suffered financial hardships, may have had to move, or no longer felt safe in their own homes.

Even some drug crimes—often referred to as "victimless" because the criminal took part willingly—have real victims. Clearly, too many inmates are behind bars for "simple" drug crimes, such as marijuana possession or the sale of small quantities. But some drug crimes are not solely matters of private behavior and do bring harm to others. So here too, the issue is more complicated.

As long as the distribution and sale of drugs is illegal, these activities give rise to illegal markets, which are governed by violence and intimidation. As Albert Reiss wrote:

> Not only do the market's entrepreneurs seek market shares by violent means, but their use of violence may result in community residents becoming the victims of violence as in, for example, drive-by shootings and gang warfare. Moreover, the concentration of sales in dwellings as well as on street locations opens residential housing and communities to nonresidential as well as residential users who engage in the crimes of prostitution, robbery, burglary, and theft to obtain money to purchase drugs. It seems reasonable to conclude that ordinary citizens in these communities are the victims of so-called victimless crimes. In these instances, crime not only induces public fear, but also destroys community life. (Reiss 1999, p. 60)

Imprisonment may or may not be the appropriate punishment for drug offenders, but many of their crimes produce real victims. Their victims are just less visible. To ignore that fact is simply wrong.

The crime victims' movement can be credited with many policy and legislative changes. Victims' rights activists—many of them survivors themselves—have had a profound impact on legislative reforms, the expansion of victims' assistance and compensation programs, and the creation of new laws that articulate and enforce crime victims' rights. Numerous local victims' advocacy organizations have been formed, perhaps the most well known being Mothers Against Drunk Driving (MADD). These organizations have successfully lobbied for tougher penalties for offenders and greater victim involvement in all phases of the criminal justice system.

In 1990, the Crime Control Act established a new framework for victims' rights by creating the first federal bill of rights for victims of crime. This legislation, referred to as the Victims' Rights and Restitution Act of 1990, or the Victims' Rights Act, requires law enforcement officers, prosecutors, and correctional officers to ensure that victims receive basic rights and services, including the right to be reasonably protected from the accused, to be notified of court proceedings, to be present at all public court proceedings unless the court determines otherwise, and to information about the offender's imprisonment and release.

In 1994, passage of the Violent Crime Control and Law Enforcement Act created new rights for victims of sexual assault, domestic violence, and child abuse. This legislation also included significant funding for a variety of new crime prevention programs for victims. In 1997, Congress passed the Victims' Rights Clarification Act, asserting that victims should have the right to both attend proceedings and deliver or submit a victim impact statement. As Karmen recently wrote: "No set of ideas has had a more profound impact on the criminal justice system in the last 30 years than has the institutionalized public concern about the victim of crime" (Karmen 2001, p. xvi).

Early state victims' rights legislation focused largely on the rights and services afforded during the prosecution of a criminal case. The police hired victim advocates and prosecutors to assure that victims' needs were considered and that victims stayed involved in the legal proceedings. Virtually no attention was paid in these early years to the role victims might play in postconviction or parole proceedings. The first major report on crime victims, The President's Task Force on Victims of Crime's *Final Report* (1982) contained 68 recommendations, only 5 of which pertained to parole. The first 4 task force recommendations urged parole boards to (1) notify victims of parole hearings; (2) allow victims to attend parole hearings and provide input; (3) reincarcerate parolees who committed new crimes; and (4) not apply the exclusionary rule to parole revocation hearings.

The lack of attention paid by victim advocates and prison officials to victim issues is understandable. Most crime victims never come into contact with prison or parole systems. This is because most perpetrators, even if they are convicted, do not end up in prison. While the odds of a conviction leading to imprisonment increased for many kinds of crime during the 1990s, they are still fairly low overall. In 1998, 44 percent of all convicted felons were sentenced to state prisons (Durose 2001). Violent offenders have a higher probability of a prison sentence: 70 percent of those convicted of rape will receive a prison term, but just 46 percent of those convicted of aggravated assault. If one examines the odds that an arrest will lead to a prison term, the figures are much lower: only about 28 percent of all those arrested for robbery end up in prison; for burglary, the figure is about 17 percent.

The fifth and major corrections recommendation of the 1982 presidential task force was that the parole system in the United States be eliminated. The task force characterized parole as "early release" and noted that victims bitterly resent any practice that "lets inmates out early." In the ensuing years, victims' groups urged legislatures to abolish discretionary parole altogether, and as discussed in chapter 3, 16 states did.

Unfortunately, abolishing parole does *not* serve to increase victim safety. In fact, it does just the opposite. It removes the major incentive that inmates have for participating in rehabilitation programs. It also eliminates most formal parole hearings, the major method by which victims can provide details of the crimes to corrections officials, making sure that their needs are considered in the release decision and in the assignment of special parole conditions. As Mario Paparozzi, past president of the American Probation and Parole Association and former chair of the New Jersey Parole Board, put it: "No-parole schemes sounded tough but eliminated the opportunity for citizen-oriented boards to review convicts' cases." Paparozzi argued that parole review hearings provide a chance for crime victims to have their say, which they normally do not in the plea bargains that end most cases (Gest 2001, p. 209).

When states abolish parole or reduce the discretion of parole authorities, they replace a rational, controlled system of earned release for selected inmates with automatic release for nearly all inmates (Burke 1995). No-parole systems remove a gatekeeper role that can protect victims and communities. And, as shown in chapter 2, inmates actually serve longer prison sentences in states retaining discretionary parole, and prisoners released through discretionary parole have higher success rates than those released mandatorily.

Today, victim advocates are working to assure that they are notified of the inmate's release status and about key criminal justice proceedings in which they might participate. They are also working collaboratively with parole officials to assign parole supervision conditions that might increase their sense of safety and reduce their sense of risk (e.g., no-contact orders). And, for those who wish to be involved directly with the offender, some are participating in victim-offender mediation and other educational programs designed to educate the offender about the harm he caused the victim and the community. To a much lesser extent, victims are participating in the new reentry partnership projects or reentry courts initiatives, which are discussed in chapter 9.

The Victim's Opportunity to Participate in Parole Hearings

The 1982 president's task force recommended that parole boards "allow victims of crime, their families, or their representatives, to attend parole hearings and make known the effect of the offender's crime on them" (p. 83). In the ensuing years, nearly all parole boards have opened up their decision-making process by granting victims, prosecutors, and judges the opportunity to provide input at the parole hearing. Parole boards historically received input only from prison staff regarding an inmate's suitability for release. A survey conducted in 1994 by the Association of Parole Authorities, International found that, of all of the types of individual inputs that parole boards consider, victim statements are ranked the most important (Rhunda, Rhine, and Wetter 1994).

Victim input into the parole process is one of the few areas of victims' rights in which nearly all states have enacted legislation. Thirty-two of the 50 states have amended their state constitutions to include victims' rights, usually including the rights to be informed, present, and heard at critical stages in the criminal justice process, including prisoner release. However, just 15 states notify all victims that a parole hearing has been scheduled. In the remaining states, notice is provided only if the victim so requests (Rhunda, Rhine, and

Wetter 1994). Only 6 states do not permit victims to appear at the parole hearing (Arkansas, Georgia, Hawaii, Kansas, North Carolina, and Wyoming).

Most states (32) identify the "victim" as the actual victim, the victim's family, or a victims' group, and all of these are allowed to provide input. Thirteen states do not identify victims' groups as the victim, and they are excluded from providing testimony (Association of Parole Authorities, International 2001b). Of the states that let victims comment on offender requests for parole, 46 states allow statements to be submitted in person; 42 states allow written statements. In 5 states (Alabama, South Carolina, Nebraska, Tennessee, and West Virginia), members of the general public—not just the victim—can testify against the release of a prisoner.

Victim statements are confidential in 32 states, however, in 7 states, inmates can obtain the information provided by victims to the board. In the remaining jurisdictions, the inmate may obtain such information if the hearing is conducted as a public open meeting. Most parole boards notify the victim of the parole board's decision, but the victim usually must formally request in writing that he wishes to be notified. Alabama, Oregon, and South Dakota are the only states that do not notify the victim of all parole release decisions.

In some states, state law requires victim notification. In 1990, Arizona passed a state constitutional victims' bill of rights, which guarantees victims the right to notice of and to be heard at parole hearings. State law also provides a remedy if a victim's rights were ignored. In 1993, Patricia Pollard's assailant, Eric Mageary—who had been convicted of kidnap and rape—was released, and Ms. Pollard was not notified. Ms. Pollard filed a lawsuit, and a parole rehearing was ordered. After she testified, the board reversed its decision and denied Mageary's release (Office for Victims of Crime 1998).

Why Are So Few Victims Involved in Parole Matters?

Today, nearly every state has procedures for soliciting victim input at parole hearings and notifying victims of inmate release dates. However, parole agencies report that less than half of parole hearing cases filed have victim notification requests and that victims attend only one-fourth of parole hearings (Seymour 1997).

There are several reasons why victim involvement is poor. In most states, victims must *request* to be notified of parole hearings and release dates, and many simply fail to ask that this information be sent to them. Also, if during the course of the prison stay, the victim moves, it is the victim's responsibility to notify the parole board of her change of address. And while parole boards may provide the date, time, and location of the hearing, most victims are not told how to provide information or present testimony. An excellent recent publication, *The Victim's Role in Offender Reentry: A Community Response Model* (Seymour 1997), provides guidelines for preparing a victim impact statement (VIS). It includes a checklist for preparing a VIS and encourages justice system officials to complete it so that it becomes part of the inmate's official prison record. At the time of the parole hearing, parole board members can review this VIS even in the absence of the victim.

Some parole boards (e.g., South Carolina, Virginia, Pennsylvania, Massachusetts) have appointed a victim member to the board. This helps assure that the victim's perspective is considered in release decisions and also serves to make the parole-hearing environment more sensitive to victims' fears and needs. One such victim member said that she hopes that when victims testify before the board of which she is a part, even if they do not know that she too has been victimized, they will be able to feel the support and empathy she brings to the questions she asks and the respect she gives them. It is also true that parole hearings are usually located in geographically remote areas, during the week, and victims often have neither the time nor resources to travel to such locations.

However, the emotional difficulties surrounding victim testimony are more important than these practical concerns. Victims understandably avoid having to relive the victimization once again. Crime victims often fear that the offender will retaliate if the source of the information becomes known—and, as noted above, some states permit the inmate to have access to victim statements.

Victims also fear that they may have a face-to-face confrontation with the offender. Unfortunately, this is a realistic concern. Parole boards in 20 states allow both the victim and inmate to be present during the parole hearing. Other authorities report that they take the victim's testimony separately, and some schedule separate hearings. However, parole authorities almost never provide different waiting areas that separate victims and their offenders (or the offender's family, who might have come to testify on the offender's behalf). As

Karmen (2001, p. 180) wrote: "Victims can feel especially endangered by a vengeful, violent ex-offender if their cooperation and testimony was a crucial factor leading to conviction." Research has shown that victims who have concerns about their safety and security—at any point throughout the justice process—are less inclined to actively participate in justice proceedings.

Most victims knew their assailants, particularly in violent crimes, and the inmate often knows where the victim and the family continue to work or live. In 1999, almost 7 out of 10 rapes or sexual assaults were committed by an intimate, relative, friend, or acquaintance. Statistics on violent crimes against juveniles show that, in 80 percent of cases, victims know their perpetrators. Surprisingly, just 55 percent of juvenile correctional agencies even notify victims of their offenders' release (Office for Victims of Crime 2000).

While nearly all states now permit victims to testify at parole hearings, some parole board members have voiced concern that the emotional appeal of a victim's verbal testimony may cause them to lose the neutrality necessary to make important decisions about inmates. However, most board members say they try to stay objective about the process, recognizing the impact of the crime, but trying not to get too lost in the emotion of it. As Steve Baker, a parole board member in New Jersey put it: "When you listen to the inmates describing how sorry they are and how well they have behaved in prison, and the defense attorney describing the fact that the criminal is a changed man, you tend to forget why the inmate is here to begin with. The victim[s] and their families tell us the impact of the crime on their lives, and we definitely listen to them a lot." Another parole board member added: "We have the police version of the crime, the inmate version of the crime. We would like to think inmates tell us the truth, but we know they don't. The victim might tell us a totally different version. Victim testimony helps us assess the credibility of what the inmate is telling us. Yes, it costs us money to have victims participate in the process, but it is definitely worth it" (Office for Victims of Crime 2000).

It is also true that not all victim testimony is unsympathetic to offenders. Herman and Wasserman, from the National Center for Victims of Crime, note, "The common perception of victims as people with no relationship to offenders, and without sympathy for offenders, upon closer examination reveals that victims of crime are highly diverse" (2001, p. 429). In many instances, victims know their offenders well and want them helped.

The Impact of Victim Testimony on Parole Outcomes

Research has shown that victim impact statements are not associated with harsher sentences and that their absence does not correlate with more lenient sentences. Generally, victim impact statements have not been shown to produce significant effects upon sentence lengths or sentencing patterns (Erez and Roger 1995). However, it should be noted that most of this research has focused on sentencing rather than on parole decision making, and no scientific studies have looked at the effect of victims' testimony on release decisions.

The lack of a relationship between victim input and sentencing decisions is not as surprising as it might first appear, because information from victims is only one factor among many that determine sentencing and parole outcomes. Karmen writes:

> The potential impact of victim input into parole board decisionmaking is limited. The boards review statements from victims, prosecutors, judges, and other concerned parties. They interview the inmates themselves and review their criminal behavior. Boards are often subject to intense pressures either to keep convicts confined longer or to let some out ahead of schedule to make room for new arrivals. (Karmen 2001, p. 181)

Parole decision making has always been highly political (as nearly all parole board members are appointed by governors) and is the primary mechanism for controlling prison population levels (and associated litigation and fines due to overcrowding).

Rhunda and colleagues conducted a survey in 1994 of U.S. parole boards and found that nine factors are important in their decision making. The most important factor in deciding whether to grant parole release is the nature of the offender's current crime. This is followed rather closely by prior violent criminal record and prior felony convictions. The possession of a firearm ranks fourth among the nine factors. The remaining five items are previous incarceration, prior parole adjustment, prison disciplinary record, psychological report, and victim input, although these last five do not carry as much significance as the top four factors.

It is important to recognize that, by soliciting victim impact statements, the victim's role in the criminal justice system is validated, and it may aid some victims' ability to reconstruct their lives in the aftermath of the crime. Research suggests that when victims are given the opportunity to provide information about the effect of the crime, it can improve their overall opinion of the criminal justice system (Godwin and Seymour 1999).

While most victims do not choose to testify at parole hearings, and their testimony may not strongly predict the release–no release decision, parole boards and victims still have a critically important collaboration to foster. Victims strongly desire to be notified of inmates' release dates and release plans, and victims can play a vital role in helping the parole board to decide the most appropriate conditions of release.

Victim Concerns about Prisoner Reentry

Notifying victims when prisoners are released can be a matter of life and death. There are numerous documented cases of victims being killed by offenders recently released from prison. In many of these cases, the victims were unable to take precautions to save their lives because they had not been notified of the inmates' release. As Seymour wrote: "Often called 'the threshold right' from which all other victims' rights and services emanate, victim notification takes on added importance within the context of offender reentry" (Seymour 1997, p. 15).

The American Probation and Parole Association (APPA) recently mailed a survey to its members asking them to identify and prioritize crime victims' rights, needs, and concerns with offender reentry Table 8.1 shows that victims most want *more* information—to be told whom to contact if they have concerns and to be notified of the offender's location (either in prison or in the community). They are significantly less concerned or interested in financial restitution, participating in any victim-offender mediation, or referrals to social service agencies for their own recovery.

Victims also want the justice system to provide this information to them automatically. As a survivor of a violent crime recently stated, victims should not have to request to be notified of an inmate's release—it should be automatic—and it is not only formal notice of the release date that is critical, but also the inmate's reentry plans. A survivor of a kidnap and sexual assault said:

> I need information, not just on the status of the offender, but about his mindset, his intentions, his mental health status, and

Table 8.1. Victims' concerns and needs about prisoner reentry

Victim need or concern	Percentage
Information about whom to contact if the victim has concerns	75
Notification of offender location	75
Notification of offender status	65
Protective or no-contact orders	64
Input into conditions of release	33
Financial/legal obligations	29
Information about referrals	22
Offender programming that creates awareness	19
Victim-offender programming and mediation	12

Source: Seymour 2001.

> his future plans. Where will he be living? What kind of work will he be doing? Who will be supervising information? Recently, I discovered that this information may be available if the victim writes a letter to the Department of Corrections and it is determined that the victim's need to know this information outweighs the offender's right. But victims should not have to write a letter defending their right to receive it! Rather, it should be provided as part of the victim's core right to information and notification. (Seymour 2001, p. 15)

Pennsylvania has one of the more comprehensive systems for involving victims in postconviction decisions. Crime victims are notified of their right to participate by the county district attorney. The district attorney provides the victim with a registration card at the time of sentencing. The victim must complete the registration form and send it to the state Office of the Victim Advocate (OVA). Once a victim is registered, the OVA is legally mandated to notify her of prerelease programming (e.g., movement to a halfway house), inmate escape, inmate transfer to a mental health facility outside the jurisdiction of the Department of Corrections, and the opportunity to provide oral and written comments on parole decisions. By policy, the OVA also notifies victims of the death of an inmate, general information regarding the inmate's status when requested, and special conditions of prerelease participation.

Pennsylvania also posts on the Internet the names of all persons currently in prison, so victims can check to see if their offenders have been released. As discussed in chapter 6, 25 states now allow the public to access the names and release dates of all prisoners through the Internet. Data from Pennsylvania's OVA show that, in 2000, 10,187 notifications were sent to registered crime victims; victim comments were received in 2,268 (22 percent) cases; and petitions to deny parole were submitted by 329 victims (3 percent). Fewer than 5 percent of all registered crime victims have chosen to submit petitions to deny parole since the OVA began keeping statistics in 1996.

For a variety of reasons, victims are not playing a central role in prisoner reentry, and they should be. In 1998, the Office for Victims of Crime issued an update to the 1982 presidential task force, entitled *New Directions from the Field: Victims' Rights and Services for the 21st Century*. It focused more heavily on the victim's role in postconviction matters and recommended that all victims, upon their request, be notified at least 60 days prior to inmates' release in order to address safety concerns and prepare themselves psychologically (Fine 2000). They should also be notified of inmates' escapes or deaths. Additional recommendations included:

- Notices should be provided in a language common to the community, and they should be designed to reach victims with limited literacy as well.
- Victims should be notified if an offender on parole fails to comply with a special condition ordered by the court, absconds, or is released from supervision, including no-contact provisions.
- Victims should be notified of the name and telephone number of the parole agent and of all conditions attaching to the supervised release; procedures for contacting officials when violations of release conditions occur and for reporting acts of harassment, intimidation, or violence 24 hours a day, seven days a week; and the known address, city, and county where the offender will be released.
- Correctional agencies should follow the lead of the 31 states that recommend revocation or parole when a parolee in any way harasses, intimidates, or retaliates against a victim. Parole agencies should also develop protocols that provide for notification to victims if they appear to be in imminent danger.

Innovative technologies have emerged in recent years to augment victims' access to notification of inmate release and other information. At least 10 states report utilizing automated voice response notification systems, which place telephone calls to victims, upon request, and inform them of offenders' pending release or parole hearings. Several states (e.g., Illinois, Pennsylvania, New York, Florida) now include updates on inmates' status, location, and relevant hearings which are available to victims and the general public via the Internet. Of course, providing this information to the public also is likely to reduce the job and housing opportunities available to inmates. How to address this inherent conflict is a fundamental issue for prisoner reentry.

Some also question whether notifying victims of their offenders' activities is in their best interests. Some report that victims feel additional anxiety and fear with the new information. Victim advocates say that notifying a victim of an inmate's parole eligibility and release does not go far enough and that referrals for counseling should also be provided and paid for. State victim compensation normally reimburses psychological counseling for the victim immediately after the crime occurs but does not normally cover crisis intervention or other types of emotional support that the victim may require at the inmate's release.

As Herman and Wasserman (2001) point out, how a victim reacts to reentry depends on many factors, including the seriousness of the crime, the length of time that has passed since the crime was committed, the personal and economic circumstances of the victim, the victim's relationship to the offender, any specific dangers posed by the offender's return, and the extent and quality of community-based support services and resources. While there is great diversity in the reactions of victims to their offenders' release, they all have a common interest in programs designed to prevent recidivism and increase successful reintegration.

Involving Victims in Reentry Planning and Reentry Partnerships

Crime victims often have the most detailed knowledge of the offender and the risks he poses to public safety. As such, they are ideally suited to assisting parole authorities in assigning parole conditions. Victims should be central to parole and reentry efforts. Even if most parole boards no longer retain the discretion to set the date of release, all of them set the conditions of release. Eighty percent of all released prisoners will be supervised on parole caseloads, and victims can provide vital information to assure that authorities assign the most appropriate conditions at release. Victims—often more so than any other person—know the conditions that fostered the criminality of this individual. Victims can report the degree of violence involved in the crime, the factors that perpetrated it, and the extent of victim harm. Such information should be used by parole boards to identify the needs and risks posed by the returning inmate. If victims are informed of the assigned parole conditions, they can also help to monitor them and inform authorities if violations are occurring. Engaging the victim in this collaborative manner serves the parolee, the crime victim, and the community at large. Again, however, authorities must balance the victim's needs for vengeance and safety with the true risks posed by the returning inmate.

Victims can assist the parole board in deciding which programs and postprison conditions to require, and parole board members report relying heavily on victim statements for this task. For instance, parole boards may establish a geographic "safe zone" perimeter around the victim (for example, in California, it is 30 miles from the victim's place of residence). They may also impose no-contact conditions, where the parolee is unable to seek out this particular victim or an entire class of potential victims (e.g., children). They might also notify the parole board that the inmate is a gang member, and the parole board might attach "gang terms" to the parole, where the parolee is not able to have contact with any gang members. The victim might also give information that would suggest the parolee be required to attend sex-offender treatment or a substance abuse program. These and other special parole conditions may serve to reduce the fear the victim experiences when the parolee is released and also to help the offender succeed—thereby reducing future victimizations.

Victims also can serve as additional pairs of eyes in the community and provide vital information to authorities when parolees are violating their parole conditions (*if* they have been told what those parole conditions are). Again, because many victims will know their offenders, they are often the first to know when the offender is slipping back into old habits and committing new crimes. If parole authorities work collaboratively with victims, victims can notify authorities and provide input during the parole violation hearing. Victims are permitted to participate in parole violation hearings in 22 states. However, only 6 states notify the victim when the parolee is in violation of a parole condition and facing revocation.

It is not just that the victim could provide information *to* parole officials, but parole officials could help reduce victim fears if they were more communicative. They might tell the victim that the parolee has completed a substance abuse program, is employed full time, recently married, or will be monitored on an intensive supervision caseload—all of which might serve to increase the victim's sense of safety. Just as the victim was closest to the offender prior to incarceration, parole and corrections staff are closest to the inmate at release. They have information on the inmate's current psychological state and that information should be given to the crime victim. Parole boards can also assure victims that parole officers will assist in collecting any restitution they are owed. Restitution may be important to some victims, both financially and psychologically.

Communities across the nation are experimenting with a variety of reentry initiatives, the most popular being *reentry partnerships*, and *reentry courts*. These programs are designed to better manage the return of inmates to the community by using either the authority of the police (in reentry partnerships) or the authority of the court (in reentry courts) to encourage a broad-based coalition to support prisoner reentry. Yet, in the efforts to date, none is actively involving victims. This is unfortunate from a variety of perspectives. First, their input is vital, given the unique information they have about the offender and the incentives they have to ensure that the offender is "making good." Second, without their political support, victims can derail the initiatives. As Seymour wrote, "Crime victims can 'drive' reentry partnerships as involved and respected participants, or can just as easily derail them if their needs and interests are ignored" (Seymour 2001, p. 3). Seymour recommends that victims of an offender who is about to be released should be contacted by a victim service provider or a law enforcement official and be asked, "How are you doing? Is there anything that can be done to help you in this transition process? What are your safety and information needs, and how can we meet them?" To date, this is not happening.

Restorative justice programs, such as victim-offender mediation, may bring the victim and the offender together. This is often more for the offender's educational benefit than for the victim, although some suggest that it helps the victim to feel better as well (although there is little research on this for more serious crimes). Based on the information in table 8.1, victims have relatively little interest in participating in mediation programs with their specific offender who is in prison or on parole. As one survivor of a kidnap and sexual assault put it:

"In my particular case, I would not wish to meet with my offender under any circumstances, because I would not be able to trust his word, nor would I want to demonstrate any of my concerns. In addition, he would learn a great deal of information about me, and might see my intentions as fear or weakness. Instead of feeling empowered, I would feel vulnerable" (Seymour 1997, p. 36).

Some members of victims' groups do participate in general education sessions for prisoners, usually after a significant time has passed since their own victimization. However, restorative justice parole efforts are virtually nonexistent, so we do not know whether the victims' statements above would reflect the majority of victims of parolees. Of course, respecting victims' rights must take precedence over any educational benefits to offenders.

Conclusions

The increasingly diminished role of victims in sentencing and parole has gone largely unnoticed. Victims' advocates have celebrated a number of gains, but those gains have occurred mostly at the front end (e.g., more counseling programs, greater compensation for losses, advocates to assist with police and district attorney's offices), although, legally speaking, greater rights have been afforded the victim in parole as well. Most states now have statutes authorizing the victim to be notified of parole hearings and of parole eligibility dates. Unfortunately, this is a hollow victory: they have increasingly gained the right to appear and testify at parole hearings, but fewer states are holding such hearings. Today, nearly every state has procedures for soliciting victims' input at parole hearings and notifying victims of inmate release dates. However, parole agencies report that fewer than half of parole hearings have victim notification requests on file and that victims attend only one-fourth of parole hearings.

Crime victims have a vital role to play in managing the offender's return from prison. They should be consulted not only about the inmate's suitability for parole but also asked for input regarding the conditions of release. Special conditions (e.g., no-contact orders) can be attached to an inmate's parole term, increasing victim safety and perhaps reducing offender recidivism. Involving victims more integrally in prisoner reentry processes and programs is critical, since the political support of victims and victim advocates will be critical to implementing the reforms discussed in the next chapter.

NINE

What to Do?

Reforming Parole and Reentry Practices

The more punitive crime policies of the 1980s and 1990s resulted in states cutting inmate education and job-training programs, thereby removing a major incentive for inmates to behave well and improve themselves while in prison. The elimination of discretionary parole in many states has meant that inmates simply bide their time in prison, and there is no gatekeeper to review the inmates' preparation for release, release plans, or risk level. Laws that mandate long fixed prison terms for serious offenders have had the perverse effect of returning some of the most dangerous convicts to the community with the least supervision and control. Clearly, we can and should do better.

There are four major areas in which prisoner reintegration practices need to be reformed:

1. Alter the in-prison experience. Provide more education, work, and rehabilitation opportunities. Change the prison environment to promote life skills rather than violence and domination.
2. Change prison release and revocation practices. Institute a system of discretionary parole release that incorporates parole release guidelines. These parole guidelines should be based primarily on recidivism prediction.
3. Revise post-prison services and supervision. Incorporate better parole supervision classification systems, and target services and surveillance to those with high need and risk profiles.
4. Foster collaborations with the community and enhance mechanisms of informal social control. Develop partnerships with service providers, ex-convicts, law enforcement, family members, victim advocates, and neighborhoods to support the offender.

Most of the reform ideas discussed in this chapter are not proven programs, and most have not been sufficiently evaluated. Rather, they are promising practices, as identified by the available information and experts in the field. Unfortunately, little scientific research exists on the reentry process, parole release decision making, or the effects of variations in postprison services. Parole has never attracted much research interest, and this is even truer today, as many states have eliminated their research departments to fund prison expansion. So, even though the need for scientific data is stronger than ever, in most instances, there is no funding. There is an emerging body of research on what works in correctional treatment but less information on how parole and release policies affect subsequent behavior. Nonetheless, experts' opinions and preliminary evidence suggest that a number of strategies are worth pursuing.

Alter the In-Prison Environment

There are two primary ways to alter the prison experience so as to better address reentry issues. The first, much tried and debated, is to provide a greater number of high-quality in-prison treatment, work, and education programs. The second, new and innovative, is to fundamentally change the *culture* and activities in prison so as to teach daily living skills and values that more closely resemble those in the free world. However, prior to implementing either of these notions, prison officials must accept that prisoner reintegration is part of their core responsibilities.

Recommendation 1: Prison Administrators Should Embrace the Mission of Prisoner Reintegration

Part of the difficulty in rethinking prisoner reentry is that it is not clear who owns the problem. In recent years, most prison administrators have endorsed a "confinement model" mission, which can be summarized succinctly as "keep them in, keep them safe, and keep them in line" (Logan 1993, p. 27). In other words, the prison system does not bear responsibility for what happens to inmates *after* release. Much like in a transportation system, prison officials manage the "traffic flow" as efficiently as possible and let someone else worry about where the people are headed.

But this mentality severely affects public safety and an inmate's chances of successful transition. Preparation for release cannot begin several weeks before an inmate is released. Every facet of the correctional experience—both inside and outside prison walls—should be connected in some way to the preparation and support necessary to help the offender make a successful transition. In fact, for the prison administrator facing budget constraints, initiatives like truth-in-sentencing can be used to refocus resources and programs on release services. Previously, it was difficult to gauge exactly when an inmate would be released. With truth-in-sentencing and other determinate sentencing schemes, the day someone walks into prison, the prison staff knows exactly when she will be released. This allows more targeted release planning.

Ideally, reentry programs would be systemic in focus, starting at reception and carrying through in a seamless and coordinated fashion through the completion of parole supervision. Adopting such an approach, however, requires that prison administrators take a leadership role in prisoner reentry, and in most states, that is not happening. As Ned Rollo, an ex-convict who runs prerelease programs in several states, told the author: "Preparing inmates for the free world is frequently treated as an isolated, second-class function, rather than as a vital mid-step in an ongoing process. Administratively, the function is often viewed as low priority, a shallow institutional 'after thought' of little importance."

Corrections agencies could be expected (and funded) to create a set of systems that spans the boundaries of prison and community. For example, correctional agencies could create linkages between in-prison jobs and community-based employment and job training, and between in-prison health care and community-based health care. Corrections could be expected to link mental health services on both sides of the wall, or work with community-based domestic violence services when a prisoner is released with a history of spousal abuse. They could also be expected to assist the prisoner in securing the tools to succeed, for example, identification, driver's license, access to Social Security or other benefits, or housing upon release. Where necessary, the department of corrections would be authorized to purchase services to ensure a smooth transfer of responsibility, for example, the first few months of rent in a hotel if no other housing is available, or transitional mental health counseling if no comprehensive community-based care is available.

Just as welfare reform forced welfare agencies to shift from a dependency model to a model of transition to independence, so too a reentry perspective would force correctional agencies to take practical steps to move prisoners toward independence. In the case of welfare reform, this shift meant that welfare agencies invested in child care, job training, and employee assistance programs—whatever it took to move the client from welfare to work. Similarly, corrections agencies should make strategic investments in transitional services to move prisoners toward independence.

The necessary first step here is that prisons must embrace reintegration as a goal, and this is a matter of enormous controversy. But there are some leaders who are trying to change that. The Ohio Department of Rehabilitation and Corrections (DOC), under the leadership of Reginald Wilkinson, former president of the American Correctional Association, has officially adopted a new reentry mandate. In 2001, Ohio launched an initiative entitled "The Ohio Plan for Productive Offender Reentry and Recidivism Reduction." That plan requires personal reentry plans for each offender being released, reexamines standards for parole revocation, and dismantles ineffective prerelease programs (Wilkinson 2001). Wilkinson also created the Office of Offender Reentry and Recidivism (OORR) to collect data and assess the effectiveness of current programs.

A priority of Ohio's OORR is to create stronger linkages between the DOC and many key reentry activities that are distinctly local. For example, health, child welfare, job placement, drug treatment, and other services are usually county functions and therefore require the leadership of the mayor or other local executive. In our traditional configuration of responsibilities, we have oddly placed responsibility for reentry management in a state agency, typically a parole division or a corrections agency. Yet, we have also created community supervision functions in law enforcement, probation, or pretrial release agencies, which are often county or city based. Most mental health and substance abuse programs are also county or city based. These artificial distinctions are barriers to reentry management. Resources are not shared, and data systems that might help coordinate care are not integrated. The Ohio DOC is trying to foster links among prisons and community-based organizations and also to marshal the necessary community resources to assist in successful reintegration. Correctional leaders in Maryland, Washington, and Oregon are moving in similar directions.

If prison officials do not embrace reentry as part of their core mission, the next two policy recommendations cannot be effectively implemented.

Recommendation 2: Rehabilitate Reentry: Implement Treatment, Work, and Education Tracks in Prison

We cannot maximize recidivism reduction if we do not reinvest in treatment and work programs. It simply cannot be done. Research demonstrates that rehabilitation programs *do* reduce recidivism if they incorporate proven principles and are targeted to specific offenders. But just as the evidence is building that some programs *do* work, states are dismantling those very programs due to budget constraints. As noted in chapter 5, less than a quarter of all inmates participate in prison treatment or work programs. These programs should not be seen as benefits given to prisoners. Rather, they are opportunities available to prisoners who are willing to make productive use of them.

Not all inmates are motivated to participate in treatment, education, or work programs, nor would all likely benefit from participation (although program participation reduces prison violence and, in that sense, benefits everyone). We must recognize diversity in needs and prioritize scarce program resources where they will do the most good. In prison, often those that need job training the least (i.e., they have the highest skill levels to begin with) are given the best job opportunities. Priority should be given to those with an identified need and potential to succeed.

The cry for more programming is always met with public skepticism. The public (and hence, elected officials) simply does not believe that prison programs make a difference. This is the unfortunate legacy of the Martinson nothing-works era, discussed in chapter 3. Today, however, there is scientific evidence that prison programs *do* work, for *some* people, in *some* settings. Correctional programs can increase postrelease employment and reduce recidivism, provided the programs are well designed and implemented. At the same time, programs that are poorly targeted, poorly designed, and poorly implemented do *not* work. Inmates are not a homogeneous group, and rehabilitation depends on recognizing their diversity in needs, risks, and amenability to treatment.

What Works in Prison and Reentry Programming? There were numerous scholarly reviews of correctional treatment published during the 1990s. Their complete findings are not repeated here. Rather, readers interested in rehabilitation would do well to read these articles, as they contain useful information on program design, implementation, and costs. The most relevant research reviews for our purposes are MacKenzie and Hickman (1998), Seiter and Kadela (2003), Lawrence et al. (2002), Gaes and Kendig (2002), Gaes et al. (1999), Cullen (2002), Aos et al. (2001), and Taxman et al. (2002b). These reviews use a number of different methods to assess what works. Yet, despite differing methodologies, their findings are consistent. Importantly, all conclude that some rehabilitation programs effectively reduce recidivism.

The Gaes, Cullen, and Gaes and Kendig reviews summarize recent meta-analyses. Meta-analysis (the analysis of analysis) examines data from many different studies dealing with the same research question in order to determine general findings. Studies included in a meta-analysis are screened to meet minimum research design standards. Seiter and Kadela and MacKenzie and Hickman adopted a rating system to assess the quality of program evaluations before endorsing the published findings. Lawrence and colleagues and Taxman summarize the existing literature as well as the program experiences of selected states. In an important, methodologically sophisticated review, Aos and colleagues reviewed more than 400 research studies and considered not only treatment effects but also the costs and benefits of different programs.

Taken together, these research reviews have generally found the following prison rehabilitation programs to be effective, usually measured in terms of reductions in recidivism or increases in employment after release:

- academic skills training, including adult basic education and general equivalency diplomas, which teaches the offender how to participate in education activities and how to read, write, and utilize basic arithmetic;
- vocational skills training, which teaches how to acquire and maintain employment in order to fulfill financial obligations and how to engage in purposeful activity and postrelease employment;
- cognitive skills programs, which focus on engaging in accurate self-appraisal and goal setting, solving problems effectively, maintaining self-control, and displaying prosocial values;
- sex-offender interventions, especially cognitive restructuring, which teaches the inmate to control self- or other-destructive behavior; and

- drug abuse treatment (therapeutic community [TC] and TC-plus-aftercare, not outpatient counseling).

Despite the research evidence showing that, in general, participants in prison-based educational, vocational, cognitive restructuring, and substance abuse programs are more successful—that is, commit less crime and are employed more often and for longer periods of time after release—there are important caveats.

First, the effects are not large. Aos and colleagues reported that the best programs could be expected to deliver 20–30 percent reductions in recidivism or crime rates for the intended populations. More typical programs, on the other hand, were able to demonstrate only 5–10 percent reduction. For example, nearly 50 percent of all adult offenders leaving prison are subsequently reconvicted for another felony offense within three years of release. A 10 percent reduction from a 50 percent starting point results in a 45 percent recidivism rate, a significant, but not a huge, reduction. Second, existing program evaluations generally employ weak methodologies that limit the extent to which we can attribute improved inmate outcomes solely to program activities. Participation in most prison programs is voluntary, and generally speaking, the most motivated prisoners participate in programs. As a result, the research designs have an inherent sample selection bias, since volunteers are more motivated to succeed than the prison population at large. There is also the problem of trying to estimate how many inmates would or could be affected by these interventions. If positive program outcomes depend on volunteering (which might be a proxy for motivation to change), and only a small fraction of inmates will volunteer, then it is easy to exaggerate the benefits of expanding programs. Third, most programs have high dropout rates. Yet, evaluations often report only the recidivism rates of program completers. Again, this produces a sample selection bias. Fourth, Aos and colleagues say that some of the effective programs are not cost effective, as measured by the value to taxpayers and crime victims. In their review, they estimated the costs of avoided crime, arrests, and convictions. They argue that even if a program leads to reduced recidivism, if it costs a great deal relative to its crime reduction benefits, it may not be economical. The researchers computed two cost-benefit analyses. The first cost analysis incorporated only direct costs and benefits (savings) of a program. These include benefits to the taxpayer by reducing the marginal operating and capital costs of processing the recidivists (e.g., police, courts, corrections). The second cost analysis incorporated victim effects, which are immeasurable but include monetary costs and quality-of-life costs, such as medical expenses and reductions in the future earnings of victims. The crime victim costs were taken from Miller, Cohen, and Wiersema (1996), who used jury awards to estimate these parameters.

Table 9.1 summarizes the Aos findings pertaining to adult prison and reentry programs. It is important to note, however, that they found the largest and most consistent economic returns for certain programs designed for juvenile offenders. Several of the juvenile interventions produced benefit-to-cost ratios that exceeded $20 of benefits for each dollar of taxpayer costs. As shown in the last column in table 9.1, the cost-benefit ratios for adult programming are generally one-fourth of that. Investing in juvenile programs is clearly more cost and crime beneficial than investing in adult programs.

The first column of table 9.1 shows the average effect size that Aos and colleagues report for each program. An *effect size* is a summary statistic measuring the degree to which research evidence indicates a program can affect crime: the larger the program's negative effect size, the larger its expected affect on crime outcomes. Aos explains that, technically speaking, the effect size statistic reported in table 9.1 is not quite the same as a percentage reduction in crime rates, but for many of the programs listed, it is close to that more intuitive measure. For example, an effect size of –.13 for in-prison vocational education is roughly equivalent to a 15 percent reduction in future crime rates for that group.

The second column shows Aos and colleagues' best estimate of what these programs typically cost per participant (in year 2000 dollars). The cost estimates are termed "net" estimates because some programs have an immediate displacement of other program costs. The next two columns show the estimated economic benefits of the program, that is, the benefits that a program is expected to produce in terms of future crime reduction less the costs of the program. The first column shows an estimate for "criminal justice only," which includes the taxpayer benefits. *Taxpayer benefits* are estimates of the operating and capital costs associated with reprocessing recidivists. The second column estimates the economic benefits for both the taxpayer and the crime victim. The final column is the benefit-to-cost ratio for the program: for the in-prison therapeutic drug treatment program, for example, the ratio is $1.91 in benefits per dollar of costs.

From table 9.1, we can see that all of these programs work to lower criminal recidivism rates. Generally speaking, however, the degree to which recidivism is reduced is not large—single digit, not double digit, percentage reductions in recidivism rates should be expected. Nonetheless, with treatment typically costing $1,000 to $3,000 per participant (sex-offender treatment was more expensive), the net economics of adult programs appear positive.

There is, therefore, ample scientific evidence to suggest that treatment programs—*if* well designed and implemented—can reduce both recidivism and costs. Effective programming appears to depend heavily on both the type of intervention and the principles that guide its implementation. The most effective programs generally match offenders' needs with program characteristics, ensure that program participation is timed rather close to an inmate's release, ensure that prison programming is followed up by community-based aftercare following release, and provide programming for a minimum of six months.

It is also important to understand: simply because there is no published scientific evidence that something works, one cannot say that "nothing works." The vast majority of correctional programs have *never* been evaluated—and many correctional evaluations are of such poor quality as to be meaningless. There is a need to implement programs that incorporate empirical evidence and to build in evaluation components to help us improve future programs. Texas is engaged in just such an effort.

The Texas Rehabilitation Tier Program In 2001, Texas implemented the Texas Rehabilitation Tier Program, which brings selected rehabilitation programs back into the prison setting. The Texas legislature was motivated by research evidence showing that certain programs worked (and others did not) and also by an interest in implementing ongoing program evaluations.

Participation in rehabilitation programs is now mandatory for Texas inmates. Each inmate is assessed at intake and then is given a need score and a timing score. The developers of the system say they considered giving a motivation score as well but were discouraged from doing so since the research literature suggests that some benefits accrue even to initially unmotivated inmates. Inmates with the highest demonstrated needs, one year to release, and the highest predicted recidivism rate are given priority for treatment and work program participation. Texas retains discretionary parole for most inmates, and participation in programs affects parole release decisions.

The Texas Department of Criminal Justice identified six programs as rehabilitation tier programs:

Table 9.1. What works in adult correctional treatment and at what cost?

Offender program type	Average size of crime reduction effect	Net cost of program per participant ($)	Net benefits per participant: Criminal justice costs only ($)	Net benefits per participant: Criminal justice + victim costs ($)	Benefits per dollar spent (using CJ + victim costs) ($)
Drug treatment (compared to no treatment)					
In-prison therapeutic community, no aftercare	–0.05	2,604	–899	2,365	1.91
In-prison therapeutic community with aftercare	–0.08	3,100	–243	5,230	2.69
In-prison nonresidential substance abuse treatment	–0.09	1,500	1,672	7,748	6.17
Drug courts	–0.08	2,562	–109	4,691	2.83
Case management substance abuse programs	–0.03	2,204	1,050	1,230	1.56
Sex offender treatment (compared to no treatment)					
Cognitive-behavioral	–0.11	6,246	–778	19,534	4.13

Intermediate sanctions (compared to regular programs)					
Intensive supervision (surveillance oriented)	–0.03	3,296	–2,250	–384	0.88
Intensive supervision (treatment orientated)	–0.10	3,811	–459	5,520	2.45
Other (compared to no treatment or other programs)					
Work release	–0.03	456	507	2,351	6.16
Job counseling & search for inmates leaving prisons	–0.04	772	625	3,300	5.28
In prison adult basic education	–0.11	1,972	1,852	9,176	5.65
In-prison vocational education	–0.13	1,960	2,835	12,017	7.13
Correctional industries	–0.08	1,800	1,147	9,413	6.23

Note: Aos et al. also report the standard error associated with each effect size. For all the programs in this table, the standard errors are relatively low (0.02–0.10). The larger the standard error, the less confidence that the average effect size is the true effect size.

Source: Aos et al. 2001.

- In-Prison Therapeutic Community, a 9–12-month in-prison intensive treatment program for substance-abusing offenders, which utilizes a therapeutic community approach. An offender's parole release is tied to completion of the in-prison phase of the program.
- Substance Abuse Felony Punishment, a 9–12-month intensive treatment program for substance-abusing offenders, which utilizes a therapeutic community approach.
- Prerelease Substance Abuse Program, a 4–6-month substance abuse treatment program using a modified therapeutic community approach.
- Prerelease Therapeutic Community, which offers substance abuse treatment, vocational, and educational programs coupled with a life-skills training program delivered in a modified therapeutic community.
- Sex Offender Treatment Program, a three-phase program involving counseling to overcome offense denial, accepting responsibility for behavior, and reintegration and relapse prevention.
- Faith-Based Prerelease Program, also known as the InnerChange Freedom Initiative, which uses biblical principals to assist offenders in making good moral decisions.

Importantly, each component of the Texas Rehabilitation Tier Program also includes a funded program evaluation. Preliminary evaluation data show that several of the programs are working while others are less successful. The evaluators, however, note that the programs are new and that more meaningful evaluation data will be forthcoming. See Eisenberg (1998, 2001) for complete descriptions of the program design, implementation, and evaluation plans.

Recommendation 3: Encourage Inmate Responsibility through Parallel-Universe Concepts

Rehabilitation programs are not enough. The reason is straightforward. Offenders who acquire literacy, employability, and sobriety skills may not understand *why* these skills are essential. As Dora Schriro, former director of the Missouri DOC, explains:

> In prison, officials decide when, where, and with whom prisoners will work, live, eat, and play. Such comprehensive control serves various management aims, but disserves the goal of preparing prisoners to live in the community, where they must

> be responsible for all decisions, however important or mundane, that affect their lives. The rules and regulations of corrections and its approach to work and civic involvement discourage critical thinking and personal responsibility. Even inmates who unfailingly follow prison officials' directives often encounter difficulty as ex-offenders. Many have been "colonized" and continue to heed others' directions, whether good or bad, after release. They have not internalized the values underlying civil, productive conduct. (Schriro 2000, p. 2)

Dr. Schriro developed an innovative strategy for the Missouri prison system and entitled it Parallel Universe. Her approach was premised on the notions that life inside prison should resemble life outside prison as much as possible and that top priority must be given to assisting inmates to acquire values, habits, and skills that will help them become productive, law-abiding citizens. Essentially, the parallel universe is a corrections-based reentry program. It has four components:

- Every offender is engaged during work and nonwork hours in productive activities that parallel those of free society. In work hours, offenders go to school and work and, as applicable, to treatment for sex offenses, mental health problems, and drug and alcohol dependencies. In nonwork hours, they participate in community service, reparative activities, and recreation.
- Every offender must adopt relapse prevention strategies and abstain from unauthorized activities, including drug and alcohol consumption and sexual misconduct.
- Most offenders can earn opportunities to make choices and are held accountable for them.
- Offenders are recognized for good conduct and can improve their status by obeying the rules and regulations.

Missouri citizens also adopted the Buns Out of Bed initiative in 1993, which requires all general population inmates to participate full time in school, work, or treatment. Work is mandatory, and prison employment encompasses a variety of full-time and part-time assignments that amount to a full day's work, five days a week.

As in most other prisons, work in Missouri often involves menial assignments. However, Missouri is different in that prisoners are interviewed for the jobs, and they retain their jobs by following directions and learning to accept criticism. As in the community, education increases earning potential: when offenders earn their GEDs, their pay increases. Similarly, the GED is now the prerequisite for enrolling in vocational education and for "premium pay" work.

Outside of prison, life consists of more than work. Thus, prisoner work and treatment programs are augmented in Missouri with activities that help inmates acquire other life skills and learn the underlying values. Community service, reparation, and recreation are used to this end.

The parallel-universe concept promotes responsibility in a number of ways. For example, the management of offenders' personal affairs has been revised to promote decision making. Offenders keep track of their account balances at the canteen. They learn to manage their time. They renew their prescriptions before their supplies of medication run out. Making such decisions and accepting the consequences for not making them are no longer the responsibility of prison authorities. Decisions about other routine activities, including doing laundry and cleaning cells, have also been made the prisoners' responsibility. Schriro writes, "When personal choice is eliminated, so is personal accountability because the system makes all decisions for prisoners" (p. 3).

Missouri says that implementing these parallel-universe concepts has served to reduce prisoner recidivism. The state reports that, between 1994 and 1999, the proportion of inmates returned to prison on new felony charges decreased from 33 percent to 20 percent, the sixth lowest recidivism rate in the nation. Missouri officials also note that the number of lawsuits brought by prisoners in 1999 was less than one-fourth what it was in 1994.

Recommendation 4: Prisoners Should Participate in Comprehensive Prerelease Planning

No one argues with the critical importance of prerelease programs to prisoner reintegration. In fact, one of the major recommendations made by the President's Commission on Law Enforcement and Administration of Justice in 1967 was that prisons offer a wide range of reentry programs, including prerelease instruction, work release, education release, and home furlough.

Prerelease programs proliferated in the 1970s, but at the end of 2002, just 12 percent of all state prisoners released participated in *any* type of prerelease program—and this figure had remained stable for a decade. Moreover, what goes on in the name of prerelease programs is widely regarded as too little, too late, often only 10–15 hours of classroom instruction, over a period of several weeks, devoted to discussing "life skills." Topics discussed usually include how to fill out a job application, how to ride a bus, how to apply for a driver's license, or the legal requirements of being on parole. The prisoner may also be given the names and addresses of local public or private agencies that can be contacted for assistance.

It is not that this information is useless, but rather that it alone fails to address the prisoner's reentry needs. Moreover, prerelease programming in most prisons is given very low priority in terms of resources and staffing. Volunteers with little correctional education experience usually teach prerelease classes. Even when the instructors are qualified, many say that there is no real curriculum to guide their activities. Prerelease program guidelines are vague, generalized, and overly simplistic. Lesson plans may simply list the topics to be covered (e.g., finding a job, reuniting with family). There is no professional agreement as to what *content* should be covered in these class sessions. Curriculum is therefore left to the discretion of the individual instructors, and they are seldom given guidance as to agreed-upon best practices, or proven programs. Actual content is thus home grown and its value dependent on the knowledge, energy, and insight of each individual instructor. Moreover, prerelease programs may be spread over several weeks, be concentrated in a single week, involve small-group discussions or large-class lectures, utilize solely outside speakers or be taught by a single instructor, and so on.

The haphazard nature of current prerelease programs in prisons means that few believe they are doing much good. Studies of the effectiveness of prerelease programs (conducted in the 1970s–1980s; none have been done more recently) found few positive results. In one systematic study, participants in a five-week prerelease program were tested on a number of items before and after instruction. Although 70 percent felt the course had been beneficial, the data showed little change in the respondents' behavior. The researchers concluded that because the program sought to meet the needs of inmates as a group rather than as individuals, it failed to meet any one inmate's particular needs (Frank 1973). Lack of data on effectiveness, prison crowding, and limited resources have forced prison administrators to reduce formal prerelease programs to the point where they seem to exist only on paper in most states.

The national attention being paid to prisoner reentry is causing some states to reexamine their reentry programs. Ohio, after examining its old reentry programs, abolished them due to a lack of evidence of their effectiveness. But the state immediately appointed a task force to examine what programs might work and is investing more heavily in job fairs and other methods to foster closer partnerships between community businesses and returning prisoners. Ohio officials also are working with community agencies to assure that inmates have the required identification, including a driver's license to secure government benefits and other needed services.

Some experts say that while prisoners certainly need help finding jobs and obtaining identification, those life-skills approaches alone are insufficient. As Ned Rollo, a national expert on reentry programs, told the author (February 2002): "No matter how well intentioned, these approaches do not take into account the unique factors of client receptivity and motivation, and do not address the holistic needs of the client."

Since 1979, Rollo and his company, OPEN, Inc., have been providing direct services to inmates about to be released. In 1988, they developed "99 Days & a Get Up," a self-help prerelease and postrelease educational program. The core of the program is the adoption of prosocial values and behavior. Rollo revised his specialized training program and is now delivering the program in selected prisons nationwide (Rollo 2002).

His inmate-based prerelease training program is designed to begin six months prior to the inmate's release, to take place in small-group settings of 12–15 inmates, and to require approximately 40 contact hours to complete. Students participate in 35–40 interactive exercises, and instructors use consistent lesson plans and videotapes to guide them. The materials are designed so that there is consistency and quality in the type of program delivered and the instructor teaching it. Because the materials cover both pre- and postrelease periods, students are encouraged to use the handbooks before and after release to work through problem solving.

Rollo's 99 Days program does not focus on providing life skills but rather on working with inmates to examine how they relate to the free world and the community at large, that is, their values and attitudes. The individual must be able to honestly address his value system and mindset and work to shift those values from an antisocial to a prosocial perspective. Rollo told the author, "It takes more than mere information about how to get a driver's license and fill out a job application to turn a defined criminal into a responsible human being who feels and acts in concert with the public will. The greatest challenge following release from prison is finding something worth living for!"

Rollo's program is timed to take place when the inmate may be most willing to hear this message. Rollo believes that prerelease programs that involve the offender in the few months immediately preceding his release date are fundamentally flawed. He believes that inmates are suffering psychological "gate pains" during this time period and are not open to absorbing new information, such as how to look for a job. This information should be given to them earlier if it is to be effectively learned. Life-skills information should be given in the 6–12-month time period prior to release, and more value-based information should be concentrated in the 3–6 months directly prior to release.

Ideally, Rollo believes the group would meet three times per week, two hours per session, for the three-month period immediately preceding prison release. During the last few sessions, family members could be brought into the sessions. Including the family in prerelease activities is seldom done and critically important. A study by the Vera Institute of Justice interviewed randomly selected inmates released from New York institutions in July 1999 (Nelson, Deess, and Allen 1999). The researchers found that the most important determinant of success was family and community support. Unfortunately, the Vera study showed that most inmates return to the community without many ties: 50 out of the 66 who were interviewed at release reentered the community alone, with no one to meet them as they exited prison or as they got off the bus in New York City.

Few would disagree with the desirability of providing prerelease programs for prisoners, and it will probably surprise some readers that just 12 percent of *all* state prisoners released at the end of 2002 received such assistance. Now that we have some credible reentry programs to test, implementing them should be given high priority.

Modify Decision-to-Release Policies

Recommendation 5: Reinstitute Risk-Based Discretionary Parole Release

We should reinstitute discretionary parole release in the 16 states that have abolished it. Eliminating discretionary release reduces the incentives for inmates to try to rehabilitate themselves while incarcerated. Some inmates may recognize the intrinsic value of improving themselves, but more inmates will participate if they believe it will reduce their prison stay. Research suggests that, regardless of a prisoner's initial motivation to participate in prison programs, positive benefits accrue. So what benefits are gained by reducing motivation and participation in prison programs? Eliminating discretionary release works against our attempts at rehabilitation.

Perhaps most important, eliminating discretionary release removes the ability of state officials to prevent the release of more violent and dangerous prisoners. A case in point is Richard Allen Davis, the parolee who murdered Polly Klaas. While in prison under indeterminate sentencing, Davis had been denied parole six times. But after California passed determinate sentencing and abolished discretionary parole, Davis had to be automatically released because he had already served the amount of prison time that the new law and its mandatory release provisions demanded. He walked out of prison a free man. Less than four months later, he kidnapped and brutally murdered Polly Klaas. Abolishing discretionary parole release undermines the system's ability to target dangerous offenders for lengthy incarceration.

No one would argue for a return to the unfettered discretion that parole boards exercised in the 1960s, which led to unwarranted disparities that often reflected the personal philosophies and prejudices of parole board members, rather than the risks posed by offenders. But we threw the baby out with the bathwater when we abolished indeterminate sentencing with discretionary parole release. Corrections officials sometimes feel it is impossible to elicit cooperation from offenders who know they will be released regardless of whether they comply with certain conditions (for example, participating in treatment). Prisoners may be less well prepared for reintegration under these circumstances. Even inmates themselves often say that determinate sentencing has resulted in more dangerous prisons, since fewer inmates are in programs, and idle hands indeed fill the devil's workshop.

As discussed previously, most (nearly 60 percent) U.S. inmates do not currently appear before a parole board to have their readiness for release considered, but instead are released automatically at the end of a set prison term. Abolishing parole was a politically expedient way to appease the public, which equated parole with letting inmates out early. As Brian Callery, former chair of the Massachusetts Parole Board wrote: "On the surface that sounds fine. 'Let's keep them behind bars' goes the refrain. But the losers are the communities that inherit these maximum-security ex-offenders who come out with no mandated obligations, no responsibilities, and no supervision. It is time to realize that higher parole numbers actually mean safer streets, not softer sentences" (Callery 2001).

Instituting a system of parole release guidelines, which should incorporate both risk of recidivism and offense severity, is now strongly recommended by corrections experts. Parole guidelines were quite popular in the 1970s and 1980s, and their use was shown to provide for a measure of equity (by reducing both sentencing and parole disparities), greater consistency and fairness, and more accountability. They have fallen into disuse in many states because the parole board has lost much of its discretion, and even when the board retains discretion, its decision making is constrained by politics, prison crowding, truth-in-sentencing, and mandatory sentencing rules. Moreover, older parole guideline systems have not been validated in many years, and there is often no computerized system to facilitate their use. As offenders' characteristics changed, prediction instruments worked less well. Many parole guideline systems have been abandoned or are now used as advisory only. Ironically, as our methods of recidivism prediction have improved, fewer parole boards retain the discretion to use this vital information in prison release decisions.

The Texas legislature mandated that the Texas Board of Pardons and Paroles revise its parole guidelines. A consultant undertook a comprehensive recidivism study and redesigned the state's parole guidelines. In September 2001, the Texas legislature adopted the new guidelines. The parole guidelines score inmates eligible for parole consideration on their risk factors and on their offense rankings. Risk factors include prior incarcerations, prison disciplinary conduct, and age at release. Offense severity rankings were determined by ratings given by the Texas parole board members to nearly 2,000 felony offenses in the Texas Penal Code.

The risk and severity factors are scored separately and then merged into a composite score ranging from 1 to 7, with 1 representing the highest risk and highest offense severity. Each composite score includes a "probable parole rate." For example, offenders in the highest risk and highest severity category are scored as 1, and the approval parole probability for this level is 0–5 percent. Offenders in the lowest risk and lowest severity category are scored as 7, with an approval probability of 76–100 percent. The higher an inmate's score, the better risk he is for successfully completing parole. This score is forwarded to the parole board members, along with the inmate's case file, to use in parole board deliberations. Use of the guidelines is discretionary, and board members retain the power to vote outside the guidelines when necessary.

Texas parole board members annually review more than 60,000 offenders for release. The hope is that, by using the guidelines, the board can readily identify cases by risk level and avoid releasing high-risk inmates too early or low-risk inmates too late, while spending more time evaluating the remaining cases where a decision is tougher to reach. It is also hoped that the use of the guidelines will reduce disparity in sentencing decisions and make parole decision-making criteria more explicit and predictable to the public, the legislature, and offenders.

At the core of the Texas parole guidelines and virtually all other parole release guideline systems is an empirical assessment of the inmates' risk of recidivism. Clearly, prison officials want to deny parole to those who have a high probability of recidivating and release those who represent little risk. Risk prediction has been a core interest of criminologists since the early 1930s, and although our methods have improved, it is still an imperfect science.

Research has shown that risk prediction instruments are improved if they consider both static factors and dynamic factors. Static risk factors include variables such as age, criminal history, and gender, variables that are unchangeable. Dynamic or changeable risk predictors reflect factors that can change over time (e.g., gang affiliation, rehabilitation program participation, prison disciplinary record, prison custody level). Using both static and dynamic factors increases the accuracy of recidivism predictions. A meta-analysis of 131 studies found that, in the area of predicting reoffending, dynamic predictors performed at least as well as static domains, but that combining these factors increased recidivism prediction accuracy appreciably (Gendreau, Little, and Goggin 1996).

It is important to note, however, that although these factors are be correlated with parole recidivism, the ability to predict recidivism is rather limited. Knowing all of this information and using it to predict who will recidivate and who will not results in accurate predictions only about 70 percent of the time. Factors in the environment (for example, family support and employment) predict recidivism as well or better than the factors present at sentencing (which are usually used in recidivism prediction studies). However, actuarial recidivism prediction instruments are more accurate in predicting recidivism than human judgments. Klein and Caggiano applied six well-known risk assessment instruments to parole outcome data from Texas, California, and Michigan. A variety of recidivism measures were used. The best overall predictive items were prior criminality, youth drug abuse, and poor employment history. They concluded, however, "When all the variables were used together they [the six models] did not predict more than 10 percent of the variance on any measure of recidivism" (Klein and Caggiano 1986).

Nonetheless, when trying to protect the public and deliver just and equitable punishment to offenders, parole guidelines are an important tool; they make the release decision transparent, fair, and grounded in assessments of risk and crime severity.

The question of who should make parole release decisions is also worth rethinking. The President's Crime Commission recommended in 1967 that parole board members not be politically appointed but rather be trained, full-time correctional professionals. The commisson noted that having politically appointed laypeople in these important positions "is incompatible with the development of the kind of expertise necessary to make a decision as complex and important as that made by a sentencing judge" (President's Commission on Law Enforcement and Administration of Justice 1967, p. 181). Yet, as of 2002, governors appoint all members of the parole board in all but three states (Michigan, Minnesota, and Ohio). In two-thirds of the states, there are no professional qualifications for parole board membership. While this may increase the public accountability of parole boards, it also makes them highly vulnerable to improper political pressure. Ohio is an example of an alternative approach. There, parole board members are appointed by the director of the state department of corrections, serve in civil service positions, and must have an extensive background in criminal justice.

Recommendation 6: Encourage Victims to Submit Statements Requesting Notification of Inmates' Release and Special Parole Conditions

Crime victims are the main source of information about crimes and criminals, and they must be made an integral part of the parole process. More than one-half of all crime known to the police comes from reports by victims, in contrast to the one-third reported by witnesses and a small proportion—mostly victimless crimes—that comes from police actions. We must figure out how to use their knowledge to assist in the reentry process—not only for public safety purposes but also to enhance offender rehabilitation.

Forty-six states now let victims comment on an offender's request for parole. Victims can ask the court to attach special conditions to parole orders for safety reasons, such as requiring the parolee to live a minimum distance from the victim's residence or to refrain from contact with the victim. In most states, victims can also comment on the offender's suitability for parole, and in many they can attend the proceedings. Unfortunately, while victims are authorized to participate in such proceedings, research shows that most do not.

Victim advocates say that many victims do not know how to provide input, find the process intimidating, or just do not realize that they have to *ask* to be notified. Greater victim involvement may result from requiring parole agencies to make a more sincere effort to locate victims. Many victims will have moved by the time their offenders are released from prison, and as a result, they may never be notified. Outside sources should be used to determine current victim contact information (e.g., postal service, drivers' license bureau, Social Security).

Different methods of delivering victim impact statements should also be available to victims (e.g., written, audio, video, electronic). States might follow Florida's lead, as it now offers an automated inmate information and notification service for victims. The Victim Information and Notification Everyday (VINE) service allows victims to call a toll-free number, 24 hours a day, to receive an inmate's current location and tentative release date. This information is also publicly available on the Internet. Victims can also register to receive automated notification (by email or telephone) when an inmate is released or transferred, escapes, dies, or is placed in a work release facility. The VINE system is anonymous and kept confidential per Florida laws. Importantly, Florida permits victims, or their representatives, to submit crime-related information or requests for special parole conditions (e.g., no-contact orders) directly to the parole board via the VINE system.

Change Parole Field Services

Every day, more than 1,600 inmates walk out of prison and return home. Most (but not all) will be given $25 to $200 at the gate and a bus ticket back to their home community. About 80 percent of all releasees will be required to report to local parole authorities and begin the process of postprison parole supervision (which can last from one year to the rest of their lives).

Most parolees will return to inner-city communities and will begin the arduous process of locating a job and a place to live. They may also be required to participate in counseling programs or to begin paying victim restitution. Parole officers in many states will not be sympathetic to their plight, as parole now focuses more on providing surveillance than on services. The community at large will not be welcoming, as the public is often quite fearful of persons returning from prison. Most parolees will fail.

High parolee recidivism has led some correctional leaders to call for a new model of parole field supervision. As Joe Lehman, commissioner of the Washington Department of Corrections, told the author: "We have a broken parole system. Part of the problem is that parole can't do it alone, and we have misled the public in thinking that we can—hence the frustration, and the cries to abolish parole. We don't need to abolish parole, but a new model is sorely needed."

Interviews conducted with U.S. parole administrators and supervisors reveal a consensus that parole needs to be reinvented (a term commonly used) and that the new parole model should commit to a community-centered approach to parole supervision and should utilize technological advances to monitor high-risk and sex offenders, deliver intensive treatment to substance abusers, and establish intermediate sanctions for parole violators.

Recommendation 7: Support Greater Monitoring of High-Risk, Violent Parolees

There can be no doubt that the public, aided by private industry, will continue to demand and receive an increase in the level of control over certain violent, predatory offenders living in the community. The most visible sign of this is the expanded registration of parolees, originally begun for sex offenders, but now significantly expanded in terms of types of crimes and public accessibility to the information. The other major indicator is the growing use of technology or, to borrow a phrase from Tony Fabelo, "technocorrections" to supervise offenders in the community (Fabelo 2000).

As the Cold War wound down, the defense industry, and the developing computer and electronics industries saw the community corrections clientele as a natural place to put its energies—a growing market. Electronic monitoring, voice verification systems, inexpensive on-site drug testing, breathalyzers through the phone—all allowed parole the option of becoming more surveillance oriented.

Since the mid-1980s, the electronic monitoring industry has continued to expand, and three states (Texas, Florida, New Jersey) now use global positioning satellites (GPS) to determine whether a parolee leaves his home or enters a restricted zone, such as an area around a school or the neighborhood of a former victim. GPS can also be used to enforce no-contact victim orders. New Jersey uses the system for monitoring high-risk juveniles who have been convicted mainly of violent offenses or sexual assault. These technologies may be helpful in identifying parolees who have committed new crimes or in making community members or victims feel more secure in their homes.

Texas uses a new database and computer system to identify and track parole violators. It is called the Fugitive Apprehension Program, or Fuginet, and 300 Texas agencies are using it. Prison officials input data into the computerized system when the inmate is released from prison. Information includes gang affiliations, tattoos or identifying marks, home address, vehicle identification, prior criminal record, and so forth. In addition, up to five photos of ex-inmates are included, as well as photos of their cars. Once the parolee is in the community, parole officers update the information daily with job and family addresses and other current living information. If the parolee absconds supervision, that is immediately entered into the computer, and the police are notified. Using a password, the police are then able to retrieve all identifying information, enabling them to locate the absconder. Dallas police are using Fuginet as an investigative tool as well, entering information about a crime and comparing it with the offender database.

Parole supervision and surveillance technology is here to stay, and like any technology it can be used for good or bad. It is simply a tool. It may well reduce the costs of supervising offenders in the community and minimize the risks they pose to society. At the same time, applying the technology in a haphazard manner to parolees who represent little public risk is both unethical and raises constitutional issues. Correctional technology is developing faster than the enactment of laws to manage its use. With so many U.S. citizens under correctional control, understanding how to best utilize this fast-growing technology for public safety, rather than unnecessary intrusion, is critically important.

Recommendation 8: Provide Treatment and Work Training to Motivated Parolees after Prison

The public seems to have focused its fear and punitiveness on violent and sexual offenders and is more willing to support treatment for nonviolent offenders, particularly substance abusers. This softening of public attitudes seems to have resulted from knowledge about the high costs of prisons, combined with emerging evidence that some treatment programs are effective for some offenders under certain established conditions.

New evidence from offenders themselves suggests that there are few programs to help even those offenders who have decided to stop committing crimes. Maruna notes that we need to focus on finding programs to help those offenders who have already decided to stop offending: "This is no small thing. If personal change is a long-term, cyclical process of trial and error, treatment intervention should probably focus less on changing committed offenders and more on providing support for those who make initial efforts to change" (Maruna 2001, p. 114). He quotes a drug addict in England, who says there were many programs available to him when he was addicted, but none when he decided to go straight.

One drug abuse program that has had noted success is San Diego's Parolee Partnership Program (PPP), which is part of California's statewide Preventing Paroling Failure Program. The San Diego program, begun in 1992, provides substance abuse treatment for parolees in San Diego County. A private vendor operates the program, using principles of client selection, managed care, case management, and case follow-up. The vendor subcontracts to provide outpatient, residential, and detoxification treatment services and facilities. Support services (for example, education and vocational training and transportation) are provided directly by the vendor or through referral to other community resource agencies. Typically, the time limit is 180 days of treatment. The participant is then assigned a "recovery advocate," who motivates the offender to continue in treatment for as long as necessary and keeps the parole agent aware of the parolee's progress. The program served about 700 offenders in fiscal year 1995–1996 at a total cost of about $1.5 million (about $2,100 per parolee).

An evaluation of the program showed that the PPP was successful with its target group (characterized as hard-to-treat offenders, who on average had used drugs for about 11 years). The percentage of parolees placed in the program who were returned to prison was nearly eight percentage points lower than the return rate for the statistically matched comparison group, and this difference was statistically significant. Los Angeles County operates a similarly successful program. The success of these programs motivated the California state legislature to increase funding for parole substance abuse programs.

Research has also consistently shown that if parolees can find decent jobs as soon as possible after release, they are less likely to return to crime and to prison. A recent employer survey also showed that employers are more receptive to the idea of hiring an ex-felon if a third-party intermediary—a counseling program or other service provider in their community—is available to mentor and to help avert any problems (Wirthlin Worldwide 2000). Several parole programs have been successful at securing employment for parolees. For a recent review, see Buck (2000).

The Texas RIO (Re-Integration of Offenders) Project, begun as a two-city pilot program in 1985, has become one of the nation's most ambitious government programs devoted to placing parolees in jobs (Finn 1998c). RIO has more than 100 staff members in 62 offices who provide job placement services to nearly 16,000 parolees each year in every county in Texas (or nearly half of all parolees released from Texas prisons each year). RIO claims to have placed 75 percent of more than 200,000 ex-offenders since 1985.

RIO represents a collaboration of two state agencies, the Texas Workforce Commission, where the program is housed, and the Texas Department of Criminal Justice, whose RIO-funded assessment specialists help inmates prepare for employment and whose parole officers refer released inmates to the program. As the reputation of the program has spread, the Texas Workforce Commission has developed a pool of more than 12,000 employers who have hired parolees referred by the RIO program.

A 1992 independent evaluation documented that 60 percent of the RIO participants found employment, compared with 36 percent of a matched group of non-RIO parolees. In addition, one year after release, RIO participants had worked at some time during three-month intervals more than had comparison group members. During the year after release, when most recidivism occurs, 48 percent of the RIO high-risk clients were rearrested compared with 57 percent of the non-RIO high-risk parolees; only 23 percent of the high-risk RIO participants returned to prison, compared with 38 percent of a comparable group of non-RIO parolees. In fiscal year 1997, approximately 77 percent of Texas's ex-offenders found employment; the Texas Workforce Commission predicted that 66 percent of those employed would not return to prison (Fulp 2001). The evaluation also concluded that the program continually saved the state money—more than $5 million in 1990 alone—by helping to reduce the number of parolees who otherwise would have been rearrested and sent back to prison. These positive findings encouraged the Texas legislature to increase RIO's annual budget to more than $3 million, and other states (for example, Georgia) have implemented aspects of the RIO model.

New York City's Center for Employment Opportunities (CEO) project is a transitional service for parolees, consisting mostly of day-labor work crews. Assignment to a work crew begins immediately after release from prison, and while it is designed to prepare inmates for placement in a permanent job, it also helps to provide structure, instill work habits, and earn daily income. Most participants are young offenders, released from prison boot-camp programs, and they are required to enroll as a condition of parole. From 1992 to 1996, CEO placed 70 percent of its program participants in jobs. Those who were not placed either did not show up for services or were terminated for not following work crew rules. The average wage for job placements in 1996 was almost 50 percent above the minimum wage, and two-thirds of the jobs offered benefits. Job retention in 1996 was 75 percent after one month, 60 percent after three months, and 38 percent after six months (Dion et al. 1999).

The Safer Foundation, headquartered in Chicago, is now the largest community-based provider of employment services for ex-offenders in the United States, with a professional staff of nearly 200 in six locations in two states. The foundation offers a wide range of services for parolees, including employment, education, and housing. A 1998 evaluation shows that Safer has helped more than 40,000 participants find jobs since 1972, and nearly two-thirds of those placed kept their jobs for 30 days or more of continuous employment (Finn 1998a). Since the summer of 1997, Safer reports finding jobs for more than 3,000 ex-offenders, 73 percent of whom retained their jobs after 30 days. Safer's Youth Empowerment Program, designed for juvenile probation and parole education, enjoys comparable success. Approximately 80 percent complete training (the vast majority are placed in jobs or vocational training), and participants are 53 percent less likely than nonparticipants to be convicted of a new crime in Illinois (Tonn 1999).

Another highly successful program for released prisoners is operated by Pioneer Human Services in Seattle, Washington, a private, nonprofit organization. Pioneer Human Services provides housing, jobs, and social support for released offenders, but it also operates sheltered workshops for the hard-to-place offender. It is different from other social service agencies in that its program is funded almost entirely by the profits from the various businesses it operates and not through grants. The organization places a priority on practical living skills and job training. Most of its clients are able to maintain employment either in the free market or for Pioneer Human Services, and the recidivism rate is less than 5 percent for its work-release participants (Turner and Petersilia 1996).

There are parole programs that are effective. One of the immediate challenges is to find the money to pay for them. Martin Horn, former secretary of the Pennsylvania Department of Corrections, suggests using offender "vouchers" to pay for parole programs. At the end of the prisoner's term, the offender would be provided with vouchers with which she could purchase certain types of services upon release (for example, drug and alcohol treatment, job placement, or family counseling). Horn suggests giving $2,000 in "service coupons" for each of the two years following prison release. Offenders then could purchase the services they feel they most need. Horn's cost-benefit analysis for this plan for the state of Pennsylvania shows that it could save the state about $50 million per year—dollars that he says then could be invested in prevention programs instead of prisons (Horn 2001).

Recommendation 9: Parole Offices Should Incorporate Neighborhood Parole Supervision

One of the critical lessons learned during the 1990s was that no one program (surveillance or rehabilitation alone) or any one agency—police without parole, parole without mental health, or any of these agencies outside the community—can reduce crime, or fear of crime, on its own. Crime and criminality are complex, multifaceted problems, and real long-term solutions must come from the community and be actively participated in by the community and those that surround the offender. This model of community engagement is the foundation of community policing, and its tenets are now spreading to parole.

This new parole model is being referred to as "neighborhood parole" (Smith and Dickey 1998) or "corrections of place" (Clear and Corbett 1999). Regardless of the name, the key components are the same: strengthening parole's linkages with law enforcement and the community; offering a full-service model of parole; and attempting to change the offenders' lives through personal, family, and neighborhood interventions. At their core, these models move away from managing parolees on conventional caseloads and toward a more activist supervision, where agents are a visible presence in the community. This means that they are easily accessible to community members, and they strive to develop relations with the citizens and parolees with whom they work. They are also inclined toward a brokerage or go-between model of procuring jobs, social support, and needed treatment.

The neighborhood parole model has been most well thought out in Wisconsin, where the Governor's Task Force on Sentencing and Corrections recommended the program. Program proponents realize that neighborhood-based parole will be more costly than traditional parole supervision, but they are hopeful that reduced recidivism and revocations to prison will offset program costs. In 2000, the Wisconsin legislature allocated $8 million to fund and evaluate the Dane and Racine counties' pilot Enhanced Supervision Projects. The results have not yet been published.

Recommendation 10: Establish and Test Reentry Courts and Community Partnerships

With so many offenders exiting prison and returning to the community each year, some equate prisoner reentry with an increased public safety risk. In response to these legitimate concerns, communities have developed a number of new initiatives, including reentry partnerships, police and corrections collaborations, and reentry courts. In each of these instances, the underlying motive is the same: to engage the broader community and the justice system in monitoring and assisting prisoner reintegration. It is hoped that by doing so, the resources, political support, and responsibility for parolees will be shared.

Reentry Partnerships The U.S. Department of Justice funded the Reentry Partnership Initiative (RPI) in 2001. The participating states are Vermont, Maryland, Washington, Nevada, Missouri, Florida, South Carolina, and Massachusetts. The DOJ also awarded a grant to

Faye Taxman and her colleagues at the University of Maryland to conduct an evaluation. Taxman recently summarized the purpose of the initiative:

> The underlying premise of the reentry partnerships is that each component of the criminal justice system—police, courts, institutional and community corrections—plays a role not only in immediate offender processing and control, but also in long-term offender change. A parallel premise is that criminal justice agencies cannot do this alone, and must engage family, community service providers, the faith community and other sources of formal and informal support in reintegrating offenders. . . . The challenge is twofold: 1) how do we prepare incarcerated and recently released inmates to be productive, contributing members of the community, and 2) how do we prepare communities to support, sustain, and when necessary sanction offenders returning under a wide range of release conditions. (Taxman et al. 2002b, p. 1)

Each RPI was encouraged to bring together law enforcement, courts, corrections, and local social service agencies around issues of prisoner reentry. The reason these RPIs represent such an important development is that they involve systemwide change—moving out from prisons into communities and, ultimately, neighborhoods.

Each RPI developed programs in three distinct but intertwined phases: institutional, structured reentry, and community reintegration. The conceptual model is depicted in figure 9.1, which was originally developed by Altschuler and Armstrong (1994) for providing intensive aftercare to high-risk juveniles returning from detention. Echoing the core principles of this aftercare model, Taxman and colleagues wrote that the best RPI sites attempt to implement programs that center around a system of overarching, integrated case management, where "the collective efforts of justice agencies, service providers, family, and other community supports are devoted to enhancing the offender's accountability and productivity in the community" (2002b. p. 17). This model represents an ideal. Whether such a model can be successfully implemented or affect offender recidivism is unknown.

A subtle, but critically important point, is represented in figure 9.1. The bottom box shows the gradual shift from formal social control to informal social control. Criminologists have discovered the importance of informal social controls, or "stakes-in-conformity," for

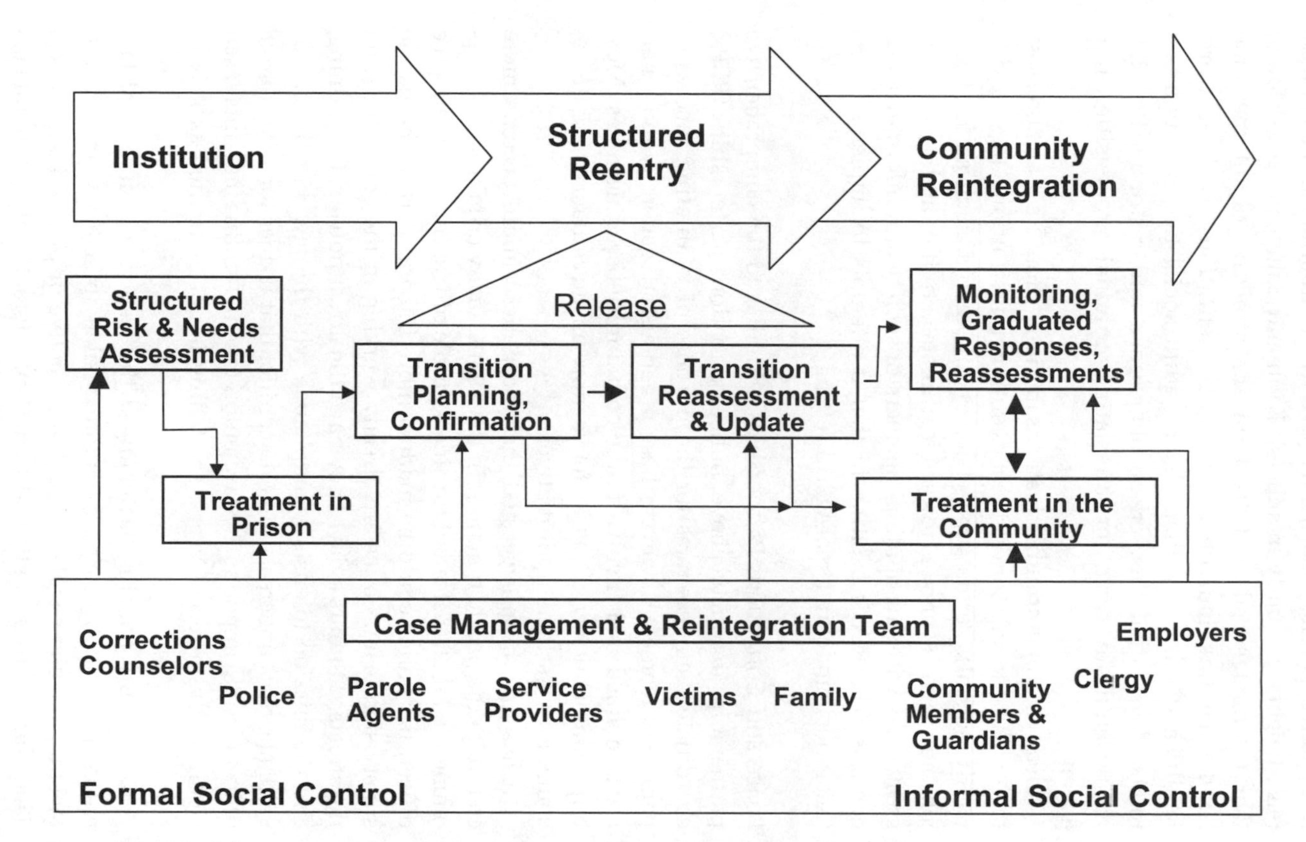

Figure 9.1. Model reentry partnership continuum. *Source*: Taxman et al. 2002b.

reducing recidivism. Ultimately, formal social control mechanisms (e.g., police, parole, judges) must give way to informal social controls (e.g., neighbors, family members). Laub and Sampson (2001) found that informal social controls form the structure of interpersonal bonds that link individuals to social institutions, such as work, family, and school. In their theory, adult social ties are important to the degree that they create obligations and restraints that impose significant costs for translating criminal propensities into action.

Ideally, formal criminal justice sanctions should act as "presses" to increase social bonds to conventional institutions (e.g., work, family, school). Parole supervision requirements, such as finding a job, may serve as presses toward legitimate activities and, ultimately, greater ties with law-abiding members of society and informal social controls. The RPI is exciting in that it attempts to implement this theoretical model in a real-world setting.

Police and Corrections Partnerships Similar to the comprehensive partnerships described above, police-corrections partnerships (PCPs) coordinate their resources for the purpose of facilitating successful parolee outcomes. However, these programs are generally more narrowly defined and involve fewer community-based agencies. Most important, however, the PCPs focus more on surveillance than do the community partnership initiatives.

It has long been suggested that the police should become more central to the parole function. In the 1980s, many criminologists recommended that, instead of turning a parole officer into a surveillance officer, the police could be made a more integral part of the parole supervision team. Police are already working in the community, on the streets, 24 hours a day. They have the arrest powers, the training, and the mission to ensure compliance with the law. For them, surveillance does not create the role conflict that it does for some parole officers. And, importantly, law enforcement funding has increased significantly in recent years, so staffing is not as limited as it is in parole.

Community policing has changed the response mentality of law enforcement. Police are now more visible in many communities, meeting neighbors and engaging in proactive or preventive policing. That change has also affected how they interact with parole officers and parolees. Advocates believe that police-corrections partnerships have the potential to reshape the way both policing and parole services are performed. For example, if PCPs are successful in preventing crimes, recidivism would decrease and the demand for incarceration would be lessened.

There are many variations of PCPs, but the ones focusing on parolees share similar goals and activities. California is typical in this regard. California's Police and Corrections Team (PACT) began in Oakland as a response to the large number of parolees at large (PALs). California has the highest parole absconding rate in the nation (20 percent), and law enforcement believed that much of the crime being committed could be attributed to PALs. Joining forces, law enforcement and the parole department began locating and returning PALs to custody.

Over time, the focal point of the PACT team in Oakland became "the Wednesday meeting," which is a two-hour orientation session that all parolees in Oakland must attend within one week of their release from prison. Some 50–75 parolees attend weekly. At the meeting, a range of service providers explains the support they offer, including drug and alcohol counseling, vocational training, anger management and domestic violence counseling, and more. The last speaker in the two-hour program is the PACT team police officer, who tells the attendees that they will be closely monitored and that parole violations will result in revocation. While all the programs presented were available prior to the PACT program, it was up to the individual parole agent to provide the information to the client and up to the client to contact the provider. Here, all parolees are exposed to the information, and they are able to make an initial contact with the provider ("one-stop shopping"). Parolee no-shows can expect home visits from their parole officers. They will be given one more chance to attend the PACT meeting, and if they fail, they may be returned to custody.

Little data exist to evaluate the impacts of PACT, although the Oakland PACT team boasts a 33 percent reduction in its PAL rate since the program began and a 16 percent reduction in crime. The California Department of Corrections is encouraged by the results, and the model has now been replicated at eight California sites.

Dale Parent of Abt Associates has reviewed police and corrections partnerships and notes that they sometimes raise critical questions. Most important, if a successful PCP emphasizes public protection by maximizing deterrence and incapacitation, the partnership might promote an atmosphere within the corrections agency that devalues treatment and causes limited programs to be scaled back even further

(Parent and Snyder 1999). This is the critical issue for parole agencies as PACT programs expand across the nation.

Reentry Courts Reentry courts are the third major program model being explored in the United States. Reentry courts are similar to drug courts, and both are judge centered. If one compares the three models discussed in this section, it could be said that the first (reentry partnerships) is parole agency centered, the second (police and corrections teams) is law enforcement centered, and the third (reentry courts) is judicially centered.

Reentry courts use judicial authority to apply graduated sanctions and positive reinforcement and to marshal community resources to support the prisoner's reintegration. Some believe the judge is in a unique position, given the prestige of the office, to confer public and official validation on the offender's reform efforts.

Reentry courts have an intuitive appeal for a number of reasons. The first is that they draw upon the popular drug court model that has proliferated in recent years. There are now more than 425 drug courts in the United States, and they are perceived to be hugely successful. The goal of reentry courts is similar to drug courts, in that both attempt to coordinate services and establish a seamless system of offender accountability and support. Drug courts usually operate prior to a prison sentence (e.g., as a diversion program), whereas reentry courts operate after prison.

Judges use a case management approach to track and supervise offenders upon release. In a sense, the judge becomes a reentry manager, as she identifies and coordinates local services that will help offenders reconnect with their families and community, including employment, counseling, education, health, mental health, and other essential services. Ideally, the judge who originally sentenced the prisoner would be the same judge who serves as his reentry manager.

Upon reentry, a "contract" is drawn up between the court and the offender. The contract lists the conditions the offender must follow, and the offender is required to appear in court every month to demonstrate how well the contract is working. These court appearances would not necessarily be long, but rather are designed to remind the offender of the conditions in the contract. Should the judge feel the offender needs more help, she can quickly mobilize the necessary resources. Should the offender fail to abide by the contract, the judge is also able to utilize a variety of intermediate sanctions to encourage compliance.

Model reentry and drug courts also involve the family and other members of the individual's support system, who are encouraged to attend the reentry court meetings. A community justice officer might also be involved. This individual would keep the court apprised of neighborhood developments involving the offender. At the end of the period of supervision, the judge would oversee a "graduation ceremony." These are actual ceremonies and are designed to celebrate the individual's successful reentry into the community. One could also imagine incorporating goal-oriented parole, where the length of time in the reentry court would be reduced as the offender met or exceeded court expectations.

Reentry courts and other problem-solving courts represent a promising development in offender reentry. Jeremy Travis has strongly endorsed this concept, writing:

> Let's imagine a world unconstrained by budgetary realities, legal conventions, or implementation considerations. If a new vision were written on a clean slate, the role of reentry management would best be assigned, in my view, to the sentencing judge, whose duties would be expanded to create a "reentry court." In this model, the judge would sentence the offender to X years, Y months of which will be served in the community under the judge's supervision. The judge would oversee the entire sentence to make sure the goals are achieved, including monitoring participation in prison prerelease programs. Many other criminal justice agencies—police, corrections, parole, probation, drug treatment, and others—would be part of the team committed to achieving these goals. If the offender follows the court contract, the judge has the power to accelerate the completion of the sentence, and return privileges that might have been lost (such as the right to hold certain kinds of jobs and your right to vote). (Travis 2000, p. 9)

Travis notes several benefits of reentry courts, saying they cut across organizational boundaries, making it more likely that offenders are held accountable and supported in their reentry attempts. Reentry courts can involve family members, friends, and others in the reentry plan. Most important, reentry courts explicitly give recognition to the fact that the offender will come back to live in the community.

The Department of Justice is now assisting reentry courts in Richard County, Ohio; El Pas County, Colorado; Des Moines, Waterloo, and Cedar Rapids, Iowa; New Castle and Sussex counties,

Delaware; and Louisville and Lexington, Kentucky. The programs all operate rather similarly (see http://www.ojp.usdoj.gov/reentry/communities.html) except for their target populations. One of the Iowa programs focuses on offenders with mental health disorders who have been dually diagnosed. Ohio's reentry court focuses on felony offenders and some offenders who are released early due to split sentencing provisions. Delaware's reentry court focuses on offenders who have served particularly long prison terms. The Kentucky programs provide an alternative to prison where nonviolent drug offenders serve a portion of their sentence in prison and then are released to an outpatient drug treatment program for one year. At present, reentry courts are largely experimental, and their results have not been studied.

Therapeutic Jurisprudence and Reintegration Ceremonies Reentry courts, along with drug courts, mental health courts, and domestic violence courts, are referred to as problem-solving courts and are part of a new movement to incorporate therapeutic jurisprudence in judicial proceedings. According to Wexler, one of the founders of the movement, *therapeutic jurisprudence* is the

> study of the role of the law as a therapeutic agent. It focuses on the law's impact on the psychological well-being or emotional life of persons affected by the law. Therapeutic jurisprudence is a perspective that regards the law as a social force that produces behavior and consequences. Sometimes these consequences fall within the realm of what we call therapeutic; other times anti-therapeutic consequences are produced. Therapeutic jurisprudence wants us to be aware of this and wants us to see whether the law can be applied in a more therapeutic way. (Wexler 2002, p. 1)

Therapeutic jurisprudence grew out of mental health law, particularly the concern over procedures pertaining to civil commitments, the insanity defense, and incompetency-to-stand-trial hearings. Observers looked at the way in which a system that is designed to help people recover or achieve mental health often causes just the opposite. Like it or not, the law and legal actors sometimes function as *anti*therapeutic agents. Therapeutic jurisprudence encourages people to think about how to lessen the negative impact of court involvement.

Wexler recently applied notions of therapeutic jurisprudence to prisoner reentry. He believes that the behavior of lawyers, judges, and other actors in the legal system can affect, both negatively and positively, how someone complies with parole conditions. He notes that judges should not simply monitor parole conditions but instead should interact with parolees in specific ways to foster prosocial activities, better problem-solving skills, and "identity reconstruction."

Current parole proceedings allow state officials to make decisions about offenders unilaterally and, as such, miss an opportunity to involve offenders in the process and to achieve some therapeutic value. The literature on the psychology of procedural justice demonstrates the psychological value of giving people the opportunity to participate in hearings they perceive to be fair. Studies in divorce and child custody hearings have shown that people who are given an opportunity to tell their part, and believe that what they said was taken seriously and respected by officials, are more likely to judge the proceedings fair and are more likely to accept and adhere to the final court disposition and conditions. Involving parolees more centrally in discussions of their parole requirements may well increase their adherence to them.

There is a long line of criminological research on desistance from crime. Laub and Sampson (2001) note that desistance is best seen as a long-term process and that changes are often due to variations in informal social control or social bonds, which in turn lead to cognitive or identity reconstruction. These informal social bonds are often triggered by salient life events, such as work, marriage, or the military. These triggering events, in turn, create new systems of social support and emotional attachment, as well as monitoring and control provided by new obligations and activities that are often repeated each day. Over time, offenders who are able to desist from crime go through "transformative action" and a "subjective reconstruction of the self," wherein they forge new commitments and find new direction and meaning in life.

Maruna describes this process as "rebiographing one's past." His findings, which are the central thesis of his book *Making Good: How Ex-Convicts Reform and Rebuild Their Lives* (2001), suggest that in order for chronic offenders to abstain from crime, they need to make sense of their past lives. Maruna interviewed a sample of active offenders (persisters) versus inactive offenders (desisters) in England. All of these men and women had extensive histories of property and drug crimes. Significantly, all of his participants also faced serious obstacles to success (e.g., economic deprivation, long criminal records, substance abuse). The differences between the two groups stemmed from the way they defined themselves within their similar social worlds. Persisters generally said they were sick of doing crime, sick of doing time, and tired of their general life situation. However, they also communicated a sense of doom and hopelessness that they tied to their lack of opportunities, poor education, drug habits, and poverty. Maruna says they repeatedly described their past through "condemnation scripts," which conveyed that they felt they had little choice but to continue in crime. Desisters, on the other hand, saw themselves in a much more positive light. Often their positive self-accounts bore little resemblance to the harsh realities of their past, but this process of "willful, cognitive distortion" helped desisters "make good." Maruna concludes that desisters employ "redemption scripts" to transform their deviant histories into the present good.

Glaser's classic 1969 study of parole in the 1960s also found these different personal perspectives critical to success, and he labeled them "differential anticipation" theories. Maruna notes that these differences in personal perspective are the basic mechanism by which the desisting self is created. It must begin by establishing the goodness of the narrator, who inevitably got involved with drugs and crime to overcome the burden of living a dismal existence. At some point, due to the help of some outside force, often someone who believed in them, they were able to turn their lives around.

Maruna found that establishing the *authenticity* of their reform, which can never be truly proven, is critical for desisters. Symbolic representations that validate the truthfulness of their change are necessary. Rituals or ceremonies are critical in this regard and should include people testifying on the desisting person's behalf. These rituals can involve respected community members, family members, and friends. Offenders sometimes interpret these judgments as being the judgment of all of society. Maruna says the courtroom provides an ideal backdrop for recasting judgment. Such redemption rituals, especially those certified by the state, can provide "a psychological turning point for ex-offenders, pulling ex-offenders more deeply into mainstream society" (2001, p. 163). Recall that desistance is best thought of as a maintenance process, and desisters—especially at the early stages of desistance—desperately need outside validation to convince *themselves* of their conversion.

Those who desist also show an overwhelming need to give back to society, therefore it follows that policies that encourage giving might affect an individual's transformation. Wexler notes, "Giving convicted offenders the option to volunteer at homeless shelters, build houses with Habitat for Humanity, or counsel juvenile offenders just might 'turn on' a few individuals to something besides criminal corruption" (Wexler 2001, p. 23). Of course, this is the core of restorative justice: helping the offender to embrace the community and vice versa.

Both Wexler and Maruna strongly endorse reentry courts. They believe they should be empowered not only to reimprison ex-felons but also to officially recognize their efforts toward reform. Through their actions, they can foster and help to sustain desistance.

Maruna notes that reformed offenders are constantly looking for reinforcement from others that they have changed. They use this information in their self-narratives to describe a change in their identities. Ex-offenders in his sample said, "I used to think of myself as being mostly like X, but *now* I think much more about myself as Y." Identity change is an essential part of personal reform.

Not surprisingly, Maruna found that "while the testimony of any convincing other will do, the best certification of reform involves a public or official endorsement from media outlets, community leaders, and members of the social control establishment" (p. 163). Maruna strongly suggests that reentry courts institute graduation ceremonies and other redemption rituals. These periodic public ceremonies are more than simply celebration; they actually reinforce and contribute to the offender's ability to rebiography his past. In a very real sense, the legal process *itself* becomes an integral part of the intervention.

Braithwaite, in his widely regarded book *Crime, Shame, and Reintegration*, also regards formal ceremonies as a means of allowing the offender to publicly adopt a repentant role. He writes, "Cultures which hold up models of adopting the repentant role will be cultures which succeed in shaming that is reintegrative" (Braithwaite 1989, p. 163). He notes that Americans are quick to label and "give free play to degradation ceremonies of both the formal and informal kind to certify deviance, while providing almost no place in the culture for ceremonies to decertify deviance." Yet, one of the most successful programs, Alcoholics Anonymous (AA), has shown that contrite and remorseful public expressions that amount to ceremonies to "decertify deviance" and signal an upward mobility and adherence to middle-class ideals, are critical to long-term success.

The research evidence also suggests that new transformative actions are not necessarily made consciously or deliberately but are often by default. Offenders do not have to make a conscious choice to change. Laub and Sampson write: "The men made a commitment to go straight without even realizing it. Before they knew it, they had invested so much in a marriage or a job that they did not want to risk losing their investment. Involvement in these institutions—work, marriage, the military—reorders inducements to crime, and over time, redirects long term commitments to conformity" (Laub and Sampson 2001, p. 51). Importantly, desistance is a process, not an event. The formation of social bonds and an investment in social relations spur changes in criminal offending, which is gradual and cumulative. When the incentives for crime-free behavior are there, coupled with a cognitive restructuring program that teaches the convict to understand the chain of events that often leads to criminality, recidivism is reduced.

Wexler and others believe that reentry courts can encourage desistance and cognitive restructuring as part of the legal process. For example, research shows that when people sign behavioral contracts, they are more likely to comply with medical advice than if they do not. Also, if they make a public commitment to comply to persons important to them, they are more likely to comply. Research also shows that if family members are informed of what patients are to do, those patients are more likely to comply. Wexler believes such principles can apply in a legal setting and, particularly, in a reentry court.

Drug courts already do this. Applause is common, and in some courts, even judicial hugs are common. Wexler writes that in one Chicago drug treatment program, upon successful completion of a drug court sentence, offenders invite their friends and family to a graduation ceremony in the courtroom. Some of the graduates make speeches, and all receive a diploma from the courts. In some courts, participants ask to have their arresting officer present at their graduation. Such a ceremony acknowledges the offenders' progress and, at the same time, may itself contribute to the maintenance of desisting behavior. The strong suggestion is that these rituals are themselves therapeutic and not merely ceremonial.

Of course, some offenders will fail to meet expectations during this period of managed reentry. Ideally, technical violations would not result in return to prison. Rather, as with drug courts, failure would result in graduated sanctions. But even if the offender commits a new crime and is returned to prison, Wexler notes that the reentry court judge can play a more positive role. If the judge takes the time to emphasize some real quality of the person, it may eventually constitute a meaningful component of the offender's self-identity. For example, even when imposing a severe sentence, a judge should not say, "You are a menace and a danger to society. Society should be protected from the likes of you." Rather, the judge might say:

> You and your friends were involved in a very serious crime, and I am going to impose a sentence that reflects just how serious. I want to add one thing, however. What I don't understand is why this happened. You are obviously very intelligent and were always a good student. Your former wife says that, until a few years ago, you were a very good, caring, and responsible father. Beneath all this, I see a good person who has gotten on the wrong path. I hope you will think about this and change that path. With your intelligence, personality, and talent, I think you can do this if you decide you really want to. (Wexler 2001, p. 21)

In this way, the judge is planting the seeds for an offender to rewrite the narrative of his life.

Maruna notes that both narrative development and desistance constitute ongoing processes. In rewriting the narratives of their lives, desisting offenders often look to instances in their pasts when their "real" selves showed and when respected members of conventional society recognized their talents and good qualities. Eventually, these are the building blocks of reform and desistance from crime.

Recommendation 11: Implement and Test Goal-Oriented Parole Terms

The parole board usually has the authority to determine, at discharge, the length of an offender's term of postrelease or parole supervision. While the period of parole supervision should be commensurate with the term of incarceration, it should also reflect the risks and needs of the individual. For example, short periods of parole should be assigned to low-risk inmates. Today, parolees are successfully discharged from parole if they adhere to their parole conditions (mostly, remain crime-free) for the length of that preassigned time period. They have virtually no opportunity to reduce the length of their parole term once it has been imposed.

The current system should be revised, as it misses a critical opportunity to reward inmates for participating in work and treatment programs while on parole. Parole terms should not solely depend on "sustaining no new arrests" but also upon completing prescribed prosocial activities. Offenders who complete activities (e.g., drug treatment) should be rewarded with a reduction in the length of the total time they are required to be on parole. Some refer to this notion as "goal parole."

Goal parole is basically an incentive system to encourage ex-inmates to earn their way off parole early. Generally speaking, parole terms are quite long in this country, usually two to five years. They are much longer in some states. For instance, Texas parole terms average 10–20 years, and can be much longer—even when there is no evidence of continued risk. As one Texas parolee told the author:

> It is now 2002. I have not committed a crime since 1987, and been totally without any incidents since 1991. I have a mortgage, have a B.S., M.A., and now am working towards my Ph.D. But I owe Texas parole monthly visits until 2017! Twenty-six years of supervision. I would submit that once I turn 57 and have not committed a crime in the last 25 years, those last years of supervision are a waste of their time. I know many guys who've been clean in excess of ten years and still have to report.

As we have seen, the risk of recidivism is highest in the first year after release. *Every* recidivism study has shown that offenders released from prison return to crime rather quickly, and if they remain arrest-free for a period of five years, they have a very low probability of rearrest after that time period. For example, Greenfeld (1985) reported on a 20-year follow-up and found that 30 percent of all those who recidivate (as measured by return to prison) do so within the first year, 60 percent within three years, 76 percent within five years, and 92 percent within ten years. Kitchener and colleagues (1977) found, using a 15-year follow-up period and the same recidivism measure, that 20 percent of those who return to prison do so within the first year, 72 percent of those who return to prison will do so within three years, 86 percent within five years, and fully 98 percent within ten years. Similar results were found for a group of young parolees tracked for six years following their release from prison. Even for this high-risk group, Beck and Shipley (1987) found that of all those who were reincarcerated within six years of parole, 62 percent were reincarcerated by the end of the second year. The rates of rearrest are even quicker, as return-to-prison recidivism measures require the significant time period necessary to process a new arrest or parole violation through the courts.

So, returns to crime happen rather quickly, if they are going to occur, and the length of parole terms should reflect that knowledge. We have shown that the stigma of being on parole is severe, limiting job opportunities and personal relationships and reinforcing the parolee's self-image as a convict. We should reduce the total length of time required on parole if the offender represents little risk of returning to crime. (On the other hand, life parole terms for predatory sex offenders may well be justified.) For example, terms of parole or postrelease supervision could range from two to six months for inmates incarcerated for 1–2.5 years; 6–12 months for inmates serving 2.5–5 years; and 12–24 months for inmates who serve more than five years. Such a proposal would take into account the seriousness of the original crime, shorten parole terms overall, and front-load scarce parole resources on those parolees who need more services and supervision. While such distinctions make logical sense, few states operate this way. Most states impose the same length of parole on the vast majority of inmates returning home.

Moreover, the initially assigned parole term should be modifiable and able to be reduced, dependent upon the completion of conditions rather than simply length of time assigned. Goal parole builds in an incentive system that encourages parolees to complete prosocial activities. It would also have the effect of redirecting parole officers to focus on positive actions and accomplishments of the parolee, in contrast to the prevalent surveillance-arrest system, which is based on enforcing compliance with conditions of parole.

The National Institute of Justice is considering a demonstration project of these ideas, and the model makes good sense. It shifts responsibility from the corrections system to the parolees by investing them with the power to affect the length of their parole terms. In goal parole, the parolee will be able to work toward early termination of parole by completing the goals established as part of his release. However, we cannot require that offenders complete more programs if programs are unavailable to them. Implementing goal parole requires a concomitant effort toward increasing program and work opportunities. Importantly, as offenders participate in work, community service, and treatment programs, connections with law-abiding citizens should increase, thereby increasing social capital and social networks, critical factors for both finding legitimate employment and fostering desistance.

Here is how goal parole might work. Let us assume that the term of parole supervision (stated at release) is a maximum of three years. At release, the inmate is told:

- Remain arrest-free for the first year, and we will subtract one month of your total parole supervision period for each arrest-free month you have in the second year. So, if you remain arrest-free for two years, we reduce your entire parole supervision period by 1 year. You have 2 years to be under supervision instead of 3.
- You can reduce that 2 years to 1.5 years, if you engage in community service.
- You can reduce that 2 years to 1 year if you participate in prosocial or self-improvement programs (drug, education) or remain fully employed.

The upshot is that a parolee who has been given three years' parole (the average in the United States) has an incentive. He can reduce that time period from three years to one by remaining arrest-free and successfully participating in work and treatment for the first year out.

The public has little to lose in this contract. Every inmate released does at least one year on parole. Recidivism studies consistently show that inmates who are going to return to crime do so very quickly. So, parolees who wish to remain criminally active are under parole supervision when they most need to be. If prisoners can remain arrest-free for the first year after release, they have very low probabilities of recidivism thereafter. Recidivism rates are even further reduced if a parolee participates in work, education, and substance abuse programs. So, the public safety risks of goal parole are rather minimal.

We have much to gain, however, from restructuring parole supervision so as to better motivate inmates to attend community work and treatment programs. Research shows that regardless of the initial motivation for enrolling in rehabilitation programs, particularly substance abuse programs, positive benefits accrue. A greater number of parolees might usefully participate in such programs if they were convinced that the duration of their parole might be appreciably reduced. Program participation not only addresses the individual's personal circumstances, but also should help the convict establish connections with law-abiding citizens, which, in turn, increase his or her social networks and legitimate opportunities. Over time, many will develop stakes in conformity and gradually reorient their assessment of the costs and benefits of crime.

Goal parole potentially represents a win-win for everyone. It saves money by not supervising those who have shown they can remain crime-free. The public assumes little risk since convicts who have remained arrest-free, are employed, and have abstained from illegal substances have very little risk of recidivism after the first year in any event. And, perhaps most important, we have empowered the offender to take control over his positive future, a factor ultimately related to long-term desistance.

Recommendation 12: Establish Procedures for Ex-Prisoners to Regain Full Citizenship

The United States allows a criminal record to scar one for life. This unforgiving attitude has been criticized by those who argue that the criminal law is largely flawed in one of its most basic aspects: it fails to provide an accessible or effective means of fully restoring the social status of reformed offenders. As Kai Erikson wrote about convicted offenders:

> He is ushered into the special position by a decisive and dramatic ceremony, yet is retired from it without hardly a word of public notice. As a result, the deviant often returns home with no proper license to resume a normal life in the community. From a ritual point of view, nothing has happened to cancel out the stigmas imposed upon him by earlier commitment ceremonies: the original verdict or diagnosis is still formally in effect. (Erikson 1962, p. 311)

The issue is of establishing some procedure by which some convicts can move beyond their criminal records is critically important. As noted in chapter 6, an increasing number of Americans now possesses a criminal record. At the end of 2002, an estimated 13 million persons (6.5 percent of all adults, and 11 percent of all adult males) had a felony conviction record. Finding out who has a criminal record is now instantaneous and widespread. Criminal records are increasingly transmitted to the general public via the Internet.

Criminal history records are notoriously incomplete and inaccurate, however. In many cases, arrests are not followed by dispositions, meaning that unfounded arrests are never "corrected." With a felony record, the chances of finding a job are significantly reduced;

government benefits and voting privileges are often denied; and the convict stigma affects many (if not most) other social interactions: buying a car or home, relationships with law-abiding citizens, involvement in church or community, and so on. From a public safety standpoint, these activities and relationships are exactly the factors that reduce long-term recidivism.

To be sure, there are valid reasons for wanting to know the criminal backgrounds of persons with whom we come in contact. Prior criminal record is one of the best predictors of future criminality, and by reducing felons' anonymity in the community, we are better able to protect ourselves against their crimes. There must be a better way simultaneously to protect the public from those criminals who wish to continue committing crimes, while not allowing those same procedures to impede ex-offenders who wish to go straight.

Procedures should be established that would allow *some* offenders to put their criminal offending entirely in the past and have the slate wiped clean. Nearly all other countries have recognized the value in doing this and have instituted laws to restore some convicts to full citizenship. Similar to sealing the criminal records for some juvenile offenders, a criminal record could also be sealed—if the crime were not particularly serious and a period of demonstrated rehabilitation had occurred. All European countries have such laws, and it is believed that they serve to increase offender employment and housing options (Metcalf, Anderson, and Rolfe 2001).

The United States has no such law. For all practical purposes, a convict is never given permission to legally move on from the past. As Maruna writes, "Without this right, ex-offenders will always be ex-offenders, hence outsiders, or the 'Other.' A correctional system that does not institutionalize such opportunities as redemption is at best an Orwellian euphemism for the reproduction of more of the same" (Maruna 2001, p. 165).

Pardons and Certificates of Rehabilitation The United States does have a system of pardons, which allows a government official to exempt a convicted offender from punishment or remove the civil disabilities associated with his conviction. Contemporary pardons are most frequently given to remedy a miscarriage of justice (e.g., a prisoner has been found to have been wrongfully convicted). In most states, pardons are given infrequently, only a handful each year. The mechanisms and conditions for obtaining a pardon vary greatly among the states, but in all cases are cumbersome and almost always apply only to first-time offenders with no prior criminal record. In New York, the only way one can receive a pardon is if evidence is provided that determines a person did not commit the offense for which she was convicted. California requires that pardons be reserved for persons who have been discharged from parole for at least 10 years and have not engaged in any further criminal activity during that time period. In 1999, federal and state authorities granted just 210 pardons to inmates in the United States. For all practical purposes, pardons are irrelevant for most inmates coming out of prison today.

The other method of restoring the rights of some offenders occurs with "certificates of good conduct" issued by a few parole boards. For example, the parole board in New York, at its discretion, may issue a Certificate of Good Conduct. By law, a prisoner is eligible for a Certificate of Good Conduct after a minimum period of time has elapsed from prison release. In the case of a felony conviction, the offender must wait a minimum of three years. This certificate restores the offender's right to vote and may remove other civil disabilities as well.

California awards Certificates of Rehabilitation, which are "court orders which declare that a person who has been convicted of a felony is rehabilitated" (Ca. PC 4852.01). Some specified sex and violent offenders are prohibited from obtaining such certificates. Persons eligible to apply for certificates of rehabilitation must demonstrate, in most cases, five to seven years of arrest-free living. The process is quite cumbersome, involving a petition, court hearing, submission of testimony and all formal records, and attorneys. Few parolees apply for such certificates, and in dozens of interviews the author conducted with parole agents and parolees, most were unfamiliar with these certificates.

England's Rehabilitation of Offenders Act England adopted the Rehabilitation of Offenders Act in 1974 to help ex-offenders live down their pasts. Where it applies, an offender will be "rehabilitated," and his convictions will be "spent." An ex-offender who becomes a "rehabilitated person" is treated for all purposes in law as "a person who has not committed or been charged with or prosecuted for or convicted of or sentenced for" the offense. This enables some criminal convictions to become spent, or ignored, after a period of time has elapsed from the date of conviction—if no felony convictions occur during this time period. If a new felony offense occurs, then neither conviction becomes spent until the rehabilitation periods for both offenses are over. Minor offenses (e.g., misdemeanors) do not affect the rehabilitation period running on the first offense. An individual's criminal history legally "expires" after a given number of years, and the act allows the offending to be put entirely in the past and the slate wiped clean. The act pertains to both juvenile and adult offenses, and the rehabilitation period is normally shorter for people aged 17 or under when convicted.

The rehabilitation period varies depending on the sentence imposed by the courts, not the type of offense (see table 9.2). Convictions receiving a prison sentence of 2.5 years or more can never become spent, and the rehabilitation period is determined from the date of original conviction.

After this rehabilitation time period, ex-offenders are not obliged to mention their criminal conviction when applying for most jobs. Even when asked directly, "Have you been convicted of a crime?" the law allows the ex-offender to say, "No." Even if they are asked less precisely if they have a "criminal record," they can answer "no" if they have no convictions or if they have been spent. Moreover, under the terms of the act, a spent conviction shall not be proper grounds for not employing—or for firing—someone.

England's act also affects civil proceedings (e.g., adoption, custody, marriage) and applications for insurance (e.g., automobile), public benefits, and housing. If any of these applications ask whether the applicant has any previous convictions, the answer can be "no" if the convictions are spent.

There are a number of jobs and professions that are exempt from the act, where employers can ask for disclosure of *all* convictions, spent and unspent. For example, all convictions must be forever revealed if the job involves supervising or training people under age 18 (e.g., teachers, social workers); providing social services to the elderly, disabled, or chronically sick; administering justice (e.g., police, probation officers).

England's act is actually more stringent than those of most other countries, where with the exception of Ireland (and Germany, for life sentences), *all* criminal offenses become spent after specified time periods. Some believe that England's act is too tough, and that the rehabilitation time period is too long, and that if it were shorter, more of the barriers would be removed earlier, and the person might have a better chance of making it. Others say that the act should not require the same time period for all people and that if someone com-

Table 9.2. England's Rehabilitation of Offenders Act (selected aspects)

	Required rehabilitation period	
Original sentence	People aged 17 or under when convicted	People aged 18 or over when convicted
Prison or youth sentences of 6 months to 2.5 years	5 years	10 years
Prison sentences of 6 months or less	3.5 years	7 years
Fines, probation, community service, drug treatment and testing	2.5 years	5 years

Source: Nacro 1998.

pletes a drug rehabilitation program, for example, he should be able to reduce his rehabilitation period. The Home Office in England is currently undertaking a review of the act.

The United States has no such system, despite the fact that we have the highest per capita rate of incarceration of any industrialized democracy. The United States incarcerates many drug and property offenders who would never be in prison in other countries—and, unlike other nations, we have no process of restoring the individual's rights. In terms of this issue, we have the worst of both worlds: higher rates of application of the criminal process combined with no way to move legally beyond its stigmatizing effects.

It is not just the practical implications that should cause concern. Shadd Maruna notes that wiping the slate clean or allowing a "legal rebiographing" is critical to offenders who have made the decision to desist from crime. He writes: "In this liberating model, an ex-offender is therefore legally enabled to rewrite his or her history to make it more in line with his or her present, reformed identity. After several years of good behavior, the State essentially says, 'You don't appear to be the sort of person who has a criminal record, therefore you needn't have one'" (Maruna 2001, p. 164).

Maruna says that without this rebiographing, ex-offenders will always be ex-offenders, hence outsiders and doomed to deviance. He also notes that we have recognized the importance of this in the juvenile justice system, where some juvenile records are destroyed or sealed upon transition to adulthood, and also in the law on bankruptcy, in which credit histories can be redeemed after a set number of years. But we have failed to enact policies for common criminals, and this selective application of the 'forgive and forget' doctrine can recreate the supposed dichotomy between Us and Them.

Whatever the specific time period or crime-related requirements, some means of allowing convicts to legally move forward and away from their criminal pasts is necessary if they are to truly become productive and free citizens.

TEN

Conclusions

When Punitive Policies Backfire

Having made this detailed analysis of parole and prisoner reentry in the United States, one must conclude that we could not have designed a more ineffective system had we set out to do so. For most offenders, corrections does not correct. Indeed, the conditions under which many inmates are handled are detrimental to successful reintegration, and many of the restrictions we place on returning prisoners prove deeply counterproductive. Clearly, we need policies that reflect the state's legitimate interests in public protection but do not at the same time, in and of themselves, diminish an individual's motivation and ability to change, which produces more crime in the long run.

The recommendations in chapter 9 will help, but they do not go far enough. They pertain to sentencing and corrections—the "back end" of the justice system. A major problem with the current system is that it fails to adequately distinguish between those who are truly dangerous and those who are not. Instead, we send far more persons to prison than need to be there for incapacitation or deterrent purposes. As a result, we end up spending a disproportionate share of our limited crime control resources on nonviolent (mostly drug) offenders, diverting resources away from violent, predatory criminals.

One of the most distinguishing characteristics of U.S. crime policy since the 1980s has been the gradual chipping away of individualized decision making and its replacement with one-size-fits-all laws and policies. We have increasingly limited discretion at every decision point in the justice system. Police now have mandated arrest policies for certain crimes; prosecutors are sometimes banned from plea bargaining; judges must impose mandatory sentences; and parole boards have abolished discretionary release in many states. Such policies may (or may not) have increased deterrence, but they certainly have sent prison populations soaring and decreased the ability of the justice system to tailor the punishment to the crime.

This is not to say that many of those imprisoned under such policies should not be there, nor that their imprisonment has not resulted in decreased crime. Nearly half (48 percent) of those now in state prisons have been convicted of a violent crime, and few would dispute the need to remove these offenders from society. But the proportion of offenders being sent to prison each year for violent crimes has actually fallen during the prison boom. In 1980, about half the people entering state prison were violent offenders; in 1996 only 26 percent of prison entrants were convicted of violent offenses. The growth in America's prison population has largely been the result of our sentencing many more convicted drug offenders to prison. In the past, less-serious offenders were granted probation or given short jail sentences. Drug offenders at the end of 2000 constituted 60 percent of the federal prison population and 23 percent of state prison populations (Government Accounting Office 2000). The nation now spends about $31 billion a year to house about 1.4 million prisoners.

Zimring and Hawkins (1999) present data showing that the crime crackdown since the late 1970s has most affected cases of marginal seriousness, rather than violent or career criminals. They found that violent offenders were not treated leniently by new policies, but rather already faced a high probability of a prison sentence, and therefore fewer of them had been spared by the previous regime and thus made available to be swept up by the crackdown. This was not the public's intent. The public most wanted to get tough with violent predators but ended up instead escalating imprisonment for marginal offenders. Zimring and Hawkins found that just 27 percent of the additional prison space added between 1980 and 1990 was for inmates who had been convicted of violent crimes.

The critical question is whether the massive increases in the imprisonment of mostly nonviolent and drug offenders has had any appreciable effect on crime in the community. The presumed relationship between stiffer sentences and lower crime is based on two distinct theories. Some argue that stiffer sentences alter a potential criminal's cost-benefit calculation, thus deterring crime. A second theory contends that, if offenders are put in prison, they are prevented, for the time of their incarceration, from committing further crimes in the community. This is referred to as the "incapacitation" benefits of imprisonment.

Certainly, there is some relationship between crime rates and the number of citizens locked up, but the relationship between crime and punishment is complex and will likely never be adequately resolved empirically. Part of the problem is that we do not know how criminals would have behaved in the *absence* of incarceration. We are also unable to simultaneously control for the many social, demographic, and economic factors—other than incarceration—that affect crime.

Discerning the relationship between imprisonment and crime has been the focus of much research, much of it poorly done. A methodologically sophisticated analysis by Spelman (2000) concluded that the prison buildup suppressed the yearly crime rate by 35 percent on average and that perhaps 25 percent of the crime drop was attributable to incarceration. This is not an inconsequential number, and we should acknowledge that an increase in the number of prisoners has contributed to the crime drop of the past few years. The more challenging issues are whether these crime-suppressing benefits are worth their social and financial costs and whether those benefits will continue as unprecedented numbers of prisoners return home.

Assessing the Unintended Consequences of Imprisonment

The costs of imprisonment are not primarily financial. In fact, the dollars associated with housing an inmate in prison are but a small part of the total price we pay for America's imprisonment policies. More significant, but often immeasurable, costs involve those relating to various interpersonal, family, economic, and political systems. It is possible that current laws and policies produce unintended consequences that, over time, contribute to higher rates of criminal violence and exacerbate the very problems they are designed to address.

Criminalization Effects of Prison

Criminologists have long suggested that prisons breed crime, act as schools for criminal learning, and produce a variety of criminogenic effects. People who serve time in prisons often return home with stronger ties to other criminals, greater criminal skills, and more antisocial attitudes. If these negative impacts of prison are real and significant, and ex-prisoners simply make up for lost time once released or escalate the seriousness and extent of their criminal involvement, then imprisonment may actually serve to increase overall levels of crime in the community.

Criminogenic effects, more broadly defined, also pertain to the stigma attached to ex-prisoners. It is possible that the offender did not change as a result of being in prison, but society's and the criminal justice system's *response* to him did. We have shown that employers are reluctant to hire ex-prisoners; landlords are hesitant to rent to them; and families and neighbors are reluctant to reconcile with them. The criminal justice system also treats ex-prisoners more harshly, increasing their probability of arrest and incarceration. If society's response makes it more difficult for the offender to resume (or establish) a noncriminal lifestyle, imprisonment may still be said to have produced criminogenic effects and increased crime in the community. In this case, the imprisonment effect is simply delayed rather than immediate.

We know these criminogenic effects are real and significant, but we seldom measure them. Petersilia, Turner and Peterson (1986) analyzed the impact of serving a prison term on future criminal behavior by studying a matched sample of California offenders, who were similar at the time of sentencing (in terms of type of crime, demographics, and criminal record) but were sentenced differently—one group to prison, one to probation. After tracking the matched groups for three years, the researchers found higher subsequent crime rates for offenders sentenced to prison. Drug offenders who had been imprisoned were 11 percent more likely than comparable probationers to have new criminal charges filed against them, violent offenders were 3 percent more likely, and property offenders were 17 percent more likely.

The higher recidivism of the imprisoned offenders can be interpreted in several ways. It may mean that, while the two groups were statistically matched, significant differences remained, and the imprisoned offenders had a greater preexisting propensity toward crime—a selection effect. Another explanation is that prison may have made offenders worse, that is, more likely to commit new crimes than they would have been without the prison experience. Given the research design, it is impossible to choose between the competing explanations. But common sense suggests that few are made better by the prison experience. If prison intensifies criminal activity, then using it to incapacitate less-serious felony offenders not only aggravates prison crowding but also increases the need for new prison space.

In medicine, the term *iatrogenic* is used to describe a situation where the treatment given by a physician exacerbates rather than helps the underlying illness. An example would be if a patient has surgery to remove his appendix, but during the operation is given AIDS-infected blood, and the patient contracts AIDS as a result. The patient leaves the surgery worse off and, if not treated for the new condition, also may pass on the infection to others. Medicine recognizes that interventions can produce both harm and benefits, and doctors therefore take the Hippocratic oath, which has as its guiding principle *primum non-nocere*, which means "first, do no harm."

In many ways, this medical analogy applies to current imprisonment policies. We are sending a great number of people to prison who would not have gone there historically. They come out worse than they would have been without the prison experience, and because few can ever get back on their feet, they pass along to others the criminal values, anger, and bitterness they developed from their imprisonment. Their imprisonment has produced a contagion effect. In a real sense, the criminal justice system has contributed to the very crime situation it seeks to address. As Abraham Lincoln once said, "The severest justice may not always be the best policy."

Ideally, we would like to send those to prison who are dangerous and have a high probability of continuing in crime if left in the community and not incarcerate those who are not dangerous and will likely be made worse from the experience—or, as is often said, we wish to imprison those "who are bad, not just those we are mad at." But today, most authorities, even some hard-line prison administrators, admit that a significant fraction of people being sent to prison today (possibly as many as a fifth to a quarter) should be diverted to specialized drug treatment programs or other well-structured alternatives to incarceration. As Frank Wood, former director of the Minnesota Department of Corrections, put it: "We have continued on a spiral of incarcerating people in this country who simply do not need to be in prison. It has forced us to spend time and resources trying to figure out how to manage large numbers of people rather than improving what we do with those that need to be or should be in prison" (cited in Riveland 1999, p. 180).

If these criminogenic or contagion effects of prisons are significant, and there is reason to expect that they are, then the revolving door of justice—with more than a half million people going to prison and being released each year—has the cumulative effect of creating more and more ex-prisoners, who have a harder and harder time of ever leading law-abiding lives. Todd Clear writes that, instead of preventing future crime, current imprisonment policies may well contain the "seeds of increases in crime" for generations to come (Clear 1996).

Collateral Damage of the War on Drugs

Drug offenders are a critical group for this discussion. The 300,000 prisoners in federal and state prisons on drug charges represent an annual operating cost of about $6 billion. Importantly, studies show that the nation gets relatively little crime reduction or incapacitation benefits from imprisoning low-level drug offenders. Although studies have shown that most criminal behavior is not organized, in the usual sense of the term, some crime, for example, car theft, fencing stolen property, and distributing illegal drugs, does appear organized as a business, where individuals fill necessary roles (Boyum and Kleiman 2002). As Blumstein notes, removing one drug dealer simply opens up an opportunity for another to enter from the queue of replacement dealers who are ready to join the industry. Since the demand for drugs does not cease with the removal of a runner or even a dealer from the drug trade, when one criminal is removed from the business, another just moves up to take over this vacant role (Blumstein 1993b). Massive drug arrests in effect create new "job openings" for drug dealers. If replacement is 100 percent, then incapacitation is not effective at all for reducing drug dealing.

In fact, over time, this practice of recruiting and replacement actually has the net effect of creating *more* drug dealers. It is possible that a young person who might otherwise have remained at the margin of crime is now recruited and initiated into the drug trade. Since we now sentence a greater number of those convicted of drug crimes to prison (rather than probation), we are creating an increasingly larger pool of mostly young minority males who carry the ex-prisoner label and its associated lifelong stigma.

Goffman (1963) describes *stigma* as an attribute that is deeply discrediting. People who are labeled "ex-prisoner" are discredited, marginalized, and, as shown in chapter 6, excluded from a variety of housing and employment opportunities. Such marginalization also has the long-term effect of weakening ties to law-abiding citizens and strengthening connections to the criminal world more generally. As Harvard economist Richard Freeman (1996) put it, "Incarceration fixes the stamp of a criminal career."

Thus, the war on drugs may well have had the unintended side effect of increasing, not decreasing, drug dealing, although some crime categories produce more significant incapacitation benefits. For example, research has shown that harsher sentencing of rapists, robbers, and burglars may be correlated with lower reported rates of those crimes (Drew 1990; Blumstein et al. 1986).

Low-level drug offenders represent a unique group whose imprisonment does not have much crime-reduction benefit, while the criminogenic costs of imprisoning them are particularly high. Most drug offenders are young minority males, and the social and psychological impacts of prison are long lasting.

Winick (1998) also suggests that officially labeling a person "criminal" may actually become a self-fulfilling prophecy, reinforce a person's antisocial behavior, and undermine the potential of any treatments he is offered. The labeling process itself may function to provide these individuals with an excuse for giving in to their criminal urges. As a result, it may be more difficult for offenders to exercise the self-control that society would like to encourage (Winick 1998).

Self-attribution and self-efficacy studies consistently show that people reframe their world experiences, expectations, and explanations for their behavior based on their self-concept, which is derived from labels others place on them. Winick suggests that the criminal label predictably diminishes the offender's potential to change and increases social and occupational ostracism when the individual is released to the community, thereby preventing successful reintegration.

Intergenerational Impacts of Imprisonment on Families and Children

It is commonly assumed that removing a criminally active parent improves the environment of the remaining family members, and for some that is certainly the case. But the incarceration of a parent is nearly always traumatizing for the child, and most children experience a sense of parental rejection, disrupted and multiple living arrangements, financial hardship, and decreased quality of care. Ultimately, children of incarcerated parents are at risk for many behaviors, including poor school performance, substance abuse, delinquency, and incarceration. But since we have no experimental studies examining the impact of parents' incarceration on their children, we are unable to establish a clear link between parental incarceration and adolescent antisocial behavior because these children often have many other risk factors for delinquency.

So, it is not entirely clear how many children are in a worse, as opposed to better, position when their parent is incarcerated, and how the positive benefits of removing a criminally active parent from a child's life weigh against the negative lifestyle changes caused by that parent's imprisonment. But, it is plausible that the massive removal of parents from their children's lives has had the counterintuitive effect of increasing the risk of delinquency among those children. This is particularly true if the parent were not so steeped in crime as to be unable to provide any nurturing.

Here again, our broad-brushed crime policies do a disservice to the complexity of the problem. True, there are parents who, by their very presence, contribute to the delinquency of their children, and removing these parents may decrease their offspring's future criminality. But by the same token, there are parents who, despite their involvement in crime, continue to provide positive parenting. Their removal from the home—and their return to the community as an ex-prisoner—will mean they are often unable to qualify for welfare, food stamps, or affordable housing. Many become homeless and live in poverty, factors ultimately increasing their children's prospects for crime.

It is sometimes hard to imagine that a criminally active parent can simultaneously provide decent parenting, but research shows that this is the case. Smith and Clear (1995) found evidence of substantial positive parenting prior to incarceration for a sample of male jail inmates. These inmates had provided significant financial support and also spent quality time with their children. After the father's imprisonment, families often had to move into cramped quarters and new school districts, new men were introduced into the family unit to replace the inmate, and there was less time for maternal parenting due to her taking secondary employment to make up for the inmate's lost income.

Several studies suggest that the adverse consequences of parental incarceration are more severe when the mother instead of the father is imprisoned. When fathers are incarcerated, mothers usually continue to serve as the primary caregivers for their children. When mothers are incarcerated, children are often relocated to another home (usually with grandparents or other relatives, not their father). In these cases, the loss of a mother not only results in emotional turmoil for the child but disrupted living arrangements and other life aspects. None of these changes causes delinquency per se, but each is associated with earlier and more active delinquent careers.

Reducing the Power of Prisons to Deter

Deterrence is one of the major goals of criminal sentencing. In theory, deterrence inhibits criminal behavior by evoking fear of punishment. Prisons are thought to produce a pain and stigma that are particularly severe, and the assumption is that people act in ways to avoid being sent to them. But Todd Clear notes that there are two ways people form impressions of a social experience such as prison: personal experience and secondhand knowledge. If the nature of these two sources were to change, perhaps the images and, consequently, their impacts, would also change (Clear 1996).

Clear suggests that as more people acquire a grounded knowledge of prison life, the power of prisons to deter crime through fear of the unknown is diminished. When imprisonment becomes common, those who directly experience it or who watch others experiencing it see that it is "survivable." He writes, "They all come to know men who go to prison and eventually come out and begin their lives again. They know and can repeat the stories of prison technique—what they do in prison in order to survive the experience. Instead of a dark fear of prison, they have a grounded image of what day-to-day life there entails. They have an expectation of survival" (Clear 1996, p. 12).

Clear cites Finckenauer's well-known evaluation of Rahway prison's Scared Straight Program as evidence of his thesis. Finckenauer (1982) found that juveniles exposed to the harsh, accusatory taunting by the lifers actually had *more* delinquency than a comparison group not exposed to the program. This was exactly the opposite of the program's intent. The theory behind the program was that first-time juvenile offenders would be so frightened by the lifers' tales that they would be "scared straight," frightened into obedience with the law in order to avoid the horrifying prison experience.

Clear believes that one explanation for the negative program results is that youths exposed to the program now had images of survival to replace preexisting images of doom. He writes:

> The youth now had a grounded experience of prison at its most brutal, and of tough men not only surviving the experience but also thriving within it. Finally, that the youth themselves survived their prison experience diminished the mystery of prison life. Fear of prison (especially from the middle class who have not experienced it) may be a real deterrent only when it is an unacquainted fear. (Clear 1996, p. 10)

Today, a far larger number of people have real life knowledge of the prison experience, which not only reduces the fear of physical deprivation but also lessens prison's stigmatizing capacity. Unfortunately, far from stigmatizing, imprisonment may actually confer status in some neighborhoods. Skolnick (1990) interviewed imprisoned gang members in California and reported that imprisonment confers a certain elevated "home boy" status, especially for gang members for whom prison and prison gangs can become an alternative site of loyalty. According to California corrections officials, inmates frequently steal state-issued prison clothing for the same reason: wearing it when they return to the community lets everyone know that they have "done hard time."

Claude Brown, who went back to the Harlem streets of his youth 30 years later, observed: "Reformatory and prison bits are still an accepted, often anticipated and virtually inevitable phase of the growing up process for young black men in this country. They have no fear of jail; most of their friends are there" (Brown 1984). Christianson (1998, p. 304) cites a reporter who was present in the South side of Chicago on the day that a young black man got out of jail after a long stay. He observed how a group of neighborhood adolescents, including the inmate's little brother, surrounded him on the stoop of his mother's porch "as if he were a rap star passing out concert tickets."

Imprisonment should not be part of a normal experience of growing up in America. It should be feared, dreaded, and have enough sting to deter. After all, depriving citizens of their freedom should have some utilitarian function. As Gibbs (1975) noted: "No legal action can deter if it is not perceived as punitive by those who are subject to it, and whether or not sanctions deter depends in part on the extent to which they are perceived as severe."

Increasing the Selectivity of Prison Sentencing

Just as it is important to get those *out* of prison who should not be there, it is equally important to keep those *in* prison who represent high risks. Reducing prison populations overall by 15–25 percent would allow us to reallocate corrections dollars so that we can focus on truly violent, predatory offenders. Such offenders should serve their full sentence, and while they are in prison, they should work and participate in education and treatment programs. When released, they should be transitioned to the community through halfway houses and work release centers, given intensive services, and be kept under surveillance. Ideally, their services would be coordinated through a reentry court.

The one-size-fits-all characteristics of current mandatory sentencing schemes mean that the system is simultaneously too lenient and too harsh. On the one hand, prisons are full of low-level, nonviolent, first-time drug offenders who historically would have gotten probation. On the other hand, we have violent offenders who often serve less time than warranted because the corrections system has neither the resources nor the staff to incarcerate these persons for their full term, treat them while in prison, or monitor them sufficiently at release.

Those who say that *most* prisoners are nonserious, nonviolent "lightweights" and should be released are just as wrong as those who say that all prisoners are vicious predators. There are significant numbers of prisoners in each of those categories, and recognizing that—and finely tailoring sentencing and corrections programs to those subpopulations—is critical to effective sentencing and reentry policy. Importantly, this more honest message is also more likely to garner public and political support.

Ultimately, we have to make finer distinctions between nonviolent and violent crime and design policies that securely imprison the violent offenders while using less costly, nonprison sanctions for nonviolent property and drug offenders. For drug offenders, we need to invest in proven rehabilitation programs. For property offenders, we know that literacy and job training can reduce their return to crime. We know that there are programs that reduce relapse and recidivism, but we refuse to invest in them. We continue to squander scarce prison resources on many offenders who represent low risks, and by doing so, we are not able to fund the community-based treatment that might have helped these offenders in the first place.

The Public's Changing Attitudes about Prisons, Drugs, and Treatment

Criminologists have long decried the nation's reliance on imprisonment, arguing forcefully that imprisonment should be used sparingly and that policymakers should create more viable alternatives to incarceration. For the most part, these experts have gone unheard. State legislatures and the U.S. Congress have continued to pass mandatory, tough-on-crime laws in the belief that such laws express the public's will. What will make the current calls for a more balanced and rational crime policy heard?

There is emerging evidence that public opinion, and that of a few political elites, is undergoing a significant transformation and that the power of the punitive response is beginning to mellow. Public opinion polls show that, although a third of the public still support tough-on-crime measures, two-thirds of the public now believe serious changes are warranted. Most of the public's desired changes are along the lines recommended above and incorporate greater individualization and flexibility. A 2002 public opinion poll conducted by Hart Research Associates concluded: "Support for long prison sentences as the primary tool in the fight against crime is waning, as most people reject a purely punitive approach to criminal justice. Instead, the public now endorses a balanced, multifaceted solution that focuses on prevention and rehabilitation in concert with other remedies" (Hart Research Associates 2002).

The Hart poll also asked opinions about what to do with people after they break the law. Nearly two-thirds of all Americans agree that the best way to reduce crime is to rehabilitate prisoners by requiring education and job training while in prison. Just one in three (28 percent) believe that keeping criminals off the street through long prison sentences would be the more effective alternative. Importantly, such progressive solutions received equally strong support across racial, education, and income groups. And the 23 percent of Americans who report that they or a close family member have been the victim of a violent crime endorse rehabilitation even *more* strongly than the general public, by a decisive 73 percent to 21 percent margin.

Perhaps the most surprising finding is the degree to which the public has now turned against previously popular mandatory sentences, such as three-strikes provisions. Fifty-six percent of adults now favor the elimination of three-strikes policies and other mandatory sentencing laws and instead favor letting judges choose the appropriate sentences. Significantly, majorities of all races and of all political party affiliations now favor eliminating three-strikes and mandatory sentencing for drug violations (Hart Research Associates 2002).

Other public opinion polls have revealed a similar pattern. The Public Agenda Foundation completed a series of focus groups in

2002 on prisoner reentry, and their results are similar (Immerwahr and Johnson 2002). They found that the public emphasizes "jobs, jobs, and more jobs," for reintegrating ex-prisoners. There was a strong belief in diversion for first-time offenders. As one focus group participant put it: "Everybody deserves a second chance . . . but not more."

The Public Agenda survey also revealed that Americans are frustrated with a prison system that releases inmates with few of the skills they need to survive. While the survey revealed the public had not yet identified "prisoner reentry" as a salient public issue, they identified with the problem. As one focus group participant in Philadelphia put it:

> You just sort of hold them in limbo for five, ten, fifteen years, and then put them right back where they started . . . the same environment, the same low employment or distressed neighborhood. I think there should be more of a balance in recognizing that there is the punishment, but at some point we have to live next door to these folks again, and they have to be reintegrated. We need to be prepared for that or we're going to continue to perpetuate a population that goes in and out of prisons. If we are willing to pay for that and be the victims of their crimes, fine, but otherwise, we need to come up with a better idea. (Immerwahr and Johnson 2002)

The voters now see the lock 'em up strategy as having failed in critical respects, and the collapse of faith in the war on drugs contributes to this perception. Three-quarters (76 percent) of those surveyed favor a proposal requiring supervised mandatory drug treatment and community service rather than prison time for people convicted of drug possession (Hart Research Associates 2002).

Americans are also frustrated with our nation's punitive approach to two other types of offenders: youth and the mentally ill. Fully 85 percent of Americans support placement of youthful offenders in community prevention programs, which teach job skills, moral values, and self-esteem, rather than prison. (However, there is also support for holding violent youth *more* accountable for their crimes.) Eight in ten Americans (82 percent) also believe that offenders with mental illnesses should receive treatment in mental health facilities instead of being sent to prison (Hart Research Associates 2002).

The public's message is clear: we want nonviolent and low-level drug offenders handled in tough community-based programs, where they will be held accountable and given access to education and job programs. We want violent offenders to go to prison, but do not want them sitting idle. And we want the prison system to not simply show inmates the door when their time is up, but provide them with resources to succeed—and surveillance to quickly identify the failures. The public wants a rational system of calibrated sentencing, where the risks and needs of the offender are matched with the costs and severity of the sanction. In short, the public wants a credible system of intermediate sanctions. *Intermediate sanctions* are punishment options that, on a continuum, fall between traditional probation supervision and incarceration.

The call for intermediate sanctions is not new. In 1990, Morris and Tonry argued in favor of a sentencing system where community-based and incarceration sentences could be regarded as interchangeable and used in combination. They noted that judges often had no choice but routine probation, which was perceived as too lenient, or full-fledged prison—there were few midrange punishment options.

Beginning in the 1980s, a coalition emerged among academics and corrections officials, which argued that intermediate sanctions better served victims and the justice system than did indiscriminate imprisonment. Over the next decade, many jurisdictions developed intermediate sanctions (for example, house arrest, electronic monitoring, community service, intensive supervision). These programs were designed to be community-based sanctions that were tougher than regular probation, but less stringent and expensive than prison (for a complete review, see Petersilia 1999a).

The hope was that prison commitments would decline as intermediate sanction programs (ISPs) spread. Offenders would be sentenced to these programs, and theoretically they would be given services that would reduce recidivism and subsequent commitments to prison. But that hope was not realized. The results showed that most ISPs did *not* reduce offender recidivism, and persons sent to ISPs had *higher* return-to-prison rates than comparison groups sent to routine probation.

The stringent conditions and strict enforcement associated with most ISP programs meant they turned up technical violators, who, in turn, were subject to revocation and reincarceration. As a result, most ISPs did not save money, and many were disbanded. Most regard the U.S. intermediate sanctions experiment as ineffective, and Reitz concluded: "No U.S. jurisdiction has succeeded in materially altering its sentencing patterns through the use of alternative punishments" (Reitz 1996, p. 159).

Could intermediate sanctions work now? The popular perception is that past intermediate sanctions programs did not work. That is not entirely true. The most important finding from the intermediate sanctions literature is that programs must deliver high "doses" of both treatment and surveillance to assure public safety and reduce recidivism. Treatment alone is not enough, nor is surveillance by itself adequate. Programs that increase offender-to-officer contacts *and* provide treatment can reduce recidivism. Petersilia and Turner (1993), the evaluators of the national ISP demonstration project, found that offenders who received drug counseling, held jobs, paid restitution, and did community service were arrested 10–20 percent less frequently than others.

Researchers and others urged a "second generation" of ISPs, incorporating the findings from the demonstration project. But by that time, the media and politicians were touting tough-on-crime measures, and there was little public or financial support for ISPs. The public has a hard time spending more than $2,000 a year for criminals sentenced to community-based programs, despite being willing to spend $23,000 per year to house them in prison.

ISP programs, if implemented now, could take advantage of the accumulated knowledge about what works in correctional programming, for which there is now a substantial body of literature. This information was reviewed in chapter 9. There are specific programs that are known to work and what both Cullen and Gendreau call "principles of effective intervention," which typically underlie effective programs. These general characteristics include providing programming for at least several months; matching offenders' needs with program offerings; focusing on skills applicable to the job market; and targeting the offenders' needs that are changeable and may contribute to crime, such as attitudes and prosocial activities. ISPs would likely be more successful if they incorporated recent knowledge about effective programming.

There is public support for revisiting intermediate sanctions programs and an accompanying body of research that would likely make the newer programs better. So, what is to stop us from charting a new, less prison-reliant course?

Will the Future Look Any Different? A Cloudy Crystal Ball

In some ways, it is quite possible to change the future of crime policy—quickly and significantly. After all, the United States dramatically increased its incarceration rates beginning in the 1970s—a quadrupling following a period of impressive stability for the five previous decades. As Blumstein and Cohen (1973) showed, the U.S. incarceration rate was strikingly stable between 1920 and 1970. But in 1980, we began to change course, and it was not due to shifts in the underlying crime problem but rather how we chose to sentence those convicted. Analysis by Blumstein and Beck (1999) shows that of the entire growth in incarceration between 1980 and 1996, just 12 percent was attributable to changes in crime rates or criminal offending. The remaining 88 percent was attributable to changes in *policy*, primarily in the decision to incarcerate (51 percent) and secondarily in the time served by those incarcerated (37 percent). So, reversing current sentencing trends is doable. Current prison practices are not driven by increasing violent crime, but rather by policy choices we have made about how to punish those who are convicted. We could just as easily make different choices.

But changing the system again will not be effortless. After all, 30 percent of Americans—a significant number—believe the current penal system is working. But public opinion polls also show that support for current incarceration policies *decreases* as knowledge of the justice system *increases*. Daniel Yankelovich, a noted public opinion researcher, also distinguishes between "raw opinion" at the early stages of a public debate on an issue, and "responsible public judgment," which occurs after the public has experienced and been educated on the alternatives and payoffs. So education about the prisoner reentry problem should help.

It would be naïve, however, to assume that crime policy is just about sentiments and public will. Even if the public is willing to retreat from some of the hard-line strategies, the incarceration boom has created a formidable foe: big businesses with a vested interest in keeping prisons full. These businesses, and the powerful unions that back them, have little interest in reducing the number of persons who go to prison.

As of the end of 2002, the American penal system consisted of 5,033 adult prisons and jails (1,558 state prisons, 110 federal prisons, and 3,365 local jails). The corrections system (including probation and parole) now employs more than 716,000 persons, with a total monthly payroll of $2.1 billion. This represents a doubling of the number of correctional employees since the mid-1980s. During the Reagan-Bush era, prisons were the second fastest growing item in state budgets, after Medicaid. The total number of U.S. citizens employed by the justice system has increased so rapidly relative to the entire U.S. employed population that approximately 1.5 percent of the nation's *entire* labor force now works in the justice system (0.2 percent for corrections). The implications of this growth and the potent political force that the criminal justice and corrections systems now yields in social policy must be acknowledged.

In the late 1950s, President Dwight D. Eisenhower warned of the strong, unwarranted influence of the "military-industrial complex." He was concerned about the extent to which the armed forces of the United States and the manufacturers of military hardware shared an interest in the ever-expanding defense budget. Today, critics point to a similar "prison-industrial complex," which is made up of special political and economic interests that encourage increasing spending on imprisonment, regardless of need.

As Eric Schlosser wrote in the *Atlantic Monthly*:

> The prison-industrial complex is not a conspiracy, guiding the nation's criminal-justice policy behind closed doors. It is a confluence of special interests that has given prison construction in the United States a seemingly unstoppable momentum. It is composed of politicians, both liberal and conservative, who have used the fear of crime to gain votes; impoverished rural areas where prisons have become a cornerstone of economic development; and private companies that regard the roughly $35 billion spent each year on corrections not as a burden on American taxpayers but as a lucrative market. (1998, p. 52)

Critics are increasingly vocal and argue that the self-interests of public and private corrections are increasingly driving U.S. penal policies.

Prison expansion has also been aided by the growth and increasing political clout of prison labor unions. Like their predecessors in criminal justice, including the police benevolent association, these organizations have spearheaded effective campaigns for more jobs and higher wages, even in the face of layoffs, hiring freezes, and revenue drops in other programs. In many states, union representatives have lobbied for prison expansion, tougher sentencing and release policies, and the curtailment of inmates' rights and privileges. Of course, all of this just assures that their ranks will continue to swell and that they remain formidable political players.

Consider the most glaring example: the California Correctional Peace Officers Association (CCPOA). A recent editorial in the *San Jose Mercury News* concluded, "Throughout the past 20 years, the California Correctional Peace Officers Association—the state's prison guard union—has achieved an unparalleled ability to dictate policy in its self-interest: the continued expansion of California's prison system" (Macallair and Schiraldi 2000). Macallair and Schiraldi note that CCPOA's massive lobbying efforts have been incredibly successful, being principally responsible for the building of 21 new prisons, the largest prison-construction effort in the history of any government. Throughout this period, the guards' union was also a primary force in promoting three-strikes legislation and mandatory prison sentences for low-level drug offenders. The union's 31,000 members each pay $60 per month to the CCPOA, generating union dues of $22 million a year, 35 percent of which goes to fund political activities. A recent editorial in the *Sacramento Bee* concluded, "[The] union is one of the most politically powerful in the state. Its endorsement—plus $2.3 million in campaign spending—helped California governor Gray Davis overcome charges in his 1998 campaign that he was soft on crime" (Weintraub 2002, p. E5). He is now paying them back.

On 13 September 2001, while the nation was fixated on the terrorist attacks that had just occurred in New York, a new CCPOA contract was signed and quickly ratified by the legislature. The public learned of the details months later, and a storm of criticism has ensued. While the state was cutting spending on health care for the poor, education, and other programs to close the state's unparalleled $12 billion budget gap, Davis approved a new prison union contract with increases in prison guard salaries of 34 percent over five years. California prison guards were already the highest paid in the nation. In addition to pay raises, he also approved huge increases in retirement benefits. The approved CCPOA contract allows a prison guard who has put in 20 years to retire at age 50 and collect an annual pension of about $43,000. An analysis of the contract for the state senator who oversees prison budget issues concluded: "The guards were given everyone else's raises" (Delsohn 2002, p. A3).

California is not alone. While collective bargaining is relatively new to U.S. corrections, at least one-third of the states now have unionized workers. A concern among criminologists is their growing influence and impact on correctional policy and rehabilitation programs—since any diversion of inmates from prison will not be viewed as in the union's self-interest.

Local communities have also found that "prison pays." Communities used to strongly oppose any siting of a prison or jail within their city boundaries, the NIMBY (not-in-my-backyard) phenomenon. But, according to Scott Christianson (1998), by the late 1980s, in harder economic times, some places, particularly sparsely populated locales, switched to lobbying to get a prospective new prison, thereby converting to a sort of PIMBY (please-in-my-backyard) phenomenon. In Texas, for instance, the competition during the early 1990s grew so fierce that some communities offered free country club memberships and other perks to prison officials as an incentive to get them to make the right siting decision (Christianson 1998).

Given their location, prisons are often the area's largest local employer, and consequently the regional economy tends to become inextricably prison based. Moreover, prisons have historically provided jobs of long duration, which seem to be inflation and recession proof, making prisons one of the few enterprises known to humankind that thrive even more in bad times than in good ones.

If communities and prisons have a vested interest in keeping their cells filled, then changes in criminal justice policies have given them a growing means to affect their personal interests and drive their own growth. As shown in figure 7.3, the reasons for the growth of the nation's prison population have shifted in recent years. New admissions from court used to drive most prison growth, but growth is now increasingly due to the readmission of parole violators. In 1980, parole violators constituted 17 percent of prison admissions, but in 1999, they constituted 35 percent. In 1991, about 140,000 parole violators were returned to prison; seven years later, that number had risen to more than 200,000, a 45 percent increase.

Parole officers have nearly unfettered discretion to revoke the parole of individuals under their supervision. Technical violations sometimes include a new offense. If a parolee has committed a new crime, it is administratively easier and less costly to send her back to prison for violating parole conditions rather than charging a new offense. So, the "technical violation" label can cover a variety of violations, from trivial to serious.

The special legal status of parolees, one of limited rights and freedom, allows for parole revocation decisions to take place in a less-than-open proceeding, sometimes without counsel present. In fact, the Supreme Court in *Morrissey v. Brewer* denied full due process rights to parolees facing revocation on the grounds that parole authorities, unlike prosecutors, have strong incentives to exercise their discretion for the *benefit* of their subjects. But given that parole officers are increasingly surveillance- rather than service-oriented, one must question whether these diminished legal rights best serve the public's interest. Parole officer discretion is an important part of the complex decision of whether to elevate a detected violation to the next level and whether to recommend to a supervisor that the parolee be returned to prison. Clearly, any effort to understand, or reverse, prison growth must examine how parole officers use this discretionary power—and whether their decisions are in the public's or their own best interests.

There is enormous variation in revocation practices among states. In 1999, for example, 66 percent of offenders admitted to California's prisons were parole violators. In Florida, parole violators account for just 7 percent of new admissions. In fact, California accounts for fully 42 percent of *all* parole revocations in the United States. New York state accounts for just 4 percent of the nation's total.

What is going on in California? Perhaps California parolees are more criminally active than parolees in other states. Or maybe they are subjected to more intensive surveillance and drug testing, both of which are likely to uncover more technical violations. But there is no empirical evidence to suggest either of these explanations is true. It may well be that the powerful correctional officers' union plays a role here too, although this is conjecture. Several people interviewed during the course of the writing of this book noted that this explanation held true to their experiences. Parole officers are also members of the CCPOA, so their incentives to keep prisons full are similar to those of prison guards. Once a hybrid of police officer and social worker, California parole agents increasingly see their jobs as enforcers rather than counselors. The reason is simple: a majority of parole officers hired in the last decade have come directly from the state's prison system.

It appears that California's prison and parole systems may have created a powerful feedback loop. Whether or not a self-interested feedback loop occurs in reality is unknown, but we should question the extent to which a growing prison-industrial complex should be that much in charge of its own intake. Parole revocations occur outside of public scrutiny and are the result of a highly discretionary administrative hearing. The public can pass (or rescind) new laws, but prison populations will not decrease dramatically as a result, since decisions made by parole officials can continue to feed the prison intake pipeline.

Caplow and Simon make another important observation. They write that "not only can the administrative procedures available to parole officers accelerate the speed of imprisonment, but these low-friction procedures can also feed the perception that criminality is spiraling out of control" (1999, p. 106). When the public hears that 50 percent of all prisoners return to prison, it fosters a sense of pessimism that anything we do can make a difference and the belief that all prisoners are committed career criminals. But, in looking behind these statistics, one learns that parole practices heavily influence the level of criminality the system confronts.

The unprecedented expansion of the prison population has been good not only for prison personnel but also for the industries that build prisons, such as architects, contractors, hardware companies, and electronic firms, and those that provide food, clothing, health care, toiletries, and telephones to inmates. A single maximum-security prison cell costs about $80,000 to build—about what it takes to build a typical middle-class suburban house. Christianson (1998) explains that prisons are so expensive because they include as standard features modular steel toilets and beds, crash-resistant gates, abuse-resistant wall and ceiling products, electronic locking systems, unbreakable glass, X-ray inspection machines, tamper-proof ceilings, and so on.

Once a prison is built, it requires huge amounts of funding to keep it running. In fact, operating costs vastly exceed building costs. As we have shown elsewhere, money does not go to work and rehabilitation programs but to personnel, building maintenance, and health care. Labor represents 60–80 percent of the costs of running a prison. As those personnel costs increase, the pressure to dismantle the few remaining prison work and education programs will rise. And, importantly, once a prison is built, it is virtually never shut down.

Between 1990 and 1998, 410 new prisons were opened by state and federal agencies. Of the nearly 1,000 state and federal prisons now in the United States, half have been built since 1980. Even though prison commitments slowed somewhat in 2001, most experts believe that virtually all of these prisons will remain open and relatively full. Once the capital commitment to prisons is made, and prisons become entrenched in the economic and social life of communities, the correctional system loses flexibility, and the pressures are to keep prisons full once they are constructed. Most prisons, even those opened a century and a half ago, remain active today.

Private prisons are the most controversial component of the prison-industrial complex. The prison boom and the favorable economics of operating prisons encouraged a number of private companies to invest in them. In the mid-1980s, private prisons were unheard of; today, 91,828 prisoners (6.5 percent of all state and federal prisoners) are held in them. The population in private prisons grew faster in 2001 (up 1.4 percent) than that in state prisons (up 1.1 percent). Three states had at least 30 percent of their inmates in privately operated facilities: New Mexico (44 percent), and Montana (33 percent), and Alaska (32 percent). In 2001, the District of Columbia had 36 percent of its inmates in private facilities.

Critics claim that the punishment of offenders should not be delegated to nonpublic agencies. At this point, the U.S. Supreme Court has not clearly established whether government can transfer the correctional function to the private sector. There is also the basic philosophical issue of whether private companies should be allowed to make a profit out of incarcerating offenders. Critics suggest that private prisons are able to operate with less public scrutiny and accountability and that they can build and fill prisons without having to go through the public debate that accompanies a state's proposal to build and fund new prisons. Proponents argue that private prisons save money, are cleaner and less crowded, house some of the more successful rehabilitation programs, and foster program innovation. Some evaluations do find that inmates released from private prisons have lower recidivism rates (for a review, see Harding 2001).

This is not the place to debate private-versus-public prisons, but for our purposes it is important to note that incentives for profit (or, in the case of public corrections, incentives to keep the cells full) might well skew the public discourse away from a search for viable prison alternatives.

Joe Hallinan's book *Going Up the River* explores how prisons have become one of the nation's biggest growth industries. He writes: "With more than 1.4 million people behind bars in this country, companies are scrambling to cash in on a market estimated to be worth $37.8 billion a year, one that is bigger than major league baseball, bigger than the porn industry. . . . Prisons are tremendous public works projects, throwing off money as a wet dog throws off water" (2001, p. 156). He describes how AT&T gives some prisons a legal kickback on every phone call placed by inmates. On a $1 phone call, the prison might make 50 cents. These commissions have meant big money for corrections. In 1997, New York alone received $21 million from phone-call commissions. Hallinan writes: "Right behind AT&T in the prison line are companies like Procter & Gamble, maker of Crest, and Helene Curtis, the shampoo and deodorant people. It seemed that there are no limits to the ways American executives could devise to cash in on the prison boom" (2001, p. xiv).

The implications are far reaching, as Hallinan describes small towns left behind by the current economic boom becoming ever more dependent on prisons (both publicly and privately operated) to replace jobs lost from disappearing factories and military bases. He asks a rhetorical question: "Are more people being put in jail, and for longer, because it's big business?" (2001, cover jacket).

The economic benefits of investing in prisons, and the political pressure to continue their expansion, means that we have to spend every available dollar on them, with none left to fund alternative programs or intermediate sanctions. The problem is that we are caught in a quagmire. We spend so much of our tax money—4 percent of state budgets in 2001—to fund prisons that we have nothing left to invest in community-based programs. As former governor James Thompson of Illinois used to say, "A dollar for corrections is a dollar that doesn't go somewhere else."

States have shifted money away from education and social services to fund prisons, and prisons increasingly shift money out of programs to pay staff and fund new construction. Of course, this ultimately backfires. Persons who fail to become educated in an ever more technologically sophisticated economy get squeezed out and are unable to compete in a more competitive job market; consequently, they face higher unemployment rates and downward mobility, which in turn is associated with poverty, substance abuse, female-headed households, and homelessness—all associated with increased crime. Once released from prison, they are now both uneducated and have the stigma of a prison record. Our short-term need to fund prisons at the expense of community corrections and rehabilitation programs is bad policy and just assures that the next generation remains unemployed and that the prison cells remain filled.

Concluding Remarks

The future is seen through a clouded crystal ball. On the one hand, there are some indications that Americans' support for prisons is waning. Public opinion polls indicate that three-quarters of Americans approve of sentencing nonviolent offenders to probation instead of imprisonment, and a substantial majority of the public supports eliminating mandatory sentencing laws. Nationwide, the number of inmates continues to grow but at slower rates. Some political leaders and public opinion makers are questioning the value of three strikes and draconian penalties for certain drug crimes. Taxpayers are growing weary of the massive costs of prisons, especially given the recent recession and the revenue loss associated with the 11 September 2001 terrorist attacks and their aftermath. With a slowing economy, the tax burden prisons place on local areas interferes with their capacity to fund schools, provide health care, and maintain basic services.

Ultimately, however, whether we choose to chart a new course on who goes to prison and how inmates are returned to communities will depend not on economics but on whether we embrace the noble idea that we have a responsibility to help offenders make new lives for themselves. It is mostly our changed value system that has led to more punitive crime policies, not changes in crime rates.

Social historians chronicle a growing divide—financially, politically, and socially—among Americans. Americans spend a large fraction of their time in gated communities, on freeways, and in the virtual world of television and cyberspace. As a result, we are increasingly disconnected from one another. Robert Putnam of Harvard, in his book *Bowling Alone*, describes the growing anonymity of Americans and the negative effect this isolation has on a number of social problems, including crime and punishment.

Putnam shows that modern Americans have fewer personal connections to others unlike themselves, and as a result, they have shallow social support systems and a diminished collective responsibility for the plight of their neighbors. Familiarity breeds an understanding of one another, community sympathy, and a willingness to help in time of need. Anonymity fosters just the opposite. He writes that we do not feel the pain (or joy) of one another's experiences like our forefathers did, because we have fewer opportunities to directly experience it or to work and socialize with those experiencing it.

Similarly, Robert Sampson discovered that "collective efficacy" was a robust predictor of lower rates of violence. His construct of collective efficacy included not only a measure of informal social control but also a measure of "cohesion and trust" among residents (Sampson, Raudenbush, and Earls 1997). Sampson and colleagues found that two characteristics—mutual trust and altruism among neighbors and their willingness to intervene when they see children misbehaving—explained why some Chicago neighborhoods were less crime-prone than others. Indeed, a neighborhood's collective efficacy was a better predictor than was its poverty or residential instability of whether a person was likely to be victimized in the neighborhood. The authors conclude: "Reduction in violence appears to be directly attributable to informal social control and cohesion among residents" (Sampson et al. 1997, p. 923).

Social support and collective efficacy are not only related to levels of crime but also to choices about how to punish wrongdoers and policies regarding social reintegration. The experience of providing social support to one another creates sentiments and compassion that are generally incompatible with harsh crime policies. In societies lacking strong, socially supportive bonds, unrealistic fear of one another is more common, and the cultural distance and stereotyping between the classes widens. Caplow and Simon (1999) suggest that this is exactly what has occurred in the United States, and it essentially explains the nation's increasing reliance on imprisonment. They write: "The greater the social and cultural distance that separates the underprivileged from the body of society, the more punitive that management is likely to be" (Caplow and Simon 1999, p. 89).

The irony is that more punitive crime policies, particularly ones that rely heavily on prisons, contribute further to the declines in social support that produced crime in the first place and that are critical for successful reintegration. As Braithwaite (1989, p. 179) wrote: "Prisons are warehouses for outcasts; they put problem people at a distance from those who might effectively shame them and from those who might help reintegrate them. Imprisonment is a policy both for breaking down legitimate interdependencies and for fostering participation in criminal cultures."

If prison is judged necessary, then maximum effort should be made to encourage ties with the family and community throughout the prisoner's stay, and prerelease programs should focus on actively connecting the prisoner to the host community (e.g., work release, study release, and so on). *Every* known study that has been able to directly examine the relationship between a prisoner's legitimate community ties and recidivism has found that feelings of being welcome at home and the strength of interpersonal ties outside prison help predict postprison adjustment.

Parole and reentry services of the future must focus on linking offenders with community institutions. This means that we have to reach outside the criminal justice system to other units of government and the community: churches, ex-prisoner self-help groups, families, and nonprofit programs. We have to share the responsibility for transitioning offenders to the community *with* the community. Community partnerships not only help the offender connect with the community, but just as important, help the community connect with the offender. If an inmate does not have a naturally occurring family support system, then reentry courts, reentry partnerships, and reintegration ceremonies can help serve this vital role.

The author hesitates to call for more programs, because such calls are quickly dismissed as being liberal on crime and are likely to be disregarded as irrelevant to the current public mood and national policy trends. In matters of prison policy, liberals who want more programs are pitted against conservatives who want more cells. This is a false dichotomy, and the honest answer is that we need both. We have to create enough prison space to incarcerate the truly violent and at the same time create programs to reduce the flood of criminals that current conditions keep creating.

In response to the call for more programs, the public's answer is likely to be "we tried all that before and it didn't work." In fact, as discussed in chapter 3, it was exactly this notion—that rehabilitation did not work—that led to the abandonment of indeterminate sentencing in the mid-1970s. So, how then can an empirically oriented criminologist, like the author, make a legitimate case for investing in more prison programming?

There are two principal arguments. Martinson (1974) was simply wrong when he—and others who summarized his research—concluded that nothing works in corrections. His "evaluation" of programs implemented in the 1960s—which was simply a tally of reported program-evaluation findings with no consideration of sample size or methodological rigor—would not pass for science using today's higher standards.

Data from meta-analysis of tens, if not hundreds, of studies confirm that treatment can work to reduce recidivism. However, treatment effects are heterogeneous; some interventions, especially those that are punitively oriented (e.g., boot camps) do not work, while others, especially those reflecting principles of effective treatment, do reduce recidivism. Scholars interpret these findings with differing degrees of optimism, but the case against the nothing-works doctrine is now pretty convincing. In a review of this literature, Cullen (2002) suggests that the nothing works doctrine is itself a fiction based far more on ideology than science. He concludes, "The empirical evidence is fairly convincing—and growing stronger as time passes—that treatment interventions are capable of decreasing recidivism" (2002, p. 287).

In retrospect, it was naïve and simplistic to ask or answer such global questions about correctional treatment effectiveness. We would not consider such questions useful in relation to medical, psychiatric, or environmental measures. As Michael Tonry points out, "We do not ask, 'Does medical treatment work?' but instead whether a particular treatment delivered in a particular way helps a particular ailment according to particular criteria" (1995, p. 202). Better questions generate better answers, and we are now getting them. Today, our knowledge of program effectiveness argues for providing treatment on demand for all drug-dependent offenders who want it and compulsory treatment for many drug-dependent offenders who do not. From both crime-control and cost perspectives, successful treatment of drug-involved offenders is, like prevention, an unequivocal winner.

Second, and most important, is that we have little choice. We now have more than 2 million citizens incarcerated in prisons and jails on any one day, including fully a third of all young black men living in the United States. In some inner cities, more than half the male residents have been incarcerated. Prisons have become vast learning centers for crime and are magnifying the social problems these communities face. Common sense suggests that many prisoners return home more desperate, more violence-prone, and more of a menace to society. The multiplier effect is certain to exact a staggering, but as yet unmeasured, future toll.

The nation faces enormous challenges in managing the reintegration of increasing numbers of individuals who are leaving state and federal prisons. It is time to do the hard work of developing more effective responses to these challenges. We should do this not only because it will be good for prisoners returning home, but because it will ultimately be good for their children, their neighbors, and the community at large. Given the magnitude of the expected prison exodus over the next decade, focusing on prisoner reintegration may be our best hope for keeping crime rates down as nearly 600,000 inmates a year—1,600 a day—leave prison to return home.

Bibliography

Abadinsky, Howard. 1997. *Probation and Parole*. 6th ed. Upper Saddle River, N.J.: Simon & Schuster.

Adams, Devon B. 2002. *Summary of State Sex Offender Registries, 2001*. Washington, D.C.: Bureau of Justice Statistics.

Adams, William, and Jeffrey Roth. 1998. *Federal Offenders under Community Supervision, 1987–96*. Washington, D.C.: Bureau of Justice Statistics.

Allard, Patricia. 2002. *Life Sentences: Denying Welfare Benefits to Women Convicted of Drug Offenses*. Washington, D.C.: Sentencing Project.

Allard, Patricia, and Marc Mauer. 2000. *Regaining the Vote: An Assessment of Activity Relating to Felon Disenfranchisement Laws*. Washington, D.C.: Sentencing Project.

Altschuler, David, and Troy L. Armstrong. 1994. *Intensive Aftercare for High-Risk Juveniles: A Community Care Model*. Washington, D.C.: Office of Juvenile Justice and Delinquency Prevention.

American Correctional Association. 2002. *Directory*. Lanham, Md.: American Correctional Association.

———. 2001. "Parole Survey." *Corrections Compendium*, 8–9.

———. 2000. *Vital Statistics in Corrections*. Lanham, Md.: American Correctional Association.

Anderson, Elijah. 1999. *Code of the Street: Decency, Violence, and the Moral Life of the Inner City*. New York: Norton.

———. 1990. *Streetwise: Race, Class, and Change in an Urban Community*. Chicago, Ill.: University of Chicago Press.

Andrews, Don A., and James Bonta. 1995. *The Level of Service Inventory–Revised*. Toronto: Multi-Health Systems.

Anglin, M. Douglas, and Yih-Ing Hser. 1990. "Treatment of Drug Abuse." In *Drugs and Crime*, edited by M. Tonry and J. Q. Wilson, 393–460. Chicago, Ill.: University of Chicago Press.

Aos, Steve, Polly Phipps, Robert Barnoski, and Roxanne Lieb. 2001. *The Comparative Costs and Benefits of Programs to Reduce Crime*. Seattle: Washington State Institute for Public Policy.

Association of Parole Authorities, International. 2001a. "Does the Parole Board Have Discretion in Parole Release?" Retrieved 26 July 2001 from http://www.apaint1.org/Pub-ParoleBoardSurvey1999.html

———. 2001b. "Parole Board Survey 2000." Retrieved 20 February 2002 from www.apaintl.org

———. 2000. "Parole Board Survey 1999." Retrieved 20 February 2002 from http://www.apaint1.org/Pub-ParoleBoardSurvey1999.html

Austin, James. 2001. "Prisoner Reentry: Current Trends, Practices, and Issues." *Crime & Delinquency* 47, no. 3:314–34.

Bartollas, Clemens. 2002. *Invitation to Corrections*. Boston, Mass.: Allyn & Bacon.

Beatty, Phillip, Barry Holman, and Vincent Schiraldi. 2000. *Poor Prescription: The Costs of Imprisoning Drug Offenders in the United States*. Washington, D.C.: Justice Policy Institute.

Beck, Allen. 2002. Personal interview. 23 January.

———. 2000. *State and Federal Prisoners Returning to the Community: Findings from the Bureau of Justice Statistics*. Washington, D.C.: Bureau of Justice Statistics.

———. 1999. "Trends in U.S. Correctional Populations." In *The Dilemmas of Corrections*, edited by Kenneth Haas and Geoffrey Alpert, 44–100. Prospect Heights, Ill.: Waveland.

Beck, Allen J., and Paige M. Harrison. 2001. *Prisoners in 2000*. Washington, D.C.: Bureau of Justice Statistics.

Beck, Allen J., Jennifer Karberg, and Paige M. Harrison. 2002. *Prison and Jail Inmates at Midyear 2001*. Washington, D.C.: Bureau of Justice Statistics.

Beck, Allen J., and Laura Maruschak. 2001. *Mental Health Treatment in State Prisons, 2000*. Washington, D.C.: Bureau of Justice Statistics.

Beck, Allen, and Bernard Shipley. 1989. *Recidivism of Prisoners Released in 1983*. Washington, D.C.: Bureau of Justice Statistics.

———. 1987. *Recidivism of Young Parolees*. Washington, D.C.: Bureau of Justice Statistics.

Berecochea, John E. 2002. "California Recidivism Rate." Paper presented at the California District Administrators' Training, Diamond Bar, Calif., 10 January.

———. 2001. *An Outcome Evaluation of Correctional Programs in the California Department of Corrections*. Sacramento: California Department of Corrections.

BI Incorporated. 2002. *Overview of the Illinois DOC High-Risk Parolee Re-Entry Program and 3-Year Recidivism Outcomes of Program Participants*. Boulder, Colo.: BI.

Bloom, Barbara, and D. Steinhart. 1993. *Why Punish the Children? A Reappraisal of the Children of Incarcerated Mothers in America*. San Francisco, Calif.: National Council on Crime and Delinquency.

Blumstein, Alfred. 2001. "Race and Criminal Justice." In *America Becoming: Racial Trends and Their Consequences*, edited by Neil

Smelser, William Julius Wilson, and Faith Mitchell, 21–31. Washington, D.C.: National Academy Press.

———. 1993a. "Making Rationality Relevant." *Criminology* 31:1–16.

———. 1993b. "Racial Disproportionality of U.S. Prison Populations Revisited." *University of Colorado Law Review* 64:743–60.

Blumstein, Alfred, and Allen J. Beck. 1999. "Population Growth in U.S. Prisons: 1980–1996." In *Prisons: A Review of Research*, edited by M. Tonry and J. Petersilia, 17–62. Chicago, Ill.: University of Chicago Press.

Blumstein, Alfred, and Jacqueline Cohen. 1973. "A Theory of the Stability of Punishment." *Journal of Criminal Law, Criminology, and Police Science* 62, no. 2:198–207.

Blumstein, Alfred, Jacqueline Cohen, Jeffrey Roth, and Christy Visher. 1986. *Criminal Careers and "Career Criminals."* Vol. 1. Washington, D.C.: National Academy Press.

Bonczar, Thomas P., and Allen J. Beck. 1997. *Lifetime Likelihood of Going to State or Federal Prison.* Washington, D.C.: Bureau of Justice Statistics.

Bonczar, Thomas, and Lauren Glaze. 1999. *Probation and Parole in the United States, 1998.* Washington, D.C.: Bureau of Justice Statistics.

Bonta, James. 1996. "Risk-Needs Assessment and Treatment." In *Choosing Correctional Options That Work*, edited by Alan T. Harland, 18–32. Thousand Oaks, Calif.: Sage.

Boone, Harry B. 1995. "Mental Illness in Probation and Parole Populations: Results from a National Survey." *Perspectives* 19:14–26.

Bottomley, Keith A. 1990. "Parole in Transition: A Comparative Study of Origins, Developments, and Prospects for the 1990s." In *Crime and Justice: A Review of Research*, edited by Michael Tonry and Norval Morris, 319–74. Chicago, Ill.: University of Chicago Press.

Boyum, David A., and Mark Kleiman. 2002. "Substance Abuse Policy." In *Crime: Public Policies for Crime Control*, edited by J. Q. Wilson and J. Petersilia, 331–82. San Francisco, Calif.: ICS Press.

Bradley, Katharine, and Michael Oliver. 2001. *The Role of Parole.* Boston: Community Resources for Justice.

Bradley, Katharine, R. B. Oliver, N. Richardson, and E. Slayter. 2001. *No Place Like Home: Housing and the Ex-Prisoner.* Boston: Community Resources for Justice.

Braithwaite, John. 1989. *Crime, Shame, and Reintegration.* New York: Cambridge University Press.

Brown, Claude. 1984. "Manchild in Harlem." *New York Times Magazine*, 16 September, p. 44.

Buck, Maria. 2000. *Getting Back to Work: Employment Programs for Ex-Offenders.* Philadelphia, Pa.: Public Private Ventures.

Bureau of Justice Statistics. 2002a. *Annual Parole Survey, 2000*. Washington, D.C.: Bureau of Justice Statistics.

———. 2002b. *Survey of Inmates in State Adult Correctional Facilities, 1997*. Washington, D.C.: Bureau of Justice Statistics.

———. 2002c. *Improving Criminal History Records for Background Checks*. Washington, D.C.: Bureau of Justice Statistics.

———. 2001a. *Use and Management of Criminal History Record Information: A Comprehensive Report, 2001 Update*. Washington, D.C.: U.S. Department of Justice.

———. 2001b. "Victim Characteristics 2001." Retrieved 5 February 2001 from http://www.ojp.usdoj.gov/bjs/cvict_v.htm

———. 1999. *Mental Health and Treatment of Inmates and Probationers*. Washington, D.C.: Bureau of Justice Statistics.

———. 1997. *National Corrections Reporting Program, 1996*. Washington, D.C.: Bureau of Justice Statistics.

———. 1993a. *Prisoners in 1992*. Washington, D.C.: U.S. Government Printing Office.

———. 1993b. *Sentencing in the Federal Courts: Does Race Matter?* Washington, D.C.: Bureau of Justice Statistics.

———. 1993c. *Use and Management of Criminal History Record Information: A Comprehensive Report*. Washington, D.C.: Bureau of Justice Statistics.

———. 1984. *Returning to Prison*. Washington, D.C.: Bureau of Justice Statistics.

Burke, Peggy B. 1995. *Abolishing Parole: Why the Emperor Has No Clothes*. Lexington, Ky.: American Probation and Parole Association.

Bushway, Shawn, and Peter Reuter. 2002. "Labor Markets and Crime." In *Crime: Public Policies for Crime Control*, edited by J. Q. Wilson and J. Petersilia, 191–224. San Francisco, Calif.: ICS Press.

California Department of Corrections. 1997. *Preventing Parolee Failure Program: An Evaluation*. Sacramento: California Department of Corrections.

Callery, Brian A. 2001. "State Needs a Parole Policy That Benefits All." *Boston Globe*, 14 July, editorial section.

Camp, Camille, and George Camp. 2001. *The Corrections Yearbook 2000*. Middletown, Conn.: Criminal Justice Institute.

Caplow, Theodore, and Jonathan Simon. 1999. "Understanding Prison Policy and Population Trends." In *Prisons*, edited by M. Tonry and J. Petersilia, 63–120. Chicago, Ill.: University of Chicago Press.

Centers for Disease Control. 1997. *Reported Tuberculosis in the United States, 1996*. Atlanta, Ga.: Centers for Disease Control.

Chaiken, Jan, and Marcia Chaiken. 1982. *Varieties of Criminal Behavior*. Santa Monica, Calif.: Rand.

Christianson, Scott. 1998. *With Liberty for Some: 500 Years of Imprisonment in America.* Boston: Northeastern University Press.

Citizens' Inquiry on Parole and Criminal Justice. 1974. *Report on New York Parole.* New York: Citizens' Inquiry.

Clear, Todd. 1996. "The Unintended Consequences of Incarceration." Paper presented at the Sentencing and Corrections Workshop, National Institute of Justice, Washington, D.C., 14 February. Retrieved 25 September 2002 from www.ncjrs.org/txtfiles/sentcorr.txt

———. 1994. *Harm in American Penology: Offenders, Victims, and Their Communities.* Albany: State University of New York Press.

———. 1992. Foreword. In *Dangerous Men: The Sociology of Parole,* edited by Richard McCleary, vii–x. New York: Harrow and Heston.

Clear, Todd R., and Anthony Braga. 1995. "Community Corrections." In *Crime,* edited by J. Q. Wilson and J. Petersilia, 421–44. San Francisco, Calif.: Institute for Contemporary Studies.

Clear, Todd, and George Cole. 2000. *American Corrections.* 5th ed. Belmont, Calif.: Wadsworth.

Clear, Todd, and Ronald Corbett. 1999. "Community Corrections of Place." *Perspectives* 23, no. 1:24–32.

Cook, Dave. 2000. "Transition for Success." In *Correctional Best Practices: Directors' Perspectives,* edited by Reginald Wilkinson. Middletown, Conn.: Association of State Correctional Administrators.

Corrections Compendium. 1997a. "Educational Opportunities in Correctional Settings." *Corrections Compendium* 22, no. 9:4–14.

———. 1997b. "Work and Educational Release." *Corrections Compendium* 22, no. 5:8–23.

———. 1994. *Education in U.S. Prisons: Survey Summary.* Lanham, Md.: American Correctional Association.

Covington, Stephanie. 2002. "A Woman's Journey Home: Challenges for Female Offenders and Their Children." Paper presented at the Urban Institute's From Prison to Home conference, Washington, D.C., 30–31 January.

Cullen, Francis T. 2002. "Rehabilitation and Treatment Programs." In *Crime: Public Policies for Crime Control,* edited by James Q. Wilson and Joan Petersilia, 253–91. Oakland, Calif.: Institute for Contemporary Studies.

Cullen, Francis, Bonnie Fisher, and Brandon Applegate. 2000. "Public Opinion about Punishment and Corrections." In *Crime and Justice: A Review of Research,* edited by Michael Tonry, 1–79. Chicago, Ill.: University of Chicago Press.

del Carmen, Rolando, Maldine Barnhill, Gene Bonham, Lance Hignite, and Todd Jermstad. 2000. *Civil Liabilities and Other Legal Issues for Probation/Parole Officers and Supervisors.* Washington, D.C.: National Institute of Corrections.

Delsohn, Gary. 2002. "A Legislative Panel Raises Questions about the Deal with His Biggest Contributors." *Sacramento Bee*, 18 May, p. A3.

Dickey, Walter J., and Michael Smith. 1998. *Rethinking Probation: Community Supervision, Community Safety*. Washington, D.C.: U.S. Department of Justice.

Dion, Robin, Michelle Der, Jacquelyn Anderson, and LaDonna Pavetti. 1999. *Reaching All Job-Seekers: Employment Programs for Hard-to-Employ Populations*. Boston: Mathematica Policy Research.

Ditton, Paula. 1999. *Mental Health and Treatment of Inmates and Probationers*. Washington, D.C.: Bureau of Justice Statistics.

Ditton, Paula, and Doris James Wilson. 1999. *Truth in Sentencing in State Prisons*. Washington, D.C.: Bureau of Justice Statistics.

Donziger, Steven R. 1996. *The Real War on Crime*. New York: Harper Collins.

Drew, Candace Cross. 1990. "Forcible Rape in California in the 1980s." In *Crime and Delinquency in California, 1980-1989*, 141–44. Sacramento: California Bureau of Criminal Statistics, California Department of Justice.

Durose, Matthew. 2001. *Felony Sentences in State Courts, 1998*. Washington, D.C.: Bureau of Justice Statistics.

Eisenberg, Michael. 2001. *Evaluation of the Performance of the Texas Department of Criminal Justice Rehabilitation Tier Programs*. Austin, Tex.: Criminal Justice Policy Council.

———. 1998. *Implementation of the TDCJ Rehabilitation Tier Treatment Programs: Progress Report*. Austin, Tex.: Criminal Justice Policy Council.

Erez, E., and L. Roger. 1995. "The Effect of Victim Impact Statements on Sentencing Patterns and Outcomes: The Australian Experience." *Journal of Criminal Justice* 23:413–33.

Erikson, Kai. 1962. "Notes on the Sociology of Deviance." *Social Problems* 9:307–14.

Fabelo, Tony. 2000. *"Technocorrections": The Promises, the Uncertain Threats*. Washington, D.C.: National Institute of Justice.

Fagan, Jeffrey, F. E. Zimring, and June Kim. 1998. "Declining Homicide in New York City: A Tale of Two Trends." *Journal of Criminal Law & Criminology* 88:1277–323.

Feely, Malcolm, and Jonathan Simon. 1992. "The New Penology: Notes on the Emerging Strategy of Corrections and Its Implications." *Criminology* 30:449–74.

Fellner, Jamie, and Marc Mauer. 1998. *Losing the Vote: The Impact of Felony Disenfranchisement Laws in the United States*. Washington, D.C.: Sentencing Project.

Finckenauer, James O. 1982. *Scared Straight: The Panacea Phenomenon*. Englewood Cliffs, N.J.: Prentice Hall.

Fine, Janet. 2000. *Victim Issues for Parole Boards.* Washington, D.C.: Office for Victims of Crime.

Finkelhor, D., and R. Ormrod. 2000. *Characteristics of Crime against Juveniles.* Washington, D.C.: Office of Juvenile Justice and Delinquency Prevention.

Finn, Peter. 1998a. *Chicago's Safer Foundation: A Road Back for Ex-Offenders.* Washington, D.C.: National Institute of Justice.

———. 1998b. *Successful Job Placement for Ex-Offenders: The Center for Employment Opportunities.* Washington, D.C.: National Institute of Justice.

———. 1998c. *Texas' Project Rio (Re-Integration of Offenders).* Washington, D.C.: National Institute of Justice.

Flanagan, Timothy, and Dennis Longmire, eds. 1996. *Americans View Crime and Justice: A National Public Opinion Survey.* Thousand Oaks, Calif.: Sage.

Fogel, David. 1975. *We Are the Living Proof.* Cincinnati, Ohio: Anderson.

Frank, B. 1973. "Graduated Release." In *Contemporary Corrections,* edited by B. Frank. Reston, Va.: Reston.

Freeman, Richard B. 1996. *Why Do So Many Young American Men Commit Crimes and What Might We Do About It?* Cambridge, Mass.: National Bureau of Economic Research working paper no. 5451.

Fulp, Elmer. 2001. "Project Rio: Reintegration of Offenders." In *State of Corrections: Proceedings, Annual Conference 2000.* Lanham, Md.: American Correctional Association.

Gabel, S. 1992. "Children of Incarcerated and Criminal Parents: Adjustment, Behavior and Prognosis." *Bulletin of the American Academy of Psychiatry & the Law* 20:33–45.

Gaes, Gerald, Timothy J. Flanagan, Laurence L. Motiuk, and Lynn Stewart. 1999. "Adult Correctional Treatment." In *Prisons,* edited by M. Tonry and J. Petersilia, 361–426. Chicago, Ill.: University of Chicago Press.

Gaes, Gerald, and Newton Kendig. 2002. "The Skill Sets and Health Care Needs of Released Offenders." Paper presented at From Prison to Home conference, Washington, D.C., 10 January.

GAINS. 1997. *Just the Facts.* Delmar, N.Y.: National GAINS Center for People with Co-Occurring Disorders in the Justice System.

Gagnon v. Scarpelli. 1973. 411 U.S. 778.

Gallup Organization. 1998. Special Request.

Garland, David. 2001. *The Culture of Control: Crime and Social Order in Contemporary Society.* Chicago, Ill.: University of Chicago Press.

Gendreau, Paul, Tracy Little, and Claire Goggin. 1996. "A Meta-Analysis of Adult Offender Recidivism: What Works?" *Criminology* 34, no. 4:575–607.

Gerstein, Dean R., and Henrick Harwood, J., eds. 1990. *Treating Drug Problems*. Vol. 1. Washington, D.C.: National Academy Press.

Gest, Ted. 2001. *Crime & Politics: Big Government's Erratic Campaign for Law and Order*. New York: Oxford University Press.

Gibbs, Jack P. 1975. *Crime, Punishment, and Deterrence*. New York: Elsevier.

Gifford, Sidra. 2002. *Justice Expenditure and Employment in the United States, 1999*. Washington, D.C.: Bureau of Justice Statistics.

Glaser, Daniel. 1969. *The Effectiveness of a Prison and Parole System*. Indianapolis, Ind.: Bobbs-Merrill.

Godwin, Tracy, and Anne Seymour. 1999. *Promising Victim-Related Practices and Strategies in Probation and Parole*. Washington, D.C.: Office of Victims of Crime.

Goffman, Erving. 1963. *Stigma: Notes on the Management of Spoiled Identity*. Englewood Cliffs, N.J.: Prentice Hall.

Gondles, James A. 2000. "Technology: Changing the Face of Corrections." *Corrections Today* 62, no. 4:6–8.

Gottfredson, Denise, David B. Wilson, and Stacy Najaka. 2002. "The Schools." In *Crime: Public Policies for Crime Control*, edited by J. Q. Wilson and J. Petersilia, 149–90. San Francisco, Calif.: ICS Press.

Gottfredson, Stephen, and Don Gottfredson. 1994. "Behavioral Prediction and the Problem of Incapacitation." *Criminology* 32, no. 3:441–74.

Government Accounting Office. 2001. *Prisoner Releases: Trends and Information on Reintegration Programs*. Washington, D.C.: Government Accounting Office.

———. 2000. *State and Federal Prisoners: Profiles of Inmate Characteristics in 1991 and 1997*. Washington, D.C.: Government Accounting Office.

———. 1999. *Foster Care: States' Early Experiences Implementing the Adoption and Safe Families Act*. Washington, D.C.: Government Accounting Office.

Greene, Judith, and Vincent Schiraldi. 2001. *Cutting Correctly: New Prison Policies for Times of Fiscal Crisis*. Washington, D.C.: Justice Policy Institute.

Greenfeld, Larry. 1985. *Examining Recidivism*. Washington, D.C.: Bureau of Justice Statistics.

Hairston, Creasie F. 2002. "Prisoners and Families: Parenting Issues during Incarceration." Paper presented at the Urban Institute's From Prison to Home conference, Washington, D.C., 30–31 January.

———. 1991. "Family Ties during Imprisonment: Important to Whom and for What?" *Journal of Sociology and Social Welfare* 18, no. 1:87–104.

Hallinan, Joseph. 2001. *Going up the River: Travels in a Prison Nation*. New York: Random House.

Hammett, Theodore M., Patricia Harmon, and Laura M. Maruschak. 1999. *1996–1997 Update: HIV/AIDS, STDs, and TB in Correctional Facilities*. Washington, D.C.: Bureau of Justice Statistics.

Hammett, Theodore, Patricia Harmon, and William Rhodes. 2002. "The Burden of Infectious Disease among Inmates and Releasees from Correctional Facilities." In *The Health Status of Soon-to-Be-Released Inmates*, 15–28. Vol. 2. Washington, D.C.: National Institute of Justice.

Haney, Craig. 2002. "The Psychological Impact of Incarceration: Implications for Post-Prison Adjustment." Paper presented at the Urban Institute's From Prison to Home conference, Washington, D.C., 30–31 January.

Harding, Richard. 2001. "Private Prisons." In *Crime and Justice: A Review of Research*, edited by M. Tonry, 265–346. Chicago, Ill.: University of Chicago Press.

Harlow, Caroline Wolf. 1999. *Prior Abuse Reported by Inmates and Probationers*. Washington, D.C.: Bureau of Justice Statistics.

Harris, Mary Belle. 1936. *I Knew Them in Prison*. New York: Viking.

Harrison, Paige M., and Allen J. Beck. 2002. *Prisoners in 2001*. Washington, D.C.: Bureau of Justice Statistics.

Hart Research Associates. 2002. "Changing Public Attitudes toward the Criminal Justice System." Retrieved 25 October 2002 from www.soros.org/crime/CJI-Poll

Hawker v. New York. 1968. 170 U.S.

Henderson, Martha. 2001. "Employment and Crime: What Is the Problem and What Can Be Done about It from the Inmate's Perspective?" *Corrections Management Quarterly* 5, no. 4:46–52.

Herman, Susan, and Cressida Wasserman. 2001. "A Role for Victims in Offender Reentry." *Crime & Delinquency* 47, no. 3:428–45.

Hinton, Mick. 2001. "Pace of Processing Keeping Parolees on Prisons' Budget." *Oklahoman*, 1 March.

Hirsch, Amy E., Sharon Dietrich, Rue Landau, Peter Schneider, and Irv Ackelsberg. 2002. *Every Door Closed: Barriers Facing Parents with Criminal Records*. Washington, D.C.: Center for Law and Social Policy.

Hoffman, Peter B. 1994. "Twenty Years of Operational Use of a Risk Prediction Instrument: The United States Parole Commission's Salient Factor Score." *Journal of Criminal Justice* 22, no. 6:477–94.

Holt, Norman. 1998. "The Current State of Parole in America." In *Community Corrections: Probation, Parole, and Intermediate Sanctions*, edited by J. Petersilia, 28–41. New York: Oxford University Press.

Holzer, Harry J. 1996. *What Employers Want: Job Prospects for Less-Educated Workers*. New York: Sage.

Holzer, Harry, Steven Raphael, and Michael Stoll. 2002. "Can Employers Play a More Positive Role in Prisoner Reentry?" Paper presented at the Urban Institute's Reentry Roundtable, Washington, D.C., 20–21 March.

Home Office. 2002. "A Review of the Rehabilitation of Offenders Act 1974." Retrieved 27 April 2002 from http://www.homeoffice.gov.uk/roareview/index.htm

Horn, Martin. 2001. "Rethinking Sentencing." *Corrections Management Quarterly* 5, no. 3:34–40.

Hughes, Timothy, Doris James Wilson, and Allen J. Beck. 2001. *Trends in State Parole, 1990–2000*. Washington, D.C.: Bureau of Justice Statistics.

Iguchi, M. Y., J. A. London, N. G. Forge, Laura J. Hickman, and K. Riehman. 2002. *Elements of Well-Being Affected by Criminalizing the Drug User: An Overview*. Washington, D.C.: Public Health Reports, National Institute of Drug Abuse.

Immerwahr, John, and Jean Johnson. 2002. "Exploring Public Opinion on Prisoner Reentry." Presentation at the Urban Institute's Reentry Roundtable, Washington, D.C., 20 March.

Irwin, John, and James Austin. 1997. *It's about Time: America's Imprisonment Binge*. Belmont, Calif.: Wadsworth.

Johnson, Eric. 2002. "U.S. Survey of Access to Criminal Records: Update." Unpublished tables. Sacramento, Calif.: SEARCH Group.

Johnson, Eric. 2001. *U.S. Survey of Access to Criminal History Records*. Sacramento, Calif.: SEARCH Group.

Karmen, Andrew. 2001. *Crime Victims: An Introduction to Victimology*. 4th ed. Belmont, Calif.: Wadsworth.

Keilin, Sharon. 2001. *An Overview of Texas Parole Guidelines*. Austin, Tex.: Criminal Justice Policy Council.

Kitchener, Howard, Annesley K. Schmidt, and Daniel Glaser. 1977. *How Persistent Is Post-Prison Success*. Washington, D.C.: Federal Probation.

Klein, Stephen, and Michael Caggiano. 1986. *The Prevalence, Predictability, and Policy Implications of Recidivism*. Santa Monica, Calif.: Rand.

Kleinknecht, William. 1997. "Juvenile Authorities Want Satellite Tracking for Felons." *Star Ledger* (Newark, N.J.), 18 November. Retrieved 2 September 1998 from www.nj.com/jersey/ledger

Kling, Jeffrey. 2002. "The Effect of Prison Sentence Length on the Subsequent Employment and Earnings of Criminal Defendants." Princeton University, Discussion Paper in Economics. Unpublished manuscript. Princeton, N.J. Retrieved 15 September 2002 from www.wws.princeton.edu

Kurki, Leena. 2000. *Racial Disparity Initiative: Collateral Effects Study*. Minneapolis, Minn.: Council on Crime and Justice.

Kurki, Leena, and Norval Morris. 2002. "The Purposes, Practices, and Problems of Supermax Prisons." In *Crime and Justice*, edited by M. Tonry and N. Morris, 385–450. Chicago, Ill.: University of Chicago Press.

Kuzma, Susan M. 1998. "Civil Disabilities of Convicted Felons: State-by-State Survey Finds Considerable Variation among States." Retrieved 5 September 1998 from http://www.corrections.com/aca.cortoday/kuzma.html

Landsberg, Mitchell. 2000. "No Simple Explanation for Jump in L.A. Murder Rate." *Los Angeles Times*, 1 December.

Langan, Patrick, and David Levin. 2002. *Recidivism of Prisoners Released in 1994*. Washington, D.C.: Bureau of Justice Statistics.

Laub, John, and Robert J. Sampson. 2001. "Understanding Desistance from Crime." In *Crime and Justice*, edited by M. Tonry and Norval Morris, 1–70. Chicago, Ill.: University of Chicago Press.

Lawrence, Sarah, Daniel Mears, Glenn Dubin, and Jeremy Travis. 2002. *The Practice and Promise of Prison Programming*. Washington, D.C.: Urban Institute.

Legal Action Center. 2001. *Housing Laws Affecting Individuals with Criminal Convictions*. New York: Legal Action Center.

———. 1996. *Study of Rap Sheet Accuracy and Recommendations to Improve Criminal Justice Recordkeeping*. New York: Legal Action Center.

Legislative Analysts Office. 1999. "Crosscutting Issues: Judiciary and Criminal Justice." Retrieved 8 February from www.lao.ca.gov/analysis

Lemert, Edwin E. 1981. "Diversion in Juvenile Justice: What Hath Been Wrought." *Journal of Research in Crime & Delinquency* 18:34–46.

Lipsey, Mark W. 1995. "What Do We Learn from 400 Research Studies on the Effectiveness of Treatment with Juvenile Delinquency?" In *What Works: Reducing Reoffending*, edited by James McQuire, 63–78. West Sussex, U.K.: Wiley.

Lipsey, M. W., and J. H. Derzon. 1998. "Predictors of Violent or Serious Delinquency in Adolescence and Early Adulthood: A Synthesis of Longitudinal Research." In *Serious and Violent Juvenile Offenders: Risk Factors and Successful Interventions*, edited by R. Loeber and David P. Farrington, 86–105. Thousand Oaks, Calif.: Sage.

Lipton, Douglas, Robert Martinson, and Judith Wilks. 1975. *The Effectiveness of Correctional Treatment and What Works: A Survey of Treatment Evaluation Studies.* New York: Praeger.

Little Hoover Commission. 1998. *Beyond Bars: Correctional Reforms to Lower Prison Costs and Reduce Crimes.* Sacramento, Calif.: State of California.

LoBuglio, Stefan. 2001. "Time to Reframe Politics and Practices in Correctional Education." In *Annual Review of Adult Learning and Literacy*, ch. 4. Vol 2. Cambridge, Mass.: National Center for the Study of Adult Learning and Literacy.

Logan, Charles. 1993. "Criminal Justice Performance Measures for Prisons." In *Performance Measures for the Criminal Justice System*, edited by John J. DiIulio, Jr., 19–60. Washington, D.C.: Bureau of Justice Statistics.

Love, Margaret Colgate, and Susan Kuzma. 1997. *Civil Disabilities of Convicted Felons: A State-by-State Survey, October 1996.* Washington, D.C.: U.S. Department of Justice.

Lurigio, Arthur J. 2001. "Effective Services for Parolees with Mental Illnesses." *Crime & Delinquency* 47, no. 3:446–61.

Lynch, James P. 2002. "Crime in International Perspectives." In *Crime: Public Policies for Crime Control*, edited by J. Q. Wilson and J. Petersilia, 5–42. San Francisco, Calif.: ICS Press.

Lynch, James P., and William J. Sabol. 2001. *Prisoner Reentry in Perspective.* Washington, D.C.: Urban Institute.

Lynch, Mona. 1999. "Waste Managers? New Penology, Crime Fighting, and the Parole Agent Identity." *Law and Society Review* 32, no. 4: 839–69.

Macallair, Dan, and Vincent Schiraldi. 2000. "If Your Job Depends on It, Throwing Non-Violent Drug Users in Jail Makes Sense." *San Jose Mercury News*, 22 June.

McDonald, Douglas C. 1999. "Medical Care in Prisons." In *Prisons*, edited by Michael Tonry and Joan Petersilia, 427–78. Chicago, Ill.: University of Chicago Press.

MacKenzie, Doris L., and Laura J. Hickman. 1998. *What Works in Corrections? An Examination of the Effectiveness of the Type of Rehabilitation Programs Offered by Washington State Department of Corrections.* College Park: University of Maryland.

Madrid v. Gomez. 1995. W.I. 17092 (N.D. Cal 1995).

Manza, Jeff, Christopher Uggen, and Marcus Britton. 2001. "The Truly Disfranchised: Felon Voting Rights and American Politics." Unpublished paper. Chicago, Ill.: Northwestern University.

Martinson, Robert. 1974. "What Works? Questions and Answers about Prison Reform." *Public Interest* 35:22–35.

Maruna, Shadd. 2001. *Making Good: How Ex-Convicts Reform and*

Rebuild Their Lives. Washington, D.C.: American Psychological Association.

Maruschak, L. M. 1999. *HIV in Prisons and Jails*. Washington, D.C.: Bureau of Justice Statistics.

Maruschak, Laura, and Allen J. Beck. 2001. *Medical Problems of Inmates, 1997*. Washington, D.C.: Bureau of Justice Statistics.

Maryland Justice Policy Institute. 2002. "Telephone Rates Charged to the Families of Maryland Prisoners." Retrieved 20 May 2002 from http://www.Md.-justice-policy-inst.org/05Simms.htm

Mauer, Marc. 1997. *Losing the Vote: The Impact of Felony Disenfranchisement Laws in the United States*. Washington, D.C.: Sentencing Project.

———. 1990. *More Young Black Males under Correctional Control in U.S. Than in College*. Washington, D.C.: Sentencing Project.

Mauer, Marc, and Meda Chesney-Lind, eds. 2002. *The Collateral Consequences of Mass Imprisonment*. New York: New Press.

Mauer, Marc, Kathy Potler, and Richard Wolf. 1999. *Gender and Justice: Women, Drugs and Sentencing Policy*. Washington, D.C.: Sentencing Project.

May, John P. 2000. "Feeding a Public Health Epidemic." In *Building Violence: How America's Rush to Incarcerate Creates More Violence*, edited by John P. May, 132–38. Thousand Oaks, Calif.: Sage.

Mears, D. P., L. Winterfield, J. Hunsaker, G. E. Moore, and R. M. White. 2001. *Strong Science for Strong Practice: Linking Research to Drug Treatment in the Criminal Justice System*. Washington, D.C.: Urban Institute.

Metcalf, Hilary, Tracy Anderson, and Heather Rolfe. 2001. *Barriers to Employment for Offenders and Ex-Offenders*. London: Department for Work and Pensions.

Miller, Ted R., Mark A. Cohen, and Brian Wiersema. 1996. *Victim Costs and Consequences: A New Look*. Washington, D.C.: National Institute of Justice.

Monahan, John. 1996. "Mental Illness and Violent Crime." *NIJ Research Review,* 1–7.

Moore, Joan. 1995. "Bearing the Burden: How Incarceration Weakens Inner-City Communities." Paper presented at the Unintended Consequences of Incarceration conference, Vera Institute, New York City, 15 June.

Morris, Norval. 2002. *Maconochie's Gentlemen: The Story of Norfolk Island the Roots of Modern Prison Reform*. New York: Oxford University Press.

Morris, Norval, and Michael Tonry. 1990. *Between Prison and Probation: Intermediate Punishments in a Rational Sentencing System*. New York: Oxford University Press.

Morrissey v. Brewer. 1972. 408 U.S. 471.

Mukamal, Debbie, and Terri Stevens. 2002. "State Legal Barriers Affecting Individuals with Criminal Records." Paper presented at the Urban Institute's Reentry Roundtable, Washington, D.C., 20 March.

Mumola, C. 2000. *Incarcerated Parents and Their Children*. Washington, D.C.: Bureau of Justice Statistics.

———. 1999. *Substance Abuse and Treatment: State and Federal Prisoners, 1997*. Washington, D.C.: Bureau of Justice Statistics.

NACRO. 1998. Law Reviews on the Web, *Rehabilitation of Offenders Act, 1974*. Retrieved 25 October from www.lawontheweb.co.uk/rehabact.htm

Nagin, D., and J. Waldfogel. 1998. "The Effect of Conviction on Income through the Life Cycle." *International Review of Law and Economics* 18:25–40.

National Center on Addiction and Substance Abuse. 1998. *Behind Bars: Substance Abuse and America's Prison Population*. New York: Columbia University.

National Center on Institutions and Alternatives. 1998. *Imprisoning Elderly Offenders: Public Safety or Maximum Security Nursing Homes?* Alexandria, Va.: NCIA.

National Coalition for the Homeless. 1997. *Homelessness in America: Unabated and Increasing, 1997*. Washington, D.C.: National Coalition for the Homeless.

National Commission on Correctional Health Care. 2002. *The Health Status of Soon-to-Be-Released Inmates*. Washington, D.C.: National Institute of Justice.

National Trust for the Development of African-American Men. 2002. Retrieved 25 September from www.keepthetrust.org.summit

Nelson, Marta, Perry Deess, and Charlotte Allen. 1999. *The First Month Out: Post-Incarceration Experiences in New York City*. New York: Vera Institute of Justice.

Office for Victims of Crime. 2000. *Victim Issues for Parole Boards*. Videotape. Washington, D.C.: Victims of Crime Resource Center.

———. 1998. *New Directions from the Field: Victims' Rights and Services for the 21st Century*. Washington, D.C.: U.S. Department of Justice.

O'Leary, Vincent, ed. 1974. "Parole Administration." In *Handbook of Criminology*, edited by Daniel Glaser, 909–48. Chicago, Ill.: Rand McNally.

Olivares, K., V. Burton, and F. Cullen. 1996. "The Collateral Consequences of a Felony Conviction: A National Study of State Legal Codes 10 Years Later." *Federal Probation* 60, no. 3:10–18.

Open Society Institute. 1997. *Education as Crime Prevention: Providing Education to Prisoners*. New York: Soros.

Parent, Dale, and Brad Snyder. 1999. *Police-Corrections Partnerships*. Washington, D.C.: National Institute of Justice.

Parke, Ross, and Alison Clarke-Stewart. 2001. "Effects of Parental Incarceration on Young Children." Paper presented at the Urban Institute's From Prison to Home conference, Washington, D.C., 30–31 January.

Peacock, Steve. 2000. "BOP Proposes Inmates Pay All Tuition Costs for College." *Corrections Journal* 4, no. 10:7.

Petersilia, Joan. 2002. *Reforming Probation and Parole*. Lanham, Md.: American Correctional Association.

———. 2000. *Challenges of Prisoner Reentry and Parole in California*. Berkeley: California Policy Research Center.

———. 1999a. "A Decade of Experimenting with Intermediate Sanctions: What Have We Learned?" *Justice Research and Policy* 11, no. 1:9–24.

———. 1999b. "Parole and Prisoner Reentry in the United States." In *Prisons*, edited by Michael Tonry and Joan Petersilia, 479–530. Chicago, Ill.: University of Chicago Press.

Petersilia, Joan, and Susan Turner. 1993. "Intensive Probation and Parole." In *Crime and Justice: An Annual Review of Research*, edited by Michael Tonry, 281–335. Chicago, Ill.: University of Chicago Press.

Petersilia, J., S. Turner, and Joyce E. Peterson. 1986. "Prison versus Probation in California: Implications for Crime and Offender Recidivism." Santa Monica, Calif.: Rand.

Pettit, Becky, and Bruce Western. 2001. "Inequality in Lifetime Risks of Imprisonment." Unpublished paper.

President's Commission on Law Enforcement and Administration of Justice. 1967. *The Challenge of Crime in a Free Society*. Washington, D.C.: U.S. Government Printing Office.

President's Task Force on Victims of Crime. 1982. *Final Report*. Washington, D.C.: U.S. Government Printing Office.

Putnam, Robert D. 2000. *Bowling Alone*. New York: Simon & Schuster.

Quinsey, V. L., M. E. Harris, A. Rice, and C. A. Cormier. 1998. *Violent Offenders: Appraising and Managing Risk*. Washington, D.C.: American Psychological Association.

Raeder, Myrna. 1993. "Gender and Sentencing: Single Moms, Battered Women and Other Sex-Based Anomalies in the Gender-Free World of the Federal Sentencing Guidelines." *Pepperdine Law Review* 20, no. 3:905-90.

Reiss, Albert J. 1999. "When and for Whom Is Violence a Crime Problem?" In *Minimizing Harm: A New Crime Policy for Modern America*, edited by Edward L. Rubin, 58–63. Boulder, Colo.: Westview.

Reitz, Kevin R. 2000. "The Disassembly and Reassembly of U.S. Sentencing Practices." In *Sentencing and Sanctions in Western Countries*, edited by M. Tonry and Richard Frase, 222–58. New York: Oxford University Press.

———. 1996. "Michael Tonry and the Structure of Sentencing Laws." *Journal of Criminal Law & Criminology* 86:1585–602.

Rhine, Edward E. 1996. "Parole Boards." In *The Encyclopedia of American Prisons*, edited by Marilyn McShane and Frank Williams, 342–48. New York: Garland.

Rhine, Edward, William Smith, Ronald Jackson, Peggy Burke, and Roger LaBelle. 1991. *Paroling Authorities: Recent History and Current Practice*. Laurel, Md.: American Correctional Association.

Rhunda, John, Edward Rhine, and Robert Wetter. 1994. *The Practice of Parole Boards*. Lexington, Ky.: Association of Parole Authorities, International.

Ripley, Amanda. 2002. "Outside the Gates." *Time*, 21 January, pp. 58–62.

Riveland, Chase. 1999. "Prison Management Trends, 1975–2025." In *Prisons*, edited by M. Tonry and J. Petersilia, 163–203. Chicago, Ill.: University of Chicago Press.

Rollo, Ned. 2002. *99 Days and a Get Up: A Guide to Success Following Release for Inmates and Their Loved Ones*. 3d ed. Dallas, Tex.: Open.

Rose, Dina, Todd Clear, and Kristen Scully. 1999. "Coercive Mobility and Crime: Incarceration and Social Disorganization." Paper presented at the American Society of Criminology, Toronto, Canada, 12–15 November.

Rossman, Shelli. 2002. "Services Integration: Strengthening Offenders and Families, while Promoting Community Health and Safety." Paper presented at the Urban Institute's From Prison to Home conference, Washington, D.C., 30–31 January.

Rothman, David. 1980. *Conscience and Convenience: The Asylum and Its Alternatives in Progressive America*. Boston: Little, Brown.

Rubinstein, Gwen. 2001. *Getting to Work: How TANF Can Support Ex-Offender Parents in the Transition to Self-Sufficiency*. Washington, D.C.: Legal Action Center.

Rudovsky, David, Alvin Bronstein, Edward Koren, and Julie Cade. 1988. *The Rights of Prisoners*. Carbondale, Ill.: Southern Illinois University Press.

Sampson, Robert J., Stephen Raudenbush, and Felton Earls. 1997. "Neighborhoods and Violent Crime: A Multilevel Study of Collective Efficacy." *Science* 227:918–24.

Schlosser, Eric. 1998. "The Prison-Industrial Complex." *Atlantic Monthly*, December, pp. 51–77.

Schmidt, Peter. 2002. "College Programs for Prisoners, Long Neglected, Win New Support." *Chronicle of Higher Education*, 8 February.

Schoeni, Robert F., and Paul Koegel. 1998. "Economic Resources of the Homeless: Evidence from Los Angeles." *Contemporary Economic Policy* 16, no. 5:295–308.

Schriro, Dora. 2000. *Correcting Corrections: Missouri's Parallel Universe.* Washington, D.C.: National Institute of Justice.

Schultz, D. 2000. "No Joy in Mudville Tonight: The Impact of Three Strikes Laws on State and Federal Corrections Policy, Resources, and Crime Control." *Cornell Journal of Law and Public Policy* 9:557–83.

Schwartz, Herman. 2002. "Out of Jail and Out of Food." *New York Times*, 21 March, opinion section.

Sechrest, Lee, Susan White, and Elizabeth Brown. 1979. *The Rehabilitation of Criminal Offenders: Problems and Prospects.* Washington, D.C.: National Academy of Sciences.

Seiter, Richard. 2002. *Correctional Administration: Integrating Theory and Practice.* Upper Saddle River, N.J.: Prentice Hall.

Seiter, Richard, and Karen Kadela. 2003. "Prisoner Reentry: What Works, What Doesn't, and What's Promising." *Crime and Delinquency* 49.

Seymour, Anne. 2001. *The Victim's Role in Offender Reentry.* Washington, D.C.: Office for Victims of Crime.

———. 1997. *National Victim Services Survey of Adult and Juvenile Correctional Agencies and Paroling Authorities, 1996.* Arlington, Va.: National Victim Center.

Shapiro, Carol. 2001. "Coming Home: Building on Family Connections." *Corrections Management Quarterly* 5, no. 3:52–62.

Shaw, George Bernard. 1946. *The Crime of Imprisonment.* Washington, D.C.: Philosophical Library.

Simon, Jonathan. 1993. *Poor Discipline: Parole and the Social Control of the Underclass, 1890-1990.* Chicago, Ill.: University of Chicago Press.

Skolnick, Jerome H. 1990. "Gangs and Crime Old as Time, but Drugs Change Gang Culture." In *Crime and Delinquency in California*, 171–79. Sacramento, Calif.: Bureau of Criminal Statistics, California Department of Justice.

Smith, Margaret, and Todd Clear. 1995. "Fathers in Prison: Interim Report." Newark, N.J.: Rutgers University. Unpublished paper.

Smith, Michael, and Walter Dickey. 1998. "What If Corrections Were Serious about Public Safety?" *Corrections Management Quarterly* 2, no. 3:12–30.

Snell, Tracy. 2001. *Capital Punishment 2000.* Washington, D.C.: Bureau of Justice Statistics, U.S. Department of Justice.

Spelman, Williams. 2000. "The Limited Importance of Prison Expansion." In *The Crime Drop in America*, edited by Alfred Blumstein and Joel Wallman, 97–129. New York: Cambridge University Press.

Stivers, Connie. 2001. "Impacts of Discretionary Parole Release on Length of Sentence Served, Percent of Imposed Sentence Served, and Recidivism." Master's thesis, University of California, Irvine.

Streeter, P. 1998. "Incarceration of the Mentally Ill: Treatment or Warehousing?" *Michigan Bar Journal* 77, no. 166:167.

Tappero, J. W., R. Reporter, and J. Wenger. 1996. "Meningococal Disease in Los Angeles County, California, and among Men in the County Jails." *New England Journal of Medicine* 335, no. 12:833–40.

Taxman, Faye, Douglas Young, and James M. Byrne. 2002a. "Offender's Views of Reentry: Implications for Processes, Programs, and Services." Unpublished manuscript. College Park: University of Maryland.

Taxman, Faye, Douglas Young, James M. Byrne, Alexander Holsinger, and Donald Anspach. 2000b. "From Prison Safety to Public Safety: Innovations in Offender Reentry." Unpublished manuscript. College Park: University of Maryland.

Terry, Don. 1992. "More Familiar, Life in a Cell Seems Less Terrible." *New York Times*, 13 September, p. 1.

Thompson, James. 1983. *Chicago Tribune*, 24 August.

Tonn, Ron. 1999. "Turning the Tables: The Safer Foundation's Youth Enterprise Program." *Corrections Today* 61, no. 1:76–78.

Tonry, Michael. 1995. *Malign Neglect: Race, Crime, and Punishment in America*. New York: Oxford University Press.

———. 1987. *Sentencing Reform Impacts*. Washington, D.C.: National Institute of Justice.

Travis, Jeremy. 2002. "Invisible Punishment: An Instrument of Social Exclusion." In *Invisible Punishment: The Collateral Consequences of Mass Imprisonment*, edited by Marc Mauer and Meda Chesney-Lind, 15–36. Washington, D.C.: New Press.

———. 2000. *But They All Come Back: Rethinking Prisoner Reentry*. Washington, D.C.: National Institute of Justice.

Travis, Jeremy, Amy Solomon, and Michelle Waul. 2001. *From Prison to Home: The Dimensions and Consequences of Prisoner Reentry*. Washington, D.C.: Urban Institute.

Turner, Susan, and Joan Petersilia. 1996. "Work Release in Washington: Effects on Recidivism and Corrections Costs." *Prison Journal* 76, no. 2:138–50.

Turner, S., J. Petersilia, and E. P. Deschenes. 1992. "Evaluating Intensive Supervision Probation and Parole for Drug Offenders." *Crime & Delinquency* 38, no. 4:539–56.

Tyler, Tom R. 1992. *Why People Obey the Law.* New Haven, Conn.: Yale University Press.

Uggen, Christopher. 2002. "Barriers to Democratic Participation." Paper presented at Prisoner Reentry and the Institutions of Civil Society: Bridges and Barriers to Successful Reintegration conference. Washington, D.C., 20–21 March.

———. 2000. "Work as a Turning Point in the Life Course of Criminals: A Duration Model of Age, Employment and Recidivism." *American Sociological Review* 65:529–46.

Uggen, Christopher, and Jeff Manza. 2001. "The Political Consequences of Felon Disfranchisement Law in the United States." Washington, D.C.: Paper presented at the annual meeting of the American Sociological Association, Washington, D.C., 12–14 August.

Uggen, Christopher, Jeff Manza, and Angela Behrens. 2002a. "Stigma, Role Transition, and the Civic Reintegration of Convicted Felons." In *After Crime and Punishment: Ex-Offender Reintegration and Desistance from Crime*, edited by Shadd Maruna and Russ Immarigeon. Albany: State University of New York Press.

Uggen, Christopher, Melisa Thompson, and Jeff Manza. 2002b. "Crime, Class, and Reintegration: The Scope and Social Distribution of America's Criminal Class." Unpublished paper. Minneapolis: University of Minnesota.

U.S. Department of Labor. 2001. *From Hard Time to Full Time: Strategies to Help Move Ex-Offenders from Welfare to Work.* Washington, D.C.: Employment and Training Administration.

Vaughn, Michael, and Leo Carroll. 1998. "Separate and Unequal: Prison versus Free-World Medical Care." *Justice Quarterly* 15:3–40.

von Hirsch, Andrew. 1976. *Doing Justice: The Choice of Punishments.* New York: Hill and Wang.

Walker, Samuel, Cassia Spohn, and Miriam DeLone. 2002. "Corrections: A Picture in Black and White." In *Exploring Corrections*, edited by Tara Gray, 13–24. Boston: Allyn & Bacon.

Weintraub, Daniel. 2002. "State Prison Guards Set to Ratify Rich New Contract." *Sacramento Bee*, 10 February, p. E5.

Western, Bruce, Jeffrey Kling, and David Weiman. 2001. "The Labor Market Consequences of Incarceration." *Crime & Delinquency* 47, no. 3:410–28.

Wexler, David. 2002. "Therapeutic Jurisprudence: An Overview." Retrieved 15 September 2002 from http://www.law.arizona.edu

———. 2001. "Robes and Rehabilitation: How Judges Can Help Offenders 'Make Good.'" *Court Review* (Spring): 19–23.

Wiebe, Doug, and J. Petersilia. 2000. "The 1996 Survey of Jail Inmates: A Comparison of the Victimization of Persons with and without Disabilities." Unpublished manuscript. Irvine: University of California.

Wilkinson, Reginald. 2001. "Offender Reentry: A Storm Overdue." *Corrections Management Quarterly* 5, no. 3:46–51.

———. 2000. *Correctional Best Practices: Directors' Perspectives.* Middletown, Conn.: Association of State Correctional Administrators.

Wilson, James. 1985. *Thinking about Crime.* New York: Basic.

Wilson, James Q., and George L. Kelling. 1982. "Broken Windows." *Atlantic Monthly*, March, pp. 29–38.

Wilson, William Julius. 1987. *The Truly Disadvantaged: The Inner City, the Underclass, and Public Policy.* Chicago, Ill.: University of Chicago Press.

Winick, Bruce J. 1998. "Sex Offender Law in the 1990s: A Therapeutic Jurisprudence Analysis." *Psychology, Public Policy, and Law* 4, nos. 1–2: 505–70.

Wirthlin Worldwide. 2000. *Member Survey: Taking the Next Step.* Welfare to Work Partnership. Vol. 1. McLean, Va. Retrieved 25 September 2002 from www.welfaretowork.org

Worth, Robert. 1995. "A Model Prison." *Atlantic Monthly*, Nov. www.theatlantic.com/issues/95nov/prisons/prisons.htm

Yankelovich, Daniel. 1994. "What Polls Say—and What They Mean." *New York Times*, 17 September.

Zimring, F. E., and Gordon Hawkins. 1999. "Public Attitudes toward Crime: Is American Violence a Crime Problem?" In *Minimizing Harm: A New Crime Policy for Modern America*, edited by Edward L. Rubin, 35–57. Boulder, Colo.: Westview.

———. 1998. *Crime Is Not the Problem: Lethal Violence in America.* New York: Oxford University Press.

Index

Gary Library - Union Inst & Univ
0 0036 00007234